PREFACE

A Handbook of MARKETING MATHEMATICS is written for you the business operator that had always wished to know how to interpret marketing ideas into accurate numbers and figures; the business teacher that needs quantitative marketing and ratios to substantiate marketing claims and reasons; the business student that cannot come to grips with how marketing concepts and strategies are turned into dollars and measurable results; and for all readers that find this book interesting and useful.

All businesses need and use mathematics. Those enterprises that know how to, and apply mathematics in making decisions are the most profitable. While other areas of business like accounting, finance, statistics, and general business have facts in one book, the marketing area is very diverse and often fragmented into more than nine subject areas and texts. Marketers waste much time searching for solutions to quantitative marketing problems. There is no one source available to look at. A Handbook of MARKETING MATHEMATICS provides more than two hundred marketing quantitative methods accumulated from marketing management, marketing research, consumer behavior, international marketing, retailing, direct marketing, salesmanship, and internet marketing.

A Handbook of MARKETING MATHEMATICS contains twenty chapters of quantitative marketing techniques that are simply explained for easy understanding and application. Each technique is defined. The importance is pointed out. A marketing problem is simulated and solved. The result is interpreted and implied, and the steps of the calculation are described.

A Handbook of MARKETING MATHEMATICS should serve as a quantitative supplement to all marketing textbooks. It is a good reference and source of exercises for marketing teachers. It is an excellent tool to train business operators on technical tools for making marketing decisions. It is a good guide for all marketing managers. A

iii

Handbook of MARKETING MATHEMATICS is for anyone that desires mathematical solutions to marketing problems.

An added value to the handbook is the **MarketMatics.** This includes the automatic spreadsheet templates that accompany the Handbook of Marketing Mathematics. MarketMatics includes more than one hundred and thirty ready-to-use worksheets that supply quick answers when you want to analyze your own data with any of the techniques illustrated in the Handbook of Marketing Mathematics using Microsoft Excel 97, 2000, and 2002. The MarketMatics is offered to buyers of the handbook at a discounted price. See the **order form** after the acknowledgement section.

A Handbook of Marketing Mathematics contains six parts with twenty chapters. Part one- Marketing Costs, is composed of chapters one through four that focus on accounting, budgeting, costs, and credit sales. Part two- Customer Decisions, includes chapters five and six that illustrate customer satisfaction and consumer behavior. Part three- Marketing Ratios, includes chapters seven through ten that have topics on market activity ratios, market leverage ratios, market liquidity ratios, and market profitability and productivity ratios. Part four- Market Attractiveness, consists of chapters eleven and twelve on market potential and market forecasting. Part five- Marketing Strategy, contains chapters thirteen and fourteen that focus on marketing research and target marketing respectively. Finally, Part six - The Four P's-contains chapters fifteen through twenty which focus on product, pricing, retailing, marketing communication, channel inventory, and sales.

Chapter one is on accounting in marketing, and shows two methods for better accounting in marketing. The cash budget illustrates how to predict or estimate sales at any time period and how to find out how much cash a business has at all times for marketing expenses. The income statement section shows how to summarize the revenue generated from sales and other sources and how to determine the amount of income available for marketing and other operations. It also shows the marketing activities that are the most profitable, and which ones are unprofitable.

Chapter two illustrates four techniques to develop effective marketing budgets. The cross elasticity budgeting shows how a marketer could measure how the demand for one product complements or substitutes another product. The next technique illustrates how to put together a direct or indirect marketing budget. The direct approach illustrates how to estimate the amount of sales that will result from a given price and marketing budget, and the indirect approach illustrates how to use benchmarks to do the estimate. The last part of the chapter shows how to compose a merchandise budgeting that enables marketers to determine the correct number of products or services to have available at a given period to meet customer demand.

Chapter three is on cost and illustrates eleven techniques for better handling the marketing costs. The cost complement technique shows how to find how much of the retail price covers the merchandise cost. The cost of credit sales illustrates how to determine the cost of offering credit to customers. The cost of forecast errors shows how to determine the amount of money a company will lose from making wrong sales forecasts. The cost-of-goods-sold ratio determines the portion of the net sales that covers the money used to make or buy the goods sold, and the cost per thousand (CPM) shows how to determine the costs for an advertisement to reach one thousand people. The sales cost/ratio analysis shows how to determine the cost difference between using a company's sales force and using a sales agency to sell the goods and services. The distribution cost analysis illustrates how to determine the amount of money spent to generate a given level of sale. The semi-fixed cost effect guides the marketer to find those costs that do not change automatically with an additional unit, but may change if substantial increase occurs in the volume of marketing activities. The fixed cost per unit shows the marketer how to find those costs that remain the same regardless of the volume of sales. The opportunity cost or optimal marketing cost illustrates how to find the foregone revenues from not using an optimal marketing mix or a combination of the marketing mix that maximizes profit. Finally, the operating expense ratio shows how to find the percentage of each sales dollar that is used to pay for marketing operations.

Chapter four focuses on credit sales and presents four techniques for better credit sales decisions. The cash discount approach illustrates how to set the reduction in price of an item to buyers for paying for the product or service in time. The credit impact on profitability helps the marketer to determine the effect of credit or delayed payment on the amount of profit the business would make. The profit impact of a quantity discount shows a marketer how to determine how profit is affected by a reduction in the cost of items based on the size of the order. The trade discount shows suppliers how to determine the amount of reduction in the list price granted to either a wholesaler or a retailer who performs functions that suppliers usually perform.

Chapter five looks at consumer satisfaction, and includes five techniques to increase consumer satisfaction. It illustrates how to determine the required increase in customer satisfaction, and this enables the marketer to know the state where buying and using the product or service meet or exceed users' expectations. The profit impact of customers' satisfaction shows the marketer how to determine the relationship between an increase in the type and amount of customers' services. The functional process development shows the marketer a step-by-step method of how to incorporate customer needs into the design of a new product or in the augmentation of existing products. Lastly, the part-worth utility approach illustrates how to estimate the utility or value of the attributes of a product.

Chapter six is on consumer behavior, and it presents two techniques to determine consumers' behavior. The attitude-toward-object method indicates how to measure customers' feelings toward the use of a product or service line, or a specific brand. The second method, the attitude toward-behavior technique illustrates the way to find out how a person feels toward an action or behavior of an object.

Chapter seven focuses on marketing ratios, and illustrates five ratios to better measure and understand activities in marketing. The account receivable turnover ratio shows marketers how to measure the average time it takes to receive the money for the sales made on credit. The fixed assets turnover ratio shows how to measure sales productivity of assets or how efficient a marketer utilizes his/her plants and equipment in selling. The total asset turnover ratio illustrates a technique that determines how effective a marketer's assets are used during a period of time. Last, the cash-flow per share ratio technique shows the marketer how to measure the discretionary funds over and above the business expenses that are available for the business to use as it wants.

Chapter eight discusses the marketing leverage ratios, and presents four techniques to measure how reliant a marketer is on debt financing to fund the operations. The fixed-charge coverage ratio technique shows the marketer how to measure his or her ability to meet all of the fixed-charge obligations. The debt-to-assets ratio approach shows how to measure the extent to which a marketer operates the activities with borrowed money. The debt-to-equity ratio illustrates how to compare the amount of marketing operation funds that is borrowed by the marketer to the amount that is provided by the stockholders or owners. Last, the time-interest earned ratio approach shows how to measure the level that a marketer's profits can decline without the business becoming unable to pay the annual interest cost.

Chapter nine centers on market liquidity ratios, and provides three ratios to measure marketers' ability to meet short-term obligations as they due. The current ratio approach shows how to determine the amount of cash assets that the marketer has to pay short-term bills as they due. The second technique, the inventory-to-net working capital ratio, shows how to measure the extent to which a marketer's working capital or operation funds are tied up in the inventory. The last technique, the quick ratio, shows the marketer the ability of the business to pay short-term bills in times of real crises without relying on the sales of inventory.

Chapter ten focuses on market productivity and profitability, and presents twenty-three methods to assess the sales or market-share consequence of a marketing strategy or the impact of various marketing strategies or programs on profit contribution. The cost-volume profit analysis illustrates how to determine how the cost and the profit of a product or service will change as the volume of sales changes. The dividend yield on common stock shows how to pro-rate the distribution of money or additional shares to common shareholders. The remaining techniques show how to find the gross margins, return on investment, variable contribution margins (VCM), percentage variable contribution margin (PVCM), earning per share, the effect of selling price on the market, and market territory performance.

Chapter eleven is on market potential, and it is illustrated with twelve techniques. The first four are market potential-consumer market, market potential-industrial market, relative market potential, and total market potential. These techniques show how to determine the number of possible users of products or service and their maximum rate of purchase. The next three techniques are category development index, brand development index, and buying power index, and these show how to use figures to measure demand gaps and sales opportunities. The product survival rate shows how to determine the rate products survive the wear and tear of customers' usage, while the replacement potential shows how to estimate the quantity of a brand of a product to produce in a period of time. The last three techniques, required total dollar sales, required total unit sales, and required market share illustrate how to find out the amount of sales or number of customers that are required in the budget to reach a target contribution margin or achieve the minimum contribution to cover cost and make profit.

Chapter twelve is on market forecasting. It presents seven techniques on how to achieve accurate forecast of the market. The first three techniques, exponential smoothing, moving average, and the straight-line projection illustrate how to forecast sales. The exponential smoothing shows how to use weighted average of past times series values to forecast future sales. The moving average shows how to use an average sale in a specific period in the past to predict the sale for a future period, and the straight line technique shows how to use "best fitting line" to forecast sales. The last four techniques, basic stock, percentage variation, stock-to-sales, and weekly supply methods illustrate how to forecast or plan the merchandise. The basic stock method shows how to determine the base or lowest level of inventory investment or the unit of merchandise to carry regardless of the predicted sales volume for every month in the year. The percentage variation method shows how to determine the amount of inventory to carry to face fluctuations in sales without having a set or given level of inventory at all times. The stock-to-sales technique shows how to determine how much inventory is needed at the beginning of each month to support that month's estimated sales. Finally, the weekly supply method shows how to plan inventory on a weekly basis.

Chapter thirteen is on marketing research. It contains eleven techniques that are used for better marketing research. Included are the analysis of variance, cluster analysis, conjoint analysis, correlation analysis, discriminant analysis, factor analysis, multidimensional analysis, multiple regression, queuing model, and strategic profit model. The chapter illustrates the situations that these techniques are appropriate for, and made efforts to calculate the problems. However, due to the complexity of the problems, most of them should be solved with the computer by using the CD provided.

Chapter fourteen focuses on target marketing. This shows how three techniques are used to better describe and understand the customers. The lifetime value of a customer shows how to measure the worth of acquiring a new customer. The second and third techniques are those to determine the size of a trading area and target market profile.

Chapter fifteen is on the product. It explains two techniques, attribute rating and brand rating. The attribute rating shows how to determine which features or attributes of a product are the most important to consumers, while the brand rating shows how to evaluate the features of identical product brands and rank them according to their importance.

Chapter sixteen focuses on pricing and shows how to use twelve techniques to set better prices. The first part of the chapter explains three general pricing methods including cost-plus pricing, retail-based pricing, and target return pricing. These are followed by six price mark-up/mark-down techniques. These include the mark-up at retail or cost, initial mark-up percentage, maintained mark-up percentage, additional retail mark-down percentage, and off-retail mark-down percentage. The remaining three techniques show how to determine the break-even point, sales variance, and price elasticity.

Chapter seventeen focuses on retailing, and presents five techniques to measure retail activities in the market. The index of retail saturation shows how to measure how many similar stores to locate in an area to satisfy the needs of the population. The retail gravitation model shows how to measure the extent that buyers are drawn to retail stores that are closer or more attractive than competitors. The retail space productivity model shows how to determine the amount of sales dollars contributed by each square foot in a retail store. The fourth technique, the retail compatibility model, shows the method to determine how much sales a store can generate by locating close to another store that sells similar or complementary products or services. The last technique is the shopper attraction model that shows how to calculate the size of the trading area in terms of the expected numbers of households that will be attracted to the retail site.

Chapter eighteen focuses on marketing communication. It presents nine techniques to select promotional activities and assess their effectiveness and efficiency. The first three techniques are advertising reach, advertising frequency, and advertising rating points. The advertising reach technique is used to find the percentage of a target audience that a business reaches with its advertisement message at least once every four weeks. The advertising frequency technique shows the average number of times a person in the target audience or group is exposed to the same advertisement message in a four-week period. The advertising rating point is the amount of advertisement that will have a marked effect in the mind and emotion of the viewers. The maximum advertising cost shows how to find the most money a firm will spend on advertising in order to achieve an operating profit goal, and the task and objective advertising budget shows how to determine the budget by stating the objectives and tasks needed to achieve the goal.

The next two techniques, the recency/frequency and monetary value segmentation 1, and the receny/frequency and monetary value segmentation 2, show how to segment the customers, find out the percentage that will order, find out the number of orders to expect, and find out the average order amount within some recent period of time based on the recency, frequency, and monetary value of the orders. The last technique is the weighted number of exposures, and this shows how to find out the amount or degree of impact an advertisement makes on the viewers.

Chapter nineteen presents twelve techniques on how to solve inventory problems in the channel of distribution. In the profitability of indirect channel section, the chapter shows the process to estimate the sales productivity of a proposed new price or expenditure by using a sales benchmark. The additional inventory cost techniques show how to find out the cost of maintaining a higher inventory level needed to meet the increase in demand. The next section presents the closing inventory at cost technique that shows how to determine the value of the goods unsold at the end of a period by basing their value on their cost price. The inventory cost technique shows how to find the cost incurred to buy and keep enough inventory. The inventory carrying cost is another technique to illustrate how to find the amount of money spent to keep enough inventory to meet the customers' demand.

The FIFO/LIFO inventory costing techniques guide the marketer to determine the cost of ending inventory. The next four techniques, inventory reorder point, inventory shortage or overage, inventory turnover, and stock turnover ratio are monitoring tools. The inventory reorder point shows how to find the level of inventory at which new orders must be placed, the inventory shortage or overage shows how to find the number by which items for sales are either more or less than the number needed for sale, the inventory turnover technique shows how to measure the rate at which the inventory is sold, while the stock turnover rate shows how to find the number of times the average inventory on hand is sold during a specific period of time. The last technique is the reduction in inventory value, and it shows how to find out the amount that the book value of the inventory should be reduced in order to give a more accurate worth or value of the inventory.

Chapter twenty is the last chapter in the handbook, and it contains five techniques that present how to determine and improve the sales efficiency. The first technique is the size of sales force model that shows how to determine the size of the sales force that a firm needs. The next technique is the required level of sales that is used to determine the amount of sales needed to achieve a minimum level of each dollar contribution to indirect cost and profit. The sales efficiency ratio shows how to compare the sales output with the cost incurred to achieve such a sales level. The sales per square foot shows how to determine the ratio of product sales to the amount of selling space used, while the last technique, the gross–margin return per square foot shows how to determine how much gross margin is generated by each square foot of a store.

I would like to hear from practitioners, educators, students, any other users of this handbook or the workbook about their likes and dislikes. Please send this to me at chidomere@wssu.edu or Marketmatics.com.

ACKNOWLEDGMENTS

Writing a book is like building your own house by yourself. The ideas and imaginations tend to be monopolized by your concepts and dreams. Deviations from set thought and patterns often dent or blunt the original visions. However, like a house, the beauty of a book depends on the admirations of the beholders. Therefore both builders and writers derive great push from the encouragements and admirations of others. Several people put forth the enthusiastic encouragement that was instrumental for me to persist to complete this handbook and its workbook.

First, I would like to express my appreciation to my family. To my wife Carolyn, I would thank for believing in my determination to write a book and for her encouragement and support. To my son Derrick, I would thank for his assistance and continuous expectation of a final output. To my son Ike, I would thank for accommodating my busy schedule and for his encouragement. And to my daughter Adamma, I would thank for her love, inquisition, and admirations of my efforts.

Second, I owe a debt of gratitude to several individuals that assisted me in my determined tasks to interpret marketing strategies in and out of mathematics and computer languages. I owe a debt of intellectual gratitude to Dr. Russell Morton, Associate Professor of MIS at Winston-Salem State University, for his useful insights whenever I called on him in my times of difficulty. I also particularly acknowledge the Faculty Development Program at Winston-Salem State University for their aid.

Third, my thanks go to several students and friends for their encouragement and support. I would like to thank Ms. Angela Martin, Ms. Jane Karonga, Ms. Yolanda Brown, Ms. Jessica Brinkley, Mr. Inman Burford, and the faculty at Winston-Salem State University for their assistance and advice.

Most of all, I would like to express my thanks and praise to God and to Jesus Christ my Savior for the knowledge, wisdom, patience and determination necessary to develop this handbook and its spreadsheets. My joy is in seeing others find these instruments useful.

Order Form For

MARKETMATICS

THE AUTOMATIC MARKETING SPREADSHEET FOR THE HANDBOOK OF MARKETING MATHEMATICS
Works with Excel 1999, 2000, & 2002

Yours at a very low price for Purchasing the Handbook.

Reduce your marketing cost

Increase your profit

Easy to use
Useful information
For marketing
Planning

chidomere@wssu.edu Marketmatics.com

_____ *Tear along the line* _____

Send $20 check or money order to:

Send my CD to:

Name: Rowland Chidomere, Ph.D.
Address: R & C Marketing
      2904 Woodhill Lane, Greensboro
      North Carolina 27406
      USA
Date of Purchase of Handbook_____

Name: _____
Address: _____
City_____ State_____
Zip Code_____ Country_____

Place of Purchase of Handbook_____

BRIEF CONTENTS

PART ONE... *1*

MARKETING COST *1*

1. ACCOUNTING.. **3**
2. BUDGETING **10**
3. COST **21**
4. CREDIT SALES **46**

PART TWO *57*

CONSUMER BEHAVIOR.................................. *57*

5. CUSTOMER SATISFACTION **59**
6. CONSUMER ATTITUDE **65**

PART THREE *73*

MARKETING RATIOS *73*

7. MARKET ACTIVITY RATIO **75**
8. MARKET LEVERAGE RATIO...................... **85**
9. MARKET LIQUIDITY RATIO **94**
10. Market Profitability/Productivity **101**

PART FOUR *145*

MARKET ATTRACTIVENESS........................... *145*

11. MARKET POTENTIAL................................. **147**
12. MARKET FORECAST.................................. **179**

PART FIVE *194*

MARKETING STRATEGY *194*

13. MARKETING RESEARCH................................. **196**
14. TARGET MARKETING **270**

PART SIX.. *274*

THE FOUR Ps *274*

15. PRODUCT.. **276**
16. PRICING **286**
17. RETAILING.. **315**
18. MARKETING COMMUNICATION **332**
19. MARKETING CHANNEL.................................. **354**
20. SALES... **381**

APPENDICES

Glossary **400**
Subject Index... **412**
References.. **426**
Photo Credits... **436**
About the Author **438**

CONTENTS

PART ONE MARKETING COST 1

CHAPTER 1 ACCOUNTING   **3**
Cash Budget 3
        Clayburn Florist Inc.
Income Statement (Profit and Loss) 6
        Greenstown Sheet Metal Inc.

CHAPTER 2 BUDGETING   **10**
Cross Elasticity Budgeting 10
        Global Computers Inc.
Marketing Budget-Direct Approach 14
        Modern Interior
Marketing Budget Indirect Approach 17
        Reliable Office Furniture

CHAPTER 3 COST   **21**
Cost Complement 21
        All Seasons Farm Supplies Inc.
Cost of credit sales 23
        Star Locks Inc.
Cost of Forecast Errors 26
        Southland Flags and Poles Inc.
Cost-of-Goods-Sold Ratio (%) 28
        Jimbus Xmas Shoppe Inc.
Cost Per Thousand (CPM) 29
        HomeBoy Fashions Inc.
Sales Cost/Ratio Analysis 32
        Pets Import Inc.
Distribution Cost Analysis 34
        Priority One Divers Supplies
Semi-fixed Cost (Step-variable cost) 36
        Children's Heaven Inc.

Fixed cost per unit.. 39
            Classic Windows Inc.
Opportunity Cost (Optimal Marketing Mix).................. 41
            Simply Unbeatable Inc.
Marketing Operating Expense Ratio (%)...................... 44
            Ideal Rent & Own Inc.

CHAPTER 4 CREDIT SALES   **46**
Cash discount.. 46
            Meats "R" Us Inc.
Credit Impact on Profitability 48
            Allied Facsimile Equipment Inc.
Profit Impact of Quantity Discount............................. 50
            Genuine Wears Inc.
Trade Discount.. 53
            Suki-Soki Orthopedic Inc.

PART TWO CONSUMER BEHAVIOR........................... *57*

CHAPTER 5 CUSTOMER SATISFACTION   **59**
Required Increase in Customers Satisfaction 59
            WEB "R" US Inc.
Profit Impact of Customer Satisfaction........................ 61
            Unique Web Works Inc.

CHAPTER 6 CONSUMER ATTITUDE   **65**
Attitude-Toward a Product 65
            UP Tiles Inc.
Attitude-Toward-Behavior... 68
            Quality Mobile X-ray Services Inc.

PART THREE MARKETING RATIOS............................ *73*

CHAPTER 7 MARKET ACTIVITY RATIO   **75**
Accounts Receivable Turnover..................................... 75
            Come & C Used Appliances Inc.

Average Collection Period.. 77
    Wesley & Wise Law Office Inc.
Fixed Assets Turnover.. 79
    Shields Glues & Adhesives Inc.
Total Assets Turnover.. 81
    A-Comfort World Inc.
Cashflow Per Share.. 83
    Goodlife Christian Bookstore Inc.

CHAPTER 8 MARKET LEVERAGE RATIO   85
Fixed-Charge Coverage 85
    Serv-Em-Up Inc.
Debt-to-Assets Ratio... 87
    Had I Known Tree Services Inc.
Debt-to-Equity Ratio 89
    Adults Pleasure Inc.
Times-Interest Earned (or coverage) Ratio.................... 91
    LuvNest Bridal Inc.

CHAPTER 9 MARKET LIQUIDITY RATIO   94
Current Ratio 94
    Woods Pro Inc.
Inventory to Net Working Capital Ratio 96
    Advanced Home Security Inc.
Quick Ratio (acid-test)... 98
    Northwest Discount Furniture Inc.

CHAPTER 10 MARKET PROFITABILITY/   101
PRODUCTIVITY RATIO
Cost-Volume Profit Analysis... 101
    LizTex's Check Printing Services Inc.
Dividend Yield On Common Stock or Equity................ 103
    Sit-In-Comfort Inc.
Dividend Pay Out to Preferred Stock or Equity 104
    Whuman Genetics
Earning per share 107
    MeriAnn Chinaware

Selling Price on Profit.. 109
       Happy Homes Funerals Inc.
Gross Margin on Inventory Investment....................................... 112
       Dick's Fruit Baskets
Gross Margin on Return Per Square Foot.................................... 115
       Little Heaven Retirement & Rehabilitation
Gross Profit Margin 117
       Kic-Jim-Kic Karate Inc.
Gross Margin Ratio (%).. 119
       A Man & A Pan Mobile Foods Inc.
Investment Turnover Ratio 121
       Advanced Vinyl Sidings
Net Profit Margin or Net Return on Sales(%) 123
       American Koast-to-Koast Inc.
Percentage Variable Contribution Margin (PVCM)..................... 125
       Amity Termite Kontrol Inc.
Price-Earnings Ratio 127
       JR Robotics
Return on Total Assets.. 129
       A World of Pets Inc.
Return on Investment (%).. 131
       Quality Personnel Inc.
Return on Investment model... 133
       American Toilet Supplies Inc.
Variable Contribution Margin (VCM)... 136
       Guminos Hand Gun Inc.
Non-traceable Cost Contribution Margin 139
       Pave-It-4-You Inc.
Territory Performance Measure... 141
       Whoz-Up Fashions Inc.

PART FOUR MARKET ATTRACTIVENESS.............................. *145*

CHAPTER 11 MARKET POTENTIAL   **147**
Market Potential – Consumer market. 147
       Perfect Shapes Inc.

Market Potential – Industrial Market................................. 149
    Bill & Sons Inc.
Relative Market Potential – Single Index Approach.................. 150
    Quality Import Cars Inc.
Total Market Potential 153
    Perfect Venture Inc.
Total Market Potential for Combined Markets...................... 155
    Jockey Products Inc.
Category Development Index (CDI) 157
    Serv-U-Fast Inc.
Brand Development Index (BDI) 160
    Tecks-Com Wireless Inc.
Buying Power Index 162
    American Nail Care & Tan Inc.
Product Survival Rate.. 164
    KompuAmerica Inc.
Replacement Potential 166
    Quality Sealed Air Inc.
Required Total Dollar Sales....................................... 169
    Carolina Standard Bank Inc.
Required Total Unit Sales... 172
    Hu-Nose Tomorrow Inc.
Required Market Share (RMS)................................... 176
    Body & Soul Inc.

CHAPTER 12 MARKET FORECAST   **179**
Sales Forecast – Exponential Smoothing 179
    Good Views Inc.
Sales Forecast –Moving Average 183
    J&J Blueprints and Supplies Inc.
Merchandise Planning-Basic Stock Method...................... 184
    Cruise-For-Fun Inc.
Merchandise Planning-Percentage Variation Method 188
    Jo-Jo Utensils Inc.
Merchandise Planning- Weekly Supply Method.................. 191
    ClearTalk Communications Inc.

Merchandise Planning-Weekly Supply Method 192
        Elm Street Antiques Inc.

PART FIVE MARKETING STRATEGY 194

CHAPTER 13 MARKETING RESEARCH   **196**
Analysis of variance (ANOVA) 196
        Elegance Mall Inc.
Cluster Analysis 204
        Fresh For-U Inc.
Conjoint analysis 222
        TCI Agric. Products Inc.
Correlation Analysis-Product Moment 230
        I Hear U Inc.
Discriminant Analysis 237
        Club Jam "O" Jam Inc.
Factor Analysis 244
        Body & Soul Recreational Inc.
Multidimensional Scaling 250
        Fresh Choice Juice Inc.
Multiple Regression 256
        Mama-Me Foods Inc.
Queuing model 263
        Edmond International Airport Inc.
Strategic Profit Model 266
        Lagos Refrigeration Services Inc.

CHAPTER 14 TARGET MARKETING   **270**
Lifetime Value of a Customer 270
        Jon Thomas Hardwood Flooring Inc.

PART SIX THE FOUR Ps 274

CHAPTER 15 PRODUCT   **276**
Attribute Rating 276
        Nic's Health Services Inc.

Brand Rating.. 283
    Peoples Brewing Inc.

CHAPTER 16 PRICING   286
Break-even Point 286
    Fantastic Tops Inc.
Cost-plus Pricing 289
    City Bar and Grill Inc.
Markup at Retail or Cost (%).. 291
    Cook's Chiropractic Center Inc.
Initial Mark-up Percentage 295
    Bush Discount Funeral Homes Inc.
Maintained Markup Percentage..................................... 297
    Smart & Associates Professional Center Inc.
Additional Retail Markdown %...................................... 299
    Global Sports Inc.
Off-Retail Markdown Percentage.................................. 302
    Jim Hardware Inc.
Sales Variance Analysis 304
    Audio Technology Systems Inc.
Price Elasticity... 306
    The Seasons Inc.
Retail-Based Pricing 310
    Adamma Quality Used Computers Inc.
Target-Return Price 313
    Affordable Homes Inc.

CHAPTER 17 RETAILING   315
Index of Retail Saturation (IRS)................................... 315
    Racquetball of Minnesota Inc.
Retail Gravitation Model 318
    Dick's Used Autos Inc.
Retail Space Productivity Model................................... 322
    Davis Eatery Inc.
Retail Compatibility Model 325
    Tobeke Fabrics Inc.

Shopper Attraction Model 328
        Adamma Reliable Fence Co. Inc.

CHAPTER 18 MARKETING COMMUNICATION   **332**

Advertising Reach.. 332
        Homeland Fashions Inc.
Advertising Frequency... 334
        The Southeastern Women Center Inc.
Advertising Gross Impression.. 336
        Don Dill Pottery Inc.
Advertising Rating Point.. 338
        Uptown Investors Inc.
        A Ride of Elegance Inc.
Maximum Advertising Cost.. 341
        Rolly's Coaches & Campers Inc.
Task and Objective Advertising Budget 343
        CTS Clinical Lab. Inc.
Recency/Frequency/Monetary Value Segmentation (1)............. 345
        Carol's Marketing & Fundraising Inc.
Recency/Frequency/Monetary Value Segmentation (2)............. 347
        Modern Furniture Inc.
Weighted Number of Exposures... 351
        Four Seasons Roofing and Siding Inc.

CHAPTER 19 MARKETING CHANNEL   **354**

Profitability of Indirect Channel Process..................................... 354
        Net Direct Inc.
Additional Inventory Cost.. 357
        Spiffy Looks Inc.
Average Inventory Investment.. 359
        Bob's Quality Autos. Inc.
Closing Inventory at Cost 361
        King's Groceries Inc.
Inventory cost... 363
        JJ Handy Homes Inc.
Inventory Carrying Cost 365
        Joe's Fine Shoes Inc.

Inventory costing - First in First out (FIFO) and Last in First out (LIFO).. 367
    Carl's Car Mart Inc.
Inventory Reorder Point 370
    A Tough Walk Inc.
Inventory Shortage or Overage...................................... 372
    Jack's Industrial Containers
Inventory Turnover.. 373
    High Roads Tires Inc.
Stock Turnover Rate 376
    Air Power Tech. Inc.
Reductions in Inventory Value 378
    Lovem Flowers & Baskets Inc.

CHAPTER 20 SALES   **381**
Size of Sales Force Model 381
    Derrick's Alarm Systems Inc.
Required Level of Sales (RLS).. 383
    Rolly's Upholstery Inc.
    Joe's Live Bait Inc.
    Pleasure Bookstore Inc.,
Sales Efficiency Ratio (%)... 393
    Yours True Exotic Cars Inc.
Sales Per Square Foot 395
    Earthly Foods Inc.
Gross-Margin Return Per Square Foot 398
    Lane Cargoes Inc.

PART ONE

MARKETING COST

Rowland Chidomere

CHAPTER 1
ACCOUNTING

Cash Budget

What is a cash budget?

It is a financial marketing tool that presents the expected cash receipt from sales and the disbursements in a period of time.

Why does a marketer need a cash budget?

1. It enables the marketer to better predict or estimate the expected sales in a time period.
2. It enables a marketer to determine how much money he/she needs to pay current bills.
3. A cash budget helps to spot a possible cash-flow problem and possible excess cash for investment on the product, pricing, promotion, and distribution.
4. It shows how much cash the company has at all times.

How does a marketer use cash budget?

Clayburn Florist Inc. (CFI), a flower wholesaler located in Blue Sky, MD was started on December 16, 1998 by Mr. Dick Clayburn, with $40,000 in inventory, and $55,000 in cash. Mr. Clayburn paid his bills promptly, and billed his customers on 30 days net (payment is due within 30 days of transaction).

Photo 1: Sledgefield Florist and Gifts

CFI made a profit of $15,000 at the end of January 1999. Mr. Clayburn was glad, and looked forward to a successful venture in 1999. At the middle of February 1999, Mr. Clayburn's accountant informed him that CFI was about to run out of cash. He was devastated. He could not imagine how such could be the case when CFI had just had a profit of $15,000. However, it happened that the customers owed CFI $47,000 from the January sales, and the company had used up the beginning cash of $55,000 to buy more inventories for an anticipated February sales of $71,000. The accountant advised Mr. Clayburn that one way to know if he would run out of money in the future is to prepare a cash budget for the rest of the year. The accountant assisted Mr. Clayburn to prepare a cash budget based on forecasted sales revenue and inventory. The first six months of the cash budget are shown on the next page.

Table 1-1
Clayburn Florist
Cash Budget (Jan-June 1999)[*]

	Jan.	Feb.	Mar.	Apr.	May.	June
Cash in						
Sales revenue	$47,000	$71,000	$90,000	$120,000	$150,000	$190,000
Cash Inflow from sales	0	$47,000	$71,000	$90,000	$120,000	$150,000
Collections of Acc Rec.	-	-	-	-	-	-
Others	-	-	-	-	-	-
Total Cash inflow	$0	$47,000	$71,000	$90,000	$120,000	$150,000
Cash out						
Cash for inventory	$55,000	$69,000	$80,000	$80,000	$100,000	$120,000
Salaries	-	-	-	-	-	-
Rent	-	-	-	-	-	-
Insurance	-	-	-	-	-	-
Capital Expenditure	-	-	-	-	-	-
Others	-	-	-	-	-	-
Cash gain or loss	($55,000)	($22,000)	($9,000)	$10,000	$20,000	$30,000
Beginning cash	$55,000	0	($22,000)	($31,000)	($21,000)	($1,000)
Ending cash	$ 0	($22,000)	($31,000)	($21,000)	($1,000)	$29,000

*MARKETMATICS includes a full year

Interpretation of the results

1. Due to the "30 days net" sales condition, the forecasted sales revenue for the last month becomes the cash inflow for the current month. Therefore, CFI had a cash-in of $47,000 in February from the January sales, and $71,000 in March from the February sales, and so on. CFI used the $55,000 beginning cash to buy inventory in January.

2. The firm bought an inventory of $69,000 in the month of February. Because CFI had a cash-in of only $47,000 in February, it had a negative balance of $22,000.

3. CFI had a cash-in of $71,000 in the month of February, and bought an inventory of $80, 000 in March. This left CFI with a loss of $9,000 in March. This amount was added to the outstanding loss of $22,000 to give a total ending cash balance of ($31,000), and so on.

4. In June, CFI realized a cash-in ending balance of $150,000 from sales, a cash outflow of $120,000 for inventory. And a first time positive balance of $29,000 was realized.

Implications of the results

1. CFI should charge lower prices in order to increase sales.
2. CFI should adjust or reduce selling expenses to increase profits and ending cash balance.
3. CFI should adjust customer credits to assure for a faster cash-in.

Calculation steps

1. Write the months that the budget will cover.
2. Find the first month's expected revenue by adding the expected sales and the outstanding credit.
3. Project the sales revenue for the first month.
4. Write down last month's sales as the cash inflow from sales for the present month.
5. Subtract the cash outflow for inventory for the month from the cash inflow to determine the cash gain or loss.
6. Subtract the cash gain or loss for the month from the beginning cash to determine the ending cash balance. *(Note: the ending cash for the previous month is the beginning cash for the following month).*

<u>*Income Statement (Profit and Loss)*</u>

What is an income statement?

It is a financial tool used by the marketer to determine how much income is available for marketing and other operations.

Why does a marketer need an income statement?

1. It summarizes the revenue generated by the marketer and the amount he/she spent to generate the revenue.
2. It shows the marketer how well he/she is doing in terms of profit and customer satisfaction.
3. It shows the marketer which marketing activities are generating the most revenue and profit.
4. It shows the marketer which marketing activities are the most expensive.
5. It guides the marketer to evaluate the success of the enterprise.

How does a marketer use an income statement?

On December 30, 1996, the Greenstown Sheet Metal Inc.'s owner Mrs. Hardrod was considering to expand her business to the northwest part of the state. The company deals in pre-engineered metal buildings, erection services, metal roofings, and wall panels. The northwest North Carolina had witnessed a rapid expansion of both residential and business occupants in the last four years. A successful retail expansion required at least $150,000. Mrs. Hardrod needed to know how much money to borrow from the bank to add to the annual profit to complete the expansion.

Photo 2: Southside Metals

The financial record for 1996 showed the following:

1. Gross sales of $393,671.79.
2. Returns and allowances of $16,300.
3. Cost of goods sold of $213,255.75.

4. Operating expenses of $118,088.
5. Profit on the rent of a parking lot of $740.47.
6. Bank interest of $3,377.48.
7. Corporate income tax 35%.

Table 1-2
Greenstown Sheet Metal
Income Statement

		Percentage
Gross Sales	$393,671.79	
(minus) Returns and Allowances	16,300	
Net Sales	$377,371.79	
(minus) Cost of Goods Sold	$213,255.75	100%
Gross Margin	$164,116.04	56.5%
(minus) Operating Expenses	$118,088.00	43.5%
Operating Profit	$46,028.04	31.3%
(plus) other income	$4,177.95	12.2%
Net Profit Before Taxes	$50,145.99	1.1%
Income Tax Expense (35% of Net Profit)	$17,551.09	13.3%
	$32,594.90	
Net Income		8.6%

Interpretation of the results

1. Greenstown Sheet Metal had a high cost of goods sold of 56.5% of sales.
2. The company had high operating expenses of 31.3% of sales.
3. The net profit before tax is low, ($50,145.99 or 13.3% of sales).
4. The net profit after tax is low, ($32,594.90 or 8.6% of sales).

Implications of the results

1. To successfully expand to the northwest, Greenstown Sheet Metal will seek a loan of $117,405.10 ($150,000-$32,594.90) from the bank.

2. The required loan amounts is 30% of its present sales or 360% of the present net income. The loan amount is too much for the company to incur.
3. Greenstown Sheet Metal should reduce the cost of goods sold and the operating expenses in order to produce a higher net income, and borrow less from the bank.

Calculation Steps

1. Determine the gross sales for the year.
2. Subtract returns and allowances from gross sales to find the net sales.
3. Subtract the cost of goods sold from the net sales to find the gross margin.
4. Subtract the operating expenses from the gross margin to find the operating profit.
5. Add other incomes to the operating income to find the net profit before taxes.
6. Multiply the net profit before taxes by the net income tax percentage to find the net income tax expense.
7. Subtract the net income tax expense from the net profit before taxes to find the net income or the "bottom line".
8. Find out the percentage makeup of each item in the net sales by dividing the item by the net sales and multiplying by 100.
9. Determine the amount of loan by subtracting the net profit from the required loan amount.

CHAPTER 2
BUDGETING

Cross Elasticity Budgeting

What is cross elasticity budgeting?

It is a technique used to forecast or project sales in units or dollars for one product or service by basing it on the demand estimate for a related major product or service. It measures how the demand for one product complements or substitutes another.

Why does a marketer need a cross elasticity budgeting?

1. It enables the marketer to effectively determine the product mix and assortments to carry by basing it on the success of related products.
2. It guides the marketer to choose the right promotion and pricing strategies for the right products.

How does a marketer use a cross elasticity budgeting?

Global Computers Inc. retails PCs, Laptops, software, printers, scanners, and accessories. Since the company's inception in 1980, Mr. Allover has noticed that attempts to increase the sales of one product line often led to increase or decrease in the sales for another product line. For example, because buyers often purchase PCs, scanners, and printers at the same time, whenever the sales of the PCs increased, the sales for printers and scanners also increased. However, an increase in the sales of PCs resulted in a decrease in the sales of the Laptops. According to Global Computers the following is the sales record for the past five years.

1. 10% of PC or Laptop buyers bought printer with them.
2. 30% of PC or Laptop buyers bought scanners with them.

3. 10% of potential PCs buyers bought Laptops whenever their preferred brands of PCs were out of stock.
4. The cost of a PC was $500 (VC=$324, FC=$176), and it sold for $1000.
5. The cost of a printer was $150 (VC=$48), and it sold for $350.
6. The cost of a scanner was $200 (VC=89), and it sold for $400.
7. The cost of a Laptop was $400 (VC=$145), and it sold for $900.
8. The unit sale in 2001 was 5000 (combination of PCs and Scanners).

Global Computers Inc. needed to know whether the company should invest the promotion money on the PCs or the Laptops, and it did the following.

Photo 3: COMPUSA

Table 2-1
Global Computers Inc.
2000 Sales Budget

	Unit Sales	Dollar Sales
PCs	5,000	$5,000,000
Total cost of PCs *(.50x 5,000,000)*		$2,500,000
Total Contribution (Total cost-Sales)		$2,500,000
a. Plus complementary effects		
Printer sales		
(5,000 x 10% x $350 x *PVCM or .86) =	500	$150,500
		($350x500x.86)
Scanners Sales		
(5,000 x 30% x $400 x PVCM or .78) =	1,500	$468,000
		($400x1,500x.78)
Total	**7,000**	**$3,118,500**
b. Minus substitution effects		
Laptops Sales		
(5,000 x 10% x $900 x PVCM or .84) =	500	$378,000
		($900x500x.84)
PCs	4,500	$3,060,000
		($1,000x4,500x .68)
Printer sales		
(4,500 x 10% x $350 x *PVCM or .86) =	450	$135,450
		($350x450x.86)
Scanners Sales		
(4,500 x 30% x $400 x PVCM or .78) =	1,350	$421,200
		($400x1,350x.78)
Total	**6,800**	**$3,994,650**

*PVCM = <u>unit price-variable cost</u>
            unit price

Interpretation of the results

1. Global Computers Inc. will make $3,118,500 if it sells only PCs, printers and scanners.
2. Global Computers Inc. will make $3,184,650 if it sells 500 Laptops in place of the same number of PCs. This is $66,150 more than if it sells only PCs, printers, and scanners.
3. The PVCM or Percentage variable contribution margin is the percentage of each additional sales dollar that will be available to help Global Computers cover its indirect costs and increase profit.

Implication of the results

1. More revenue ($66,150) is realized when more Laptops are sold in place of the PCs.

Calculation steps

1. Determine the PVCM by subtracting the variable cost from the unit price and dividing the sum by the unit price.
2. Determine the total contribution by subtracting the total cost from sales.
3. Determine the number of units of printers to be sold by multiplying the estimated PC units by the percentage of buyers of printers.
4. Determine the dollar sales for the printers by multiplying the estimated sales units by the sales price and the PVCM.
5. Determine the number of units of scanners to be sold by multiplying the estimated PC units by the percentage of buyers of scanners.
6. Determine the dollar sales for the scanners by multiplying the estimated sales units of scanners by the sales price and the PVCM.
7. Determine the number of units of Laptops sold by multiplying the estimated PC units by the percentage that buys the Laptops.
8. Determine the dollar sales for the Laptops by multiplying the estimated sales units by the sales price and the PVCM.

Marketing Budget-Direct Approach

What is a direct approach to marketing budget?

It is a technique that is used to estimate the productivity of a proposed price and marketing expenditure level in generating a company's sales by specifying the specific estimate of the sales.

Why does a marketer need a direct approach to marketing budget?

1. It guides the marketer to determine the appropriate price to charge on a product in order to reach the desired sales and profitability goals.
2. It guides a marketer to determine the marketing budget that maximizes the sales productivity.

How does a marketer use a direct approach to marketing budget?

Modern Interiors Inc. retails furniture and beds. The company is completing its tenth year of operation. The first seven years were very profitable. There was little or no competition. However, in the past two years, three ferocious competitors entered the market, and each had the intention of taking over the lead from Modern Interiors.

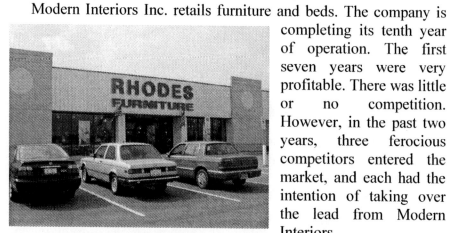

Photo 4: Rhodes Furniture

Currently, Modern Interiors has 50 percent of the Sofa-bed market share, its star product. The industry estimated a total sale of 500,000 units or $450,000,000 worth of Sofa/Beds combination in 2001. Each Sofa-Bed combination sells for $900. The unit variable cost is $150 per Sofa-Bed and the fixed cost (salaries, production etc) is $230. In order to maintain or exceed their current market share for the Sofa-Beds, Modern Interiors thought of increasing the advertising budget by 10%. However, it needed to know if the total contribution or the amount each product added to the profit will rise or fall if the advertisement budget is increased by $100,000 in 2001, so it did the following.

Table 2-2
Modern Interiors Inc.
Budget Without an Ad Increase

	Units	Dollars
Industry sales forecast for Sofa/beds =	500,000	$450,000,000
Company expected sales =	250,000	$225,000,000
(500,000 x .50 x $900)		
Variable Contribution Margin* (VCM) =	207,500	$186,750,000
(225,000,000 x .83 or PVCM (900-150/900)		
Total fixed cost = $ 57,500,000		
(250,000 x $230)		
Total direct, traceable, fixed costs		<u>$57,500,000</u>
Total Contribution		**$129,250,000**
(VCM minus TFC)		

Table 2-3
Modern Interiors Inc.
Budget With an Ad Increase

	Units	Dollars
Industry sales forecast for Sofa/beds =	500,000	$450,000,000
Company expected sales =	250,000	$225,000,000
(500,000 x .50 x $900)		
Variable Contribution Margin*	207,500	$186,750,000
(VCM)=		
(225,000,000 x .83 or PVCM (900-150/900)		

Total fixed cost(TFC) = $57,500,000
(250,000 x $230)

Advertising cost $10,250,000

Total direct, traceable, fixed costs	$67,750,000
Total Contribution	**$119,000,000**

(VCM minus TFC minus Ad cost)

Interpretation of the results

1. Sales to fifty percent of the market will give Modern Interiors a total contribution of $129,250,000, which includes the profit and any non traceable cost.

Implications of the results

1. Modern Interiors should evaluate the total contribution against the product objectives to know if it is adequate.
2. Modern Interiors could increase the total contribution amount by decreasing the variable and fixed costs.

Calculation steps

1. Find out the industry sales forecast (if possible).

2. Estimate the market share that will result from a given price and marketing expenditure(if no industry sales estimate exists, use the company's).
3. Calculate the expected company sales (market share x industry sales forecast x price per sofa- bed).
4. Calculate variable contribution margin VCM* (company sales x PVCM**).
5. Calculate total contribution (variable contribution margin minus direct and traceable fixed cost).
6. Determine whether the sales, market share, and total contribution levels meet sales objectives.

*Variable contribution margin VCM *is the sales minus variable cost of goods sold and other variable selling costs.*
**Percentage Variable Contribution Margin PVCM *(unit price-variable cost/unit price) is the percentage of each additional sales dollar that will be available to help Modern Interiors to cover its indirect costs and increase profit. In other words, how many cents are left in each dollar to cover indirect cost and profit, after paying the variable cost?*

Marketing Budget Indirect Approach

What is an indirect approach to marketing budget?

It is a technique that is used to estimate the productivity of a proposed price and marketing expenditure level in generating a company's sales by using a benchmark rather than a specific estimate of sales.

Why does a marketer need an indirect approach to marketing budget?

1. The indirect approach is used in the highest degree of uncertainty like new products.
2. It enables the marketer to find the minimum market share needed to meet the profitability objectives.

How does a marketer use an indirect approach to marketing budget?

Reliable Office Furniture Inc. wholesales desks, chairs, file cabinets, and accessories to schools, office buildings, and offices. In the past years, Reliable Office Furniture operated without a specific sales target because it was difficult for it to estimate the amount of sales that would result from a given price range or marketing budget. The company wanted its 2002 annual plan to show (1) the estimated total dollar sales for each product line, (2) the estimate of the acceptable total sales unit, and (3) the estimate of the acceptable market share for each product for the year.

Reliable Office Furniture needed to estimate the sales for the desks first, and therefore it used the following sales data from 2001:

1. Industry sales for desks in 2001 was 250,000 units.
2. Reliable Office Furniture sold 98,000 desks (39% of industry sales) in 2001 at a price of $325 per desk ($31,850,000).
3. The variable cost per desk was $45 ($4,410,000).
4. The variable contribution margin (VCM) was $27,440,000 ($31,850,000-$4,410,000).
5. The percentage-variable-contribution margin (PVCM) or the amount left in each dollar sale to cover the fixed costs and profit after paying the variable costs was 86 percent ($27,440,000/$31,850,000 or $325-$45/$325).
6. The total direct or traceable fixed cost for the desk is $7,448,000.
7. The current target total contribution is $9,992,000.
8. The industry sales forecast for desks in 2001 was 350,000 units.

Table 2-4
Reliable Office Furniture
Indirect Budgeting Approach

1. *Total dollar of sales acceptable*
   = (target total contribution) + (total direct or traceable fixed cost)
   PVCM

   Total dollar sales acceptable = $\dfrac{\$9,992,000 + 7,448,000}{.86}$

   $= \$20,279,069.77$

2. *Total unit sales acceptable*
   = (target total contribution) + (total direct or traceable fixed cost)
   PVCM per unit

   Total unit sales acceptable = $\dfrac{\$9,992,000 + 7,448,000}{\$279.5 (\$325 \times .86)}$

   $= 62,397$ units

3. *Acceptable market share* = $\dfrac{\text{Acceptable level of sales}}{\text{Industry sales forecast}}$

   Acceptable market share = $\dfrac{62397}{350,000 \text{ units}} \times 100 = 18\%$

Interpretation of the results

1. Total sales acceptable for the desks is $20,279,069.77.
2. Total unit sales acceptable for the desks is 38,345 units.
3. The acceptable market share for the desks is 11%.
4. At .31 PVCM, the total unit sales acceptable is 173,101, and the acceptable market share is 49.5%.

Implication of the results

1. Reliable Office Furniture should decide whether the estimates are suitable to its desired plan by comparing them with the specific objectives.

Calculation steps

1. Find out the industry sales for the year, and sales forecast for next year.
2. Establish the target level of contribution by the product for the year.
3. Calculate the dollar sales acceptable to achieve target total contribution at a given price and marketing cost of the product by adding the target total contribution to fixed cost, and divide by PVCM.
4. Determine the total unit sales acceptable by adding the target total contribution to fixed cost, and dividing by PVCM per unit or (price of desk x PVCM).
5. Determine the acceptable market share by dividing the acceptable level of sales by the industry sales forecast.

CHAPTER 3
COST

Cost Complement

What is a cost complement?

It is a financial marketing measure that shows how much of the retail price covers the merchandise cost.

Why does a marketer need to know the cost complement?

1. It is used to determine the costs of goods sold.
2. It shows how the cost value relates to the retail value.

How does a marketer find the cost complement?

Photo5: Southern States Co.

All Seasons Farm Supplies Inc. is a cooperative retail outlet that sells Wolverine work shoes and boots, seeds, fertilizers, and farm chemicals. The store had 300 bags of fertilizer for sale at the beginning of January 2000. It paid $10 for each bag of fertilizer,

and $80 to deliver them to the store, for a total cost of $3080. All Seasons Farm Supplies marked up each bag of fertilizer by 100% or plus $10 per bag, for a selling price of $20, and sold them in May and August for $6,000.

In September, All Seasons Farm Supplies bought another 100 bags of fertilizers for $10 per bag, and paid $35 to deliver them to the store, for a total cost of $1,035. It sold the fertilizers for $24 per bag, which was a markup of 140% and a total sale of $2,400. While preparing the end of the year records in December, All Seasons Farm Supplies needed to know the percentage of sales dollars that went to cover the cost of the fertilizer or the amount of cach retail sales dollar that is merchandise cost. It calculated it below.

Table 3-1
All Seasons Farm Supplies Inc.
Cost Complement

	Cost	Retail
Beginning inventory	$3000	$6000
Net Purchases	$1000	$2,000
Additional Markup	0	$ 400
Delivery	$ 115	0
Total inventory available for sale	**$4,115**	**$8,400**

Cost Complement = $\frac{\$4,115}{\$8,400}$ = .489 or 48.9cents of each dollar

Cost Complement = Total cost valuation/Total retail valuation

Interpretation of the results

1. Approximately 49 cents of every dollar that All Seasons Farm Supplies made from the sales of the fertilizers went to pay for the fertilizer.
2. The cost of the fertilizer is too high, and should be lowered.

Implications of results

1. About half of All Seasons Farm Supplies' revenue goes to cost. The company should put a higher mark-up on fertilizers.
2. All Season Farm Supplies should either find a low cost supplier, or increase the markup on the fertilizers.

Calculation steps

1. Record the amount of the beginning inventory under the cost column, and the retail under the retail column.
2. Record the cost of other purchases under cost, and the price they were sold under retail.
3. Record the additional markups or markdowns under the retail column.
4. Record shipping costs under the cost column.
5. Add #1 through #4 for cost and retail columns.
6. Divide the total cost by the total retail sales.

Cost of credit sales

What is the cost of credit sales?

It is a quantitative tool that is used to determine the cost of offering credit to customers.

Why does a marketer need to know the cost of credit sales?

1. To determine when it is profitable to reduce the price or to give customers credit.
2. To determine how price increases or decreases might affect the total sales.

How does a marketer find the cost of credit sales?

Star Locks Inc. is a high security locks, safes, padlocks, and master keys wholesaler located in Brazil, SD. Usually the company offers a 30-day credit to its retail customers. In 2000 Star Locks operated on a variable-contribution margin or VCM of 20 percent. Customers were given a 15% discount whenever they paid within 30 days. Star Locks anticipated a credit sales of $3m out of a total sales of $7million in 2001. It also assumed that all credit customers would pay their bills within 30 days every month or twelve times in a year. It wanted to know the cost of extending the credit to the customers in 2001, and it did as follows.

Table 3-2
Star Locks Inc.
Cost of Credit Sales

1. *Annual cost of credit*

   $= \dfrac{\text{Expected credit sales}}{\text{Annual rate of turnover}} \times$ Annual cost of credit (%)

   $= \dfrac{\$3 \text{ million}}{12 \text{ turnovers}} \times .15 = \$37,500$

Furthermore, Star Locks felt that it could generate additional sales of up to $1m in 2002 if it reduced the credit period to 20 days or eighteen times in a year. It needed to know the annual cost of such a credit.

2. *Annual cost of credit* $= \dfrac{\$4 \text{ million}}{18 \text{ turnovers}} \times .15 = \$33,333$

3. *Net effect of the change in the credit policy*
   = Increase in sales **x** Variable contribution margin – **Difference** between the costs of credit

   $= (\$1 \text{ million x } .20) - (\$37,500 - \$33,333)$
   $= \$200,000 - \$4,167$
   $= \$195,833$

24

Interpretation of the results

1. The Variable Contribution Margin is sales minus variable cost of goods sold and other variable selling costs.
2. Star Locks Inc. will lose $37,500 in 2001 from credit sales.
3. Star Locks Inc. decreased the cost of credit sales to $33,000 by changing the credit sales period from 30 days to 20 days.
4. The combined loss through credits in 2001 and 2002 is $70,833.

Implications of the results

1. Star Locks benefited from credit sales.
2. Although Star Locks Inc. may lose $70,833 in 2000 and 2001 if it offers credits, it will lose more than that amount from lost sales if it does not offer a credit.

Calculation steps

1. Set credit terms.
2. Determine the Variable Contribution Margin (VCM*).
3. Calculate the annual cost of credit by multiplying the expected credit sales by the percentage annual cost of credits, and dividing the sum by the rate of turnover.
4. To find the net effect of the change in the credit policy; (1) multiply the anticipated increase in sales by the VCM, (2) subtract the new annual cost of credit from the original annual cost of credit, (3) subtract 2 from 1.

*Variable contribution margin VCM *is the sales minus variable cost of goods sold and other variable selling costs.*
**Percentage Variable Contribution Margin PVCM *(unit price-variable cost/unit price) is the percentage of each additional sales dollar that will be available to help Star Locks Inc. to cover its indirect costs and increase profit. In other words, how many cents are left in each dollar to cover indirect cost and profit, after paying the variable cost?*

Cost of Forecast Errors

What is a cost of forecast error?

It is the amount of money a company will lose from making a wrong sales forecast.

Why does a marketer need to know the cost of forecast error?

1. It enables the marketer to develop a more accurate sales estimate.
2. It guides the marketer to a more accurate budget.

How does a marketer use the cost of forecast error?

Southland Flags and Poles Inc. is a manufacturer of US flags, state flags, national flags, church flags, message banners, pennants, and flag poles, located in Dakah, NC. In preparing its budget for 2001, the company needed to forecast or predict the number of each item to make. Based on its previous years' sales, Southland Flags and Poles predicted to make and sell 100,000 US flags at $15 per flag. They assumed that at a standard error of 5%, the company had a 95% chance of selling between 95,000 and 105,000 units of the US flags. In order to leave enough money to make the other items, the management decided to produce 95,000 US flags.

At the end of the year, the actual demand for the US flags from Southland was 98,000 or 3,000 units higher than the number the company produced. Therefore, Southland Flags and Poles wanted to know the amount of sales it lost by not making and selling up to 98,000 US flags. It did the following.

Table 3-3
Southern Flags and Poles
Cost of Forecast Errors

Cost of Forecast Error

Forecast Production Units	100,000
Standard error	- 5,000
Lower end of forecast	95,000
Actual demand	98,000
Forecast error	3,000
Cost of forecast error	**$45,000 (3000 x $15)**

Interpretation of results

1. Southland Flags and Poles lost $45,000 in sales due to inadequate inventory or not having an accurate forecast.

Implication of results

1. Southland should be better off making its production forecast. The 2,000 excess units that it would have had if it kept to its forecast would cost $30,000. The additional 3,000 units the company would have had if it made 100,000 flags would have been $45,000, which would be a profit of $15,000 ($45,000- $30,000).

Calculation steps

1. Forecast the number of units to produce.
2. Determine the low and high end of the production units based on how much standard of error you chose.
3. Determine the actual demand.
4. Multiply the shortfall or overage by the selling price.

Cost-of-Goods-Sold Ratio (%)

What is a cost-of-goods-sold ratio?

It is a financial tool that shows the portion of the net sales that covers the money used to make or buy the goods sold.

Why does a marketer need to know the cost-of-goods-sold ratio?

1. It guides to determine the right price for each product.
2. It indicates when and how the cost of the product affects profitability.

How does a marketer use the cost-of-goods-sold ratio?

Jimbus Xmas Shoppe Inc. is a specialty retailer that sells elegant Christmas trees, Christmas decorations, and ornaments at a local shopping mall. Mr. James Buris, the owner was concerned about the high lease cost at the mall. The lease took up a huge proportion of the earnings, and that hindered Jimbus' ability to invest in the business. In 2001, he was bent on increasing the store's profitability by reducing the operation costs in any way possible. He felt that a significant saving could come from reducing the cost of goods sold. In order to do this, he had to determine the cost of goods ratio or the percentage of net sales that went to the purchase of the goods or inventory in 2000. In 2000, Mr. Buris spent $390,000 to buy goods, and had a net sales of $970,000. The cost of goods ratio calculation is as follows.

Table 3-4
Jimbus Xmas Shoppe Inc.
Cost-of-Goods Sold Ratio

Cost-of-Goods-Sold Ratio (%)

$$= \frac{\text{Cost of goods sold}}{\text{Net Sales}} = \frac{\$390,000}{\$970,000} = 40\%$$

Interpretation of the results
1. Forty percent or 4 out of every 10 dollars of the store's sales is used to cover the cost of the goods.

Implications of the results
1. The ratio of the cost of goods sold to sales is high and must be reduced in order to increase profit.
2. The high cost ratio and the high lease cost leave little revenue for other expenses.
3. Mr. Buris may explore ways to significantly reduce the cost of the goods.
4. Mr. Buris may consider to significantly increase the price of goods sold.

Calculation steps
1. Determine the cost of goods sold in the purchase receipts.
2. Determine the net sales by adding sales and subtracting the cost of goods sold and other expenses.
3. Divide the cost of goods sold by the net sales, and multiply by one hundred to get the percentage.

Cost Per Thousand (CPM)

What is a cost per thousand?

It is how much it costs an advertisement to reach one thousand people.

Why does a marketer need to know the cost per thousand?

1. To determine the cost-benefit ratio of an advertisement vehicle or media.
2. To determine the appropriate advertisement cost for the sales budget.
3. To determine the advertisement media that could produce the greatest exposure of the company's message.

How does a marketer find out the cost per thousand?

Mrs. Sawyer saw the growing population of teenagers and young

adult males in Primetown, ND in the 1980s as an opportunity to start HomeBoy Fashions Inc., a trendy male clothing store that sold fashionable shirts, pants, sportswear,

Photo 6: Blumenthal's

jackets, and accessories. In 1993 Primetown had a population of two million people, and major corporations relocated into the city. The increased high income residents resulted in the high demand for good looking clothes. HomeBoy Fashions advertised in magazines every summer to introduce new lines of clothes. A four-color full-page ad in *Gents* costs $45,000, and the same ad costs $54,000 in *Golf- 4-You*. *Gents* magazine circulates to 3.8 million people, whereas *Golf -4-You* circulates to 6 million. In order to decide which magazine to advertise in, Mrs. Sawyer needed to know the cost to reach each thousand readers with each magazine, and with the television. She did the following.

Table 3-5
HomeBoy Fashions Inc.
Cost Per Thousand (CPM)

$$\textit{Cost Per Thousand (CPM)} = \frac{\text{Cost of Advertisement x } 1000}{\text{Number of Circulation}}$$

CPM (*Gents*) $= \frac{\$45,000 \text{ x } 1000}{3,800,000} = \$11.84$ per thousand

CPM (*Golf-4-You*) $= \frac{\$54,000 \text{ x } 1000}{6,000,000} = \$9.0$ per thousand

In addition, Mrs. Sawyer considered a 30 seconds spot commercial on 80/20 at a cost of \$450,000. This media reaches 60,000,000 people in Maryland and most of the neighboring states. The cost per thousand would be:

$$\text{CPM} = \frac{\$450,000 \text{ x } 1000}{60,000,000}$$

$450,000,000 \div 60,000,000 = \$7.50$ per thousand.

Interpretation of results

1. It costs .009c (\$9/1000) to reach a person using the *Golf Digest* and .012c (\$11.84/1000) by using the *Gents*.
2. Although the total expense is greater in *Golf-4-You,* the cost to reach each person is less.
3. It costs .0075c (\$7.50/1000) to reach a person by using the television advertisement.

Implication of the results

1. It costs less to reach a person using the television, but the exposure is not as long as that of magazines.

Calculation steps

1. Determine the cost of advertising in the alternative media in consideration.
2. Determine the total circulation of the alternative media.
3. Multiply the cost of advertising in each media by one thousand, and divide the result by the total circulation to get the cost of reaching one thousand.

Sales Cost/Ratio Analysis

What is a sales cost/ratio analysis?

It is a process that is used to determine the cost difference between using your own sales force and using a sales agency to sell your product or service.

Why does a marketer need to know the sales cost/ratio analysis?

1. To determine the cost effectiveness of building a company owned sales force.
2. To figure out the cost of sales force to include in the budget.

How does a marketer find out the sales cost/ratio analysis?

Pets Imports Inc. is an import wholesaler that buys rare and exotic birds and mammals from other countries and resell them to pet stores in the United States. Located in Pets' Town, Al., Pets' Import was started in 1979 by Mr. Jones. He started importing from South America and the Caribbean, and expanded to Africa,

Photo 7: COZY COUNTRY KENNELS

Asia, and Australia. In order to maintain a better control of the channel of distribution, Pets Imports used its own sales force to contact and sell to pet stores. In 1985, Pets Imports had resellers in most of the southern and southeastern United States.

In 2000, it had a gross sales of $20 million, at a cost of $5m to maintain the sales force. Mr. Jones contemplated on either using sales agencies or using his own sales force. The least cost sales agency charged 30 percent of sales to cover the territories. Mr. Jones wanted to know if utilizing an agency costs lower than using a company's sales force. Furthermore, Mr. Jones wanted to know at what sales level it costs the company more or less to use its sales force, and he did the following.

Table 3-6
Pets Imports Inc.
Sales Cost Ratio

1. *Pets' Imports Inc.'s sales force = $5m*
2. *Sales agency's sales force =   0.30 x company sales or $600,000*

Estimated sales levels	Cost of sales agency sales force
1. $15,000,000	$4,500,000
2. $16,000,000	$4,800,000
3. $17,000,000	$5,100,000
4. $18,000,000	$5,400,000
5. $19,000,000	$5,700,000
6. $20,000,000	$6,000,000

Interpretation of results.

1. At a sales volume of $20 million, it costs $6m ($1m more) to use a sales agency's sales force.
2. Pets Imports Inc. would have made about $17m in sales by paying $5m to a sales agency. Rather, it made $20m with the same amount, and a profit of $3m.

Implication of the results.

1. Pets Imports Inc. should use its own sales force at the current condition.

Calculation steps.

1. Estimate the gross sales.
2. Determine the cost of maintaining a Pets Imports' sales force.
3. Determine the cost of using a sales agency.
4. Determine the sales agency's fees by multiplying the gross sales by the agency's fees percentage.

Distribution Cost Analysis

What is a distribution cost analysis?

It is a process that is used to determine the amount of money spent to generate a given level of sale.

Why does a marketer need to know the distribution cost analysis?

1. To compare profitability in different sales levels, and decide on a method to improve it.
2. To identify possible alternatives in sales or distribution appeals or the budget.

How does a marketer find the distribution cost analysis?

Mr. Realman started Priority One Divers Supplies Inc. in Earth Land, SC in 1990 to wholesale diving equipment like wetsuits, regulators, tanks, snorkeling equipment, scubas, and instructions. With a sales force of five, Priority One called on sporting equipment retailers in North Carolina and South Carolina. For the distant states, the company used video advertising and telephones. For the customers outside the United States, Priority One made sales contact mostly through the Internet web sites. In all cases, the shipping cost is FOB plant.

The sales costs for Priority One under each distribution conditions are presented below, and Mr. Realman wanted to know how much each segment contributed to sales.

Table 3-7
Priority One Drivers' Supplies Inc.
Distribution Cost Analysis

	NC & SC (000)	Other States (000)	International (000)
Sales	$2,200	$1,500	$1,700
Labor	$300	$229	$220
Cost of Goods sold	$800	$550	$580
Var. Contri.	$1,100	$721	$900
Variable Selling Cost (VSC)			
1. **Shipping**	0	0	0
2. **Personal selling**	$300	0	0
3. **Videos and Phones**	0	$120	0
4 **Web site**	0	0	$94
5. Credit	$17	$12	$9
Total Contri. (TC)	$783	$589	$797
TC per $ sale	$.36	$.39	$.47
PVCM	50%	48%	52%

Interpretation of the results.

1. The international channel of distribution contributed the most to Priority One's profitability with a margin of 53% or 47 cent, followed by NC & SC.

Implications of the results.

1. Although not significant, the international channel of distribution was cheaper due to the lower cost of the Web site.
2. There is a great opportunity for Priority One to increase its Web site sales. At the present it is the second highest in sales, and it is expected to increase.
3. In order to reduce the credit costs, Priority One should require payments at the time of purchase on all the smaller orders.
4. Priority One could reduce the cost of personal selling in NC and SC by using alternative scheduling for the sales people.

Calculation steps.

1. Determine the total sales for each territory by adding all the sales.
2. Determine the variable contribution margin by subtracting the labor cost and the cost of goods sold from sales. (VCM=S-(CGS+L).
3. Determine the total contribution by subtracting variable selling cost, direct fixed cost, and traceable indirect costs from the variable contribution margin.
4. Calculate the total contribution per dollar sales by dividing the total contribution by sales.
5. Calculate the percentage variable contribution margin by dividing the variable contribution margin by sales.

Semi-fixed Cost (Step-variable cost)

What is a semi-fixed cost?

It is the cost that does not change automatically with an additional unit, but may change if substantial increase occurs in volume. For example, a new production plant, an additional air route, or hire a lot of supervisors in a season.

Why does a marketer need to know the semi-fixed cost?

1. It could determine when the semi-fixed forms of cost could hurt the business. For example, an international air route that is plagued with riots or a new production plant that is under utilized.

How does a marketer find the semi-fixed cost?

Children's Heaven Inc. is a day care business that was started in 1981 by Mr. Rayvins. The day care was started to take advantage of a growing population of young parents attracted to Twotuk City by the increased relocation of firms to the city. Already, Children's Heaven had three locations in the city,

Photo 8: Academy of Spoiled Children

and Mr. Rayvins was considering how to effectively compete as this market grew. Among his options was to expand the existing facilities and add one hundred extra children to their present capacity of 300, 450, and 520 respectively. However, he needed to know how this expansion will affect the average cost of each center in 2002.

Below are the various costs of the units in 2001 and the projection in 2002.

Table 3-8
Children's Heaven Inc.
Variable, Fixed, Direct, and Units costs of the Centers in 2001

	1 2001	*1 2002*	2 2001	*2 2002*	3 2001	*3 2002*
	300	*400*	450	*550*	520	*620*
Unit var. cost	$17.50	*$17.50*	$17.50	*$17.50*	$17.50	*$17.50*
Multi. by vol.	300	*400*	450	*550*	520	*620*
TVC	$5,250	*$7,000*	$7,875	*$9,625*	$9,100	*$10,850*

Total direct or traceable fixed/semifixed costs

	1 2001	*1 2002*	2 2001	*2 2002*	3 2001	*3 2002*
	$10,000	*$10,000*	$10,000	*$10,000*	$15,000	*$15,000*
Plus TVC	$5,250	*$7,000*	$7,875	*$9,625*	$9,100	*10,850*
Total cost	$15,250	*$17,000*	$17,875	*$19,625*	$24,100	*$25,850*
Divide by vol.	300	*400*	450	*550*	520	*650*
Av. Unit cost	$50.83	*$42.50*	$39.72	*$35.68*	$46.35	*$41.69*

Interpretation of the results.

1. The total variable costs, the total semi-fixed costs, and the total direct cost increased as the number of children increased.
2. An additional one hundred children to each center was enough to change the average unit cost to $42.50, $35.68, and $41.69 respectively.

Implication of the results.

1. Children's Heaven should go ahead with the expansion because the unit cost declined as the number of children in a center increased.

Calculation steps.

1. Calculate the unit variable cost (Total # of children/Total variable cost).
2. Determine the total direct or traceable cost.
3. Divide the total direct cost by sales volume to get the average unit cost.
4. Increase the number of children, and repeat step one through step three.
5. Compare the existing average unit cost on number three with the new average cost on number four.

Fixed cost per unit

What is a fixed cost per unit?

It is the cost that remains the same regardless of the volume of business, for example, salaries and electricity bills.

Why does a marketer need to know the fixed cost per unit?

1. To identify the portion of the costs that changes with volume, and the portion that does not.

How does a marketer find out the fixed cost per unit?

Classic Windows Inc. produces and wholesales custom bay windows, box windows, and casements for pictures and trophies. The windows are sold to retailers all over the world. In 1998, it sold 4million bay windows, 5.1million box windows, and 2.9million casements (a total of 12 million units). The company's largest production plant is located in Forward, CA. At this plant, Classic Windows has a huge research and development center that includes a computer graphics section. Experts from the marketing, finance, production, computer, and management departments meet to decide on the graphics. The company uses video and brochure advertising and a fleet of 60 sales force, to inform resellers of its products and services.

As the company grew, the company wanted to know a way to increase the profit margin without raising prices very high or cut the fixed marketing supports. Classic Windows needed to know the amount of the fixed cost attributed to each unit of its products. Below is the financial data from 1999.

Table 3-9
Classic Windows Inc.
Fixed Cost Per Unit

Sales		$99,000,000
Variable cost of goods sold		40,000,000
Other variable costs		5,000,000
Variable Contribution Margin(VCM)		$54,000,000
Fixed costs:		
Sales Salaries	$14,000,000	
Computer Graphics	$ 5,000,000	
Advertising	$10,000,000	
Gen. & Admin overhead	$ 4,000,000	
Total fixed cost		$33,000,000
Net operating profit		$21,000,000

Fixed cost per unit (12m units/$33,000,000) $2.75
Variable cost per unit = $3.75

Interpretation of the results.

1. The fixed cost is indirect fixed cost because it applies to the whole business.
2. The fixed cost per unit is smaller than the variable cost per unit.
3. Fixed cost is the Total Fixed Cost/Units.
4. Variable cost is the Unit sold/Total Variable Cost.

Implications of the results.

1. Classic Windows should consider lowering both the variable and fixed costs.
2. Classic Windows should hold the variable cost down while increasing the total units sold.
3. Classic Windows should find out the direct fix cost for each product line by separating the fixed cost according to product lines, and dividing it by the number of units in each product line.

Calculation steps.

1. Determine the total sales.
2. Subtract variable costs from sales to get the variable cost margin (VCM).
3. Subtract the total fixed cost from VCM to get the net operating margin.
4. Divide the total fixed cost by the total units to get the fixed cost per unit.
5. Divide the total variable cost by the total units to get the variable cost per unit.

Opportunity Cost (Optimal Marketing Mix)

What is an opportunity cost?

It is the foregone revenue from not using an optimal marketing mix or a combination of the marketing mix that maximizes profit.

Why does a marketer need to know the opportunity cost?

1. To measure the revenues a business will forgo or miss by not using a particular type of marketing strategy.

2. To guide the business to choose the most profitable strategic option or the best marketing mix.

How does a marketer find out the opportunity cost?

Simply Unbeatable Inc. is a retailer of mobile pagers, RCS mobiles, and 2-way radios located in a downtown Chicago shopping center. Simply Unbeatable was considering the best marketing strategy to use in the 2002 budget to maximize profit. The company considered using a mass marketing (MA) approach in which case it sells to everyone, or a selective marketing (SM) strategy in which it sells to a selected target market, or an exclusive marketing (EM) whereby it sells to one class of customers only. Simply Unbeatable wanted to know how much profit the company will forgo by choosing either strategy. It did the following;

Table 3-10
Simply Unbeatable Inc.
Opportunity Cost (Optimal Marketing Mix)

Alternative Marketing Mixes:

	Sales Unit Price (SP)	Sales (US)	Sales Rev (SR)	Total Prod Costs (TPC)	Adver-tising Costs (AC)	Pers. Selling Costs (PSC)	Distri-bution Costs (DC)	Total Costs (TC)	Profit (P)
MA	$5	20,000	$100,000	$40,000	$30,000	$6,000	$6,000	$82,000	$18,000

	TPC/US	AC/US	PSC/US	DC/US	TC	P/US
Unit cost/profit	$2	$1.5	.30c	.30c	$4.10	$.90

	Sales Unit Price	Sales	Sales Rev	Total Prod Costs	Adver-tising	Pers. Selling	Distri-bution	Total Costs	Profit
SM	$10	10,000	$100,000	$40,000	$3,000	$30,000	$3,000	$76,000	$24,000

	TPC/US	AC/US	PSC/US	DC/US	TC	P/US
Unit cost/profit	$4	.30c	$3	.30c	$7.6	$2.4

EM $20   5,000 $100,000 $40,000 $1,500 $30,000 $1,500 $73,000
$27,000

	TPC/US	AC/US	PSC/US	DC/US	TC	P/US
Unit cost/profit	*$8*	*.30*	*$6*	*.30*	*$14.6*	*$5.4*

Interpretation of the results.

1. The exclusive marketing approach resulted in the most profit.
2. The company will forgo a maximum of $9,000 if it uses the mass marketing.
3. The company will forgo $3,000 if it chooses to use the selective marketing.

Implication of the results.

1. Despite the high cost of production, the very high price of the exclusive products resulted to higher profit margins.

Calculation steps.

1. Add all the costs, and subtract the total cost from the total sales to determine the profit.
2. To determine the unit product cost, divide the total product cost by the unit sales.
3. To determine the unit advertising cost, divide the total advertising cost by the unit sales.
4. To determine the unit personal selling cost, divide the personal cost by the unit sales.
5. To determine the unit distribution cost, divide the distribution cost by the unit sales.
6. To determine the unit profit, divide the total profit by the unit sales.

Marketing Operating Expense Ratio (%)

What is a marketing operating expense ratio?

It is the percentage of each sales dollar that is used to pay for marketing operations.

Why does a marketer need to know the marketing operating expense ratio?

1. To know when the company is spending too much money on marketing activities.

How does a marketer find out the marketing operating expense ratio?

Ideal Rent & Own Inc. is a rental store that is located on the south side of Cincinnati, OH. It rents televisions, stereos, speakers, and household appliances to individuals and businesses. It had a net sales of $930,000 in 1999. The operating expense was $480,000. This

included 257,000 for wages; $123, 000 for promotion; $45,000 for delivery; $25,000 for security; $6,000 for replacement and warranty; and $24,000 for rent. Ideal Rent & Own needed to know the ratio of marketing costs in the operation

Photo 9: RAC Rent-A-Car

expense, and it calculated the operating ratio and the marketing expenses as follows.

Table 3-11
Ideal Rent & Own Inc.
Marketing Operating Expense Ratio

Marketing Expenses:
$$= \text{promotion} + \text{delivery} + \text{replacement and warranty}$$

$$\$123,000 + \$45,000 + \$6,000 = \$174,000$$

Marketing Operating Expense Ratio:
$$= \frac{\text{Operating expenses}}{\text{Net sales}} = \frac{\$174,000}{\$930,000} = 19\%$$

Interpretation of the results.

1. Ideal Rental is not spending too much money on marketing.
2. Marketing expenses make up 19% of sales or 19cents of each sales dollar. This is good.
3. Marketing expense consists of 36% of all the expenses ($174,000/$480,000).

Implications of the results.

1. Ideal Rental may consider increasing the marketing expenses in order to increase sales.
2. Ideal Rental should take advantage of the high marketing yield and plan the marketing mixes to maximize profit.

Calculation steps.

1. Itemize the operating expenses.
2. Determine net sales.
3. Divide net sales by the marketing related expenses to determine the marketing operating expense ratio.

CHAPTER 4

CREDIT SALES

Cash discount

What is a cash discount?

It is the reduction in price of an item to a buyer for paying for the product or service in time.

Why does a marketer have to know cash discount?

1. It is used to entice customers to pay their bills quicker.
2. It shows how the price allowance increases total sales.
3. Customers use it to take advantage of the allowance.

How does a marketer give a cash discount?

Meats "R" Us Inc. wholesales ribs, ham, turkey and chicken to

institutions and caterers. Meats "R" Us has a policy of offering cash discount as a selling strategy to increase sales, facilitate payment, and to maintain its huge loyal customers. In the month of January, the company had an invoice of $500,000 at the term of

Photo 10: ANN'S TRIAD MEATS

46

3/10/30, which means that buyers will get 3% off the price if they pay the bill within the first ten days. All the customers paid within the first ten days. The company was excited and wanted to continue the policy. However, Meats "R" Us needed to know the cost of the discount to the company. Therefore, it did the following.

Table 4-1
Meats "R" Us Inc.
Cash Discount

Cash discount = sales x % discount

$$= \$500,000 \times \frac{3}{100} = \$15,000$$

Interpretation of the results.

1. Meats "R" Us lost $15,000 in the month of January by offering a 10% discount.
2. Meats "R" Us will receive $485,000 from sales rather than $500,000.

Implication of the results.

1. Meats "R" Us might consider reducing the cash discount percentage periodically so that it does not lose a lot of cash through early payment.

Calculation steps.

1. Set the percentage discount, the discount period, and the payment deadline.
2. Determine the sales amount.
3. Multiply the sales amount by the discount rate to determine the cash discount.

Credit Impact on Profitability

What is a credit impact on profitability?

It is the effect of credit or delayed payment on the amount of profit a business would make.

Why does a marketer need to know the credit impact on profitability?

1. To determine how credit extension could affect the business profitability.

How does a marketer find out the credit impact on profitability?

Allied Facsimile Equipment Inc. is a manufacturer of high speed fax machines, plain paper fax machines, ink jet fax machines, and laser systems. The company had sales of $150,000,000 in 1999. It billed customers on the basis of 15/10/30. All the customers took advantage of the credit and paid in time, leaving an annual cost of credit of 15%.

Photo 11: Carolina Office Machines Inc.

The total contribution margin was 50% of sales. The marketing plan for the year 2000 called for the credit period to be extended to 60 days. Management believed that all the customers would take advantage of the full 60 days to pay the invoices, and sales were predicted to increase to $285 million. The company wanted to know how the credit extension to 60 days could affect the profitability, and it did the following.

Table 4-2
Allied Facsimile Equipment Inc.
Credit Impact on Profitability

(a) 15/10/30

$$\frac{\$150,000,000}{360/30\text{days or (12 turnovers)}} = \$12,500,000(\text{monthly sales}) \times .15 = \frac{\$1,875,000}{\text{monthly cost}}$$

Profit = $150,000,000 x .50 -$1,875,000 = $73,125,000

(b) 15/10/60

$$\frac{\$285,000,000}{(360/60\text{days}) \text{ or (6turnovers)}} = \$47,500,000(\text{bimonthly sales}) \times .15 = \frac{\$7,125,000}{\text{bimonthly cost}}$$

Profit = $285,000,000 x .50 -$7,125,000 = $135,375,000

(c) Net increase in credit sales
= ((b/2) - a) or $3, 562,500 - $1,875,000 = $1,687,500

(d) Increase in $ contribution
=$285,000,000 – $150,000,000) x .50 = $67,500,000

Profit Difference = $135,375,000-$73,125,000 = $62,250,000

Interpretation of the results.

1. Allied Facsimile Equipment lost $1,875,000 in credit cost on 15/10/30.
2. Allied Facsimile Equipment will lose $7,125,000 in credit cost on 15/10/60.
3. Allied Facsimile Equipment will have an increase of $62,250,000 in profit with a 60-day payment period.

Implication of the results.

1. Allied Facsimile Equipment increased sales by offering a longer payment period, and the increase resulted in a higher profit.

Calculation steps.

1. Determine the annual cost of credit for the current year by dividing sales by the credit turnover rate.
2. Determine the annual cost of sales for the future period by dividing the projected sales by the new credit turnover rate.
3. Subtract the projected credit sales from the present credit sales to find the change in the credit.
4. Determine the change in sales by subtracting future sales from the present sales.
5. Multiply the result in #4 by the total contribution percentage.
6. Subtract the result in #3 from the result in #5 to find the proposed increase or decrease in profit.

Profit Impact of Quantity Discount

What is the profit impact of quantity discount?

It is how profit is affected by a reduction in the cost of items based on the size of the order.

Why does a marketer need to know the profit impact of quantity discount?

1. It helps to understand how extending quantity discount could reduce a company's profit.
2. It helps to understand how a quantity discount could be used to increase sales and profit.

How does a marketer find out the profit impact of quantity discount?

Genuine Wears Inc. makes and sells medical uniforms to several hospitals in and around Greensboro, NC. A surgical gown sells at a regular price of $100. The largest buyer, Longlife Hospital, orders 32,400 units per year in monthly orders of 2,700 units. The annual sales-contact and order processing costs per order is $800, and the inventory carrying cost is 22 percent. The unit-variable production cost is $35. Mrs. Rears, the president of Genuine Wears, thought that if she offered the quantity discounts she termed "Double Order" whereby buyers double their orders and ordered six times in a year at the price of $95 per surgical gown, Longlife Hospital would take advantage of the discount and order more gowns six times in a year. So Mrs. Rears wanted to know how this would impact the company's profitability. She did the following.

Table 4-3
Genuine Wears Inc
Profit Impact of Quantity Discount

	REGULAR PRICE	**QUANTITY DISCOUNT**
a. Price per unit	$100	$95
b. Variable cost per unit	$35	$35
c. VCM per unit	$65 (a-b)	$60
d. Sales volume	32,400	32,400
e. $ Contribution margin	$2,106,000(c x d)	$1,944,000
f. Order Processing Cost	$800	$800
g. Number of order times	12	6
h. Total order cost	$9,600 (f x g)	$4,800
Reduction in Margin	$2,106,000 - $1,944,000 = $162,000	
Savings in order cost	$9,600 -	$4,800 = $4,800
Net profit impact		(-$157,200)

Interpretation of the results.

1. The reduction in order price by $5 amounted to a $157,200 reduction in profit due to a lower VCM.
3. The savings on order cost was not much.
4. Genuine Wears Inc. lost $157,200 with the quantity discount.
5. The savings from the reduced order frequency is not enough to cover the reduction in margin.

Implications of the results.

1. In order to break even at $60 and six orders per year, Genuine Wears has to increase the discount sales volume by 2,620 units per order.
2. The resulting dollar contribution margin of $2,110,800 subtracted from the regular margin of $2,106,000 is $4,800.
3. Any further increase in the discount sales beyond 35,180 units (32,400 + 2,780) should result in a profit.

Calculation steps.

1. Set the regular and discount prices per unit.
2. Subtract the variable cost per unit from the price per unit to find the variable contribution margin (VCM) for both regular and discount prices.
3. Multiply the VCM by the sales volume to find the dollar contribution margin for both regular and discount prices.
4. Multiply the order cost by the frequency of orders per year to find the total order costs for both regular and discount prices.
5. Subtract the dollar contribution margin for the regular price from that of the discount prices.
6. Subtract the savings in cost for the regular price from that of the discount prices.
7. Subtract #5 from #6 to find the net profit.

Trade Discount

What is a trade discount?

It is a reduction in the supplier's list price granted to either a wholesaler or retailer who performs functions such as storage, transportation and others that are normally the responsibility of the supplier.

Why does a marketer need to know of trade discount?

1. It helps one to know when and how to respond and benefit from a trade discount.
2. To establish cost effective spending and operations by performing the necessary functions as needed.

How does a marketer find the amount of the trade discount?

Suki Soki Orthopedic Inc. is a manufacturer of prosthetic equipment. It was started in 1981 to produce and distribute technologically advanced artificial limbs and orthopedic braces. Traditionally, Suki Soki had included storing and transporting as part of the wholesalers' fees, and gave them a 15% discount. However, in December 1999, the company began to charge a 5cents functional fees per dollar sales. A group of wholesalers petitioned Suki Soki, threatening to boycott its products unless it eliminated the functional fees from their accounts. Suki Soki decided to bypass these wholesalers and offered the retailers a

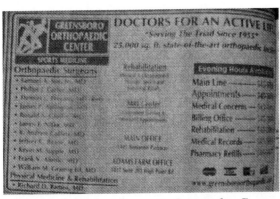

Photo 12: Greensboro Orthopaedic Center

trade discount of 20 percent if they buy directly from the company and perform the functions of promotion, storage, transportation, and financing. Suki Soki estimated to sell $70 million worth of goods in 2001 if they sell through the wholesalers, or $80 million if they sell directly to the retailers. The company was interested to know how much it would gain in either case, and it did the following.

Table 4-4
Suki Soki Orthopedic Inc.
Trade Discount

(a) Selling Through Wholesalers:

1. Estimated sales in 2001	$70,000,000
2. Functional Fees (5c per $)	$3,500,000
3. Sales and Fees (1+2)	$73,500,000
4. Trade discount ($70m x .15)	$10,500,000
5. Total Receipt (3-4)	$63,000,000

(b) Selling Directly to Retailers

1. Estimated Sales in 2001	$80,000,000
2. Trade discount ($80m x .20)	20% or $16,000,000
3. Total Receipt (1-2)	$64,000,000

Interpretation of results.

1. Suki Soki will have an increase of $1,000,000 in the total receipt by selling directly to the retailers.

Implication of results.

1. The trade discount is high in both cases. However, Suki Soki should deal directly with retailers as it is higher in receipts.

Calculation steps.

1. Estimate the annual sales.
2. Determine the percentage of trade discount.
3. Multiply the estimated sales by the percentage of trade discount.
4. Subtract discount from sales to find what the company received.

Rowland Chidomere

PART TWO

CONSUMER BEHAVIOR

Rowland Chidomere

CHAPTER 5

CUSTOMER SATISFACTION

Required Increase in Customers Satisfaction

What is customer satisfaction?

It is a state where the buying and using of the product or service meet or exceed users' expectations.

Why should a marketer know how to satisfy the customer?

1. It is necessary to retain current customers.
2. It helps to attract new customers and to increase sales.

How does a marketer know the required increase in the number of satisfied customers?

Web "R" Us Inc. does web site designs and development, Internet marketing, online catalog and store development for both residential and commercial customers. Most of the 75,000 new customers complained of the poor quality of the work and the lateness of the company in responding to technical problems. Web "R" Us observed that only 30 percent of the customers are satisfied and repeated patronage

Photo 13: WebBuilder

at least three times during a four-week period. The company figured that each sale to a customer contributes $150 to the variable contribution margin (VCM). In order to increase the number of customer patronage, Web "R" Us committed $680,000 to train the personnel, and to expand the technical services to 24 hours and seven days a week. Web "R" Us wants to know the number of satisfied customers required to get the additional funds for training, and still maintain the current level of total contribution. It used the following method.

Table 5-1
Web "R" Us Inc.
Required Increase in Customers' Satisfaction

Required increase in number of satisfied customers $=$ $\dfrac{\text{increase in direct fixed cost for customer service}}{\text{percent of satisfied} \times \text{average \#} \times \text{VCM per unit}}$ customers who repeat of repeat visits

$$= \frac{\$680,000}{.30 \times 3 \times 150} = 5{,}037 \text{ customers}$$

Web "R" Us had 34,500 satisfied customers (75,000/30%), therefore, the total number of customers required with the plan is 27,537 or 75,000 x .30 +5,037 or 22,500 + 5,037

Required % of satisfied $= \dfrac{27{,}537}{75{,}000} = 36.72\%$ satisfied and repeat
Customers   customers

Interpretation of the results.

1. Web "R" Us should increase the number of satisfied customers by 5,037 in order to cover the cost of the training.
2. The total number of customers required to support the increased cost of training is 27,537.

3. The increased training will increase the percentage of the first-time customers that are satisfied from 30% to 36.72%.

Implications of the results

1. The training cost or the direct fixed cost is extremely high, and the present level of satisfied customers is too low to offset it. Web "R" Us should reduce the training cost.
2. In addition to increasing the first-time buyers, Web "R" Us should increase the rate of repeat purchases by the existing customers.
3. Web "R" Us should pursue the proposed service training because that will increase the percentage of first-time buyers to 36.72%.

Calculation steps.

1. Determine the required increase in the number of satisfied customers by dividing the fixed cost by the number of satisfied repeat customers, the average repeat visits, and the VCM.
2. Determine the number of satisfied customers by multiplying 75,000 by 30%.
3. Determine the required percentage of satisfied first time customers by dividing the total number of customers required with the new plan by the total of new customers.
4. Find the total number of satisfied customers required for the plan to succeed by adding the existing satisfied customers to the required increase in the satisfied customers.

Profit Impact of Customer Satisfaction

What is the profit impact of customer satisfaction?

It is the relationship between an increase in the type and amount of customer service and the change in profit.

Why does a marketer have to know the profit impact of customer satisfaction?

1. It helps to determine if the right decision is made in future customer service efforts.
2. It helps to know how much to spend on customer service.

How does a marketer know the profit impact of customer satisfaction?

Unique Web Works Inc. started in May 1995. The company designs and develops web sites, and offers online marketing supports to businesses. In December 2000, Unique Web Works surveyed its customers to measure the level of their satisfaction with the company's offerings and services. The research showed that sixty-five percent of the 100,000 existing customers were first-time buyers. Forty-five percent of the first-time buyers were satisfied. Based on customer tracking, Unique Web Works sensed that thirty three percent of the satisfied customers will return on an average of three times in a month. The variable contribution margin (VCM) per customer is $500. Unique Web Works believed that spending $1.4 million to improve equipment and technical service would result in an increase in the number of satisfied first-time customers by 10 percent in 2001. The company wanted to know how much impact this increase in first-time customers will have on future profit, and it did the following.

Table 5-2
Unique Web Works Inc.
Profit Impact of Customer Satisfaction

	2000 Actual	2001 Target
1. Total buyers.	100,000	110,000
2. Multiplied. by % of 1st time buyers	x 65%	x 65%
3. Total #of new buyers.	65,000	71,500
4. Multplied by % of satisfied buyers.	x 45%	x 55% (45% +10%)
5. Total satisfied new buyers (account).	29,250	39,325
6. Multiplied by probability of repeat purchase.	x 33%	x 33%
7. Expected number of repeaters	9,652.5	12,977
8. Multiplied by the average number of repeat visits	x 3	x 3
9. Total number of visits.	28,957.5	38,931
10. Multiplied by the unit contribution margin($500)	$14,478,750	$19,465,500
11. Expected increased contribution from improved customer satisfaction ($19,456,500 -$14,478,750).		$4,986,750
12. Expenses to improve equipment and services.		$1,400,000
13. Net gain in contribution (10-11).		$3,586,750

Interpretation of the results.

1. Unique Web Works should generate $3,586,750 in future contribution to profit if it improves the percentage of satisfied first-time customers by 10% from 45 to 55 percent.

Implication of the results.

1. It is profitable for Unique Web Works to invest the $1.4m in equipment and technical service improvement.

Calculation steps.

1. Determine the total number of buyers from the sales records.
2. Multiply #1 on the table by the percent of first time buyers to find the total number of new buyers.
3. Multiply #3 by the percent of satisfied buyers to find the total number of satisfied new buyers (accounts).
4. Multiply #5 by the probability of repeat purchase to find the expected number of repeaters.
5. Multiply #7 by the average number of repeat visits and the unit contribution margin to find the increase in the contribution from repeat purchases by first-time customers.
6. Subtract the actual increase in the contribution from repeat purchases by first-time customers from the resulting future increase, to find the expected increased contribution from improved customer satisfaction.
7. To find the net gain in contributions, subtract the expenses to improve the equipment and service from the expected increased contribution by the improved customer satisfaction.

CHAPTER 6

CONSUMER ATTITUDE

Attitude-Toward a Product

What is an attitude-toward a product?

It is a measure of how a customer or a person feels toward the use of a product or a service line, and the specific brands.

Why does a marketer need to know the buyers' attitude toward the product or service?

1. It shows whether the buyers or users have favorable or unfavorable attitude or feelings towards certain brands, attributes, or features of a product or service.

How does a marketer know buyers' attitude toward the product?

UP Tiles Company Inc. is a retailer that sells tiles for kitchens, baths, countertops and sunrooms to homeowners in the city of Pointe the Great, Arkansas. Because buyers' liking for the tiles color varied greatly in the city, UP Tiles found it profitable to carry as many assorted color of tiles as it could. This attracted a lot of customers, and enabled the store to charge premium prices for the most attractive color combinations. However, because it costs more to merchandise an assorted color of tiles, the more colors UP Tiles added, the more it costs to operate. In its fourth year, UP Tiles was advised to streamline the color assortments in order to reduce the cost and maximize the profit.

As the marketing survey showed, the choice of tiles in the city of Pointe the Great was greatly influenced by the colors. Therefore, UP Tiles decided that any color elimination must be done carefully in order to minimize customer dissatisfaction. The company needed to know the customers' attitude towards each of the tile colors in the store. It conducted another survey to find out the evaluative and belief components that the buyers use to decide the color of tiles they buy. One hundred customers and potential tile buyers were asked to rate different sets of colors on a Likert scale, with 5 for mostly agree, 4 for somewhat agree, 3 for do not agree, 2 for somewhat disagree, and 1 for mostly disagree. Table 6-1 shows a sample of a completed questionnaire, and Table 6-2 shows the analysis.

Table 6-1
UP Tiles Company Inc.
A Questionnaire To Measure Attitude Toward Tile Colors

	Brand A (Black) (Blue/red)	Brand B, (White)	Brand C, (Beige)	Brand D

Evaluative component

Attitude

	Brand A	Brand B	Brand C	Brand D
1. Tiles look pretty in this color.	5	3	1	4
2. Tiles are meant to be in this color.	4	5	3	2
3. This color shines on tiles even when it fades	3	4	2	5
4. This color fits most home.	5	3	2	1
Beliefs				
1. This color is well liked in my culture	5	5	4	2
2. The color makes me lively.	5	3	1	4
3. This color hides dirt.	3	5	4	2
4. This color gives me a good luck or omen.	4	5	3	2

$$\text{Attitude(o)} = \overset{n}{\underset{i=1}{E}} \text{ biei}$$

E = the sum of bi and ei
bi = the strength of the belief that the attitude object contents
ei = the evaluative dimension associated with the object

Table 6-2
UP Tiles Company Inc.
The Hypothetical Findings of Belief and Component Analysis for the 100 respondents on four color attributes.
Beliefs(bi)

Attributes	Evaluation(ei)	Brand A,		Brand B,		Brand C,		Brand D	
	ei	bi	be	bi	be	bi	be	bi	be
1. Color beauty	5	3	15	4	20	3	15	2	10
2. Color preference	3	5	15	2	6	3	9	4	12
3. Color favor	2	5	10	2	8	2	4	2	4
4. Color impact to life	4	5	20	4	16	1	4	2	8
Overall assessment			60		50		32		34

Interpretation of results.

1. Evaluation(ei) is the average response on the evaluative components by the 100 respondents.
2. Belief(bi) is the average response on the belief components by the 100 respondents.
3. "be" is the belief multiplied by the evaluative component.
4. The higher the score, the more positive the color.
5. Brands A and B or colors black and brown received the best scores of 60 and 50 respectively. Brand A is the most preferred color.
6. Two color attributes namely; the beauty of the color and the positive impacts of the color on life, are the most important factors that determined the customers' color choice for UP Tiles.

Implications of the results.

1. UP Tiles should keep brands A and B, and discontinue brands C and D.

2. UP Tiles should create marketing strategies to takes advantage of the black and brown tiles.

Calculation steps

1. Identify the major attributes of the product brand.
2. Measure the strength of customers' evaluative and belief components or attributes on each brand's color.
3. Add up the response for each question for all the 100 respondents.
4. Calculate the evaluative(ei) by dividing the total for each question in the evaluative component by 100 or the number of respondents.
5. Calculate the belief (b) by dividing the total for each question in the belief component by 100.
6. Calculate the belief and evaluative component (be) by multiplying #4 by #5.

Attitude-Toward-Behavior

What is an attitude-toward-behavior?

It is a marketing technique that shows how a person feels toward an action or behavior of an object rather than a person's feeling towards the object itself. For example, "I know that the tiles look good in black, but I do not agree with the store manager that that is the best color for my kitchen" or "How do you feel about the nonrefundable flight ticket policy by airlines?" or "I suspect those customers that wear long coats in this store" or "I like those town homes, but it is ridiculous to pay $950 a month to own one of them".

Why does a marketer need to know an attitude-toward-behavior?

1. It is used to formulate the appropriate pricing, promotion, and distribution strategies. A friend may ask "By the way, I know that you enjoy your Sports Utility Vehicle, but how do you like the high monthly payment?", or one might say "I like

Product X, but I don't like it that much to go all the way over there to buy it", or one might say "I like those apartments, but the rent is way out of my reach".

2. To find out how much the buyers like the product and how many have the intention to buy the products.

How does a marketer know the attitude-toward-behavior?

Quality Mobile X-ray Services Inc. is located in Four Squares, Massachusetts. The company provides EKGs, Portable X-rays, and Sonograms services to individuals, hospitals, and clinics. Mr. Mobelo started the business in 1974 to take advantage of the one new hospital and three clinics that opened in the city. Quality Mobile X-ray Services goes to the locations to perform the X-rays, and provided other complementary services on demand. Both sales and profits were high during the first ten years. In 1986 the company noticed a sharp and an unusual decline in sales during the first six months.

A quick market research revealed to Quality Mobile X-rays that the office-based X-ray providers in the city gave their patients T-shirts and discount coupons that were redeemable at the drug stores. This tactic attracted Quality Mobile's customers and encroached on the market share. The company decided to survey one hundred and fifty former customers to find out why they switched to their competitors. Below is a section of the survey showing the completed items.

$$\text{Attitude(beh)} = \overset{n}{\underset{i\text{-}1}{E}}\ biei$$

E = sum of b and e
bi = strength of the belief
ei = the evaluation outcome

Table 6-3
Quality Mobile X-ray Services Inc.
Questionnaire For X-ray Users

Behavioral belief

		Mostly agree				Mostly disagree
1.	I buy from the cheapest sellers whenever the quality is similar.	5	4	3	2	1
2.	I rather visit the office and get a discount than stay at home and pay more for the service.	5	4	3	2	1
3.	Office visits appeal to me more than home services.	5	4	3	2	1
4.	I will not resume the use of the mobile service even if they offer similar deals as the in-office counterparts.	5	4	3	2	1
5.	I desire the privacy of an in-office X-ray service.	5	4	3	2	1

Evaluative components

		Mostly agree				Mostly disagree
1.	Using an X-ray service that offers a discount is better than a high price mobile service.	5	4	3	2	1
2.	Compared to a mobile service, a price discount compensates well for a trip to an office for the x-ray service.	5	4	3	2	1
3.	An office visit is better than a mobile X-ray service	5	4	3	2	1
4.	I will rather use an office X-ray service	5	4	3	2	1
5.	An office visit is more private than a home visit.	5	4	3	2	1

Table 6-4
Results of Customer Attitude Survey

Attributes	Evaluation(ei)	Behavioral belief			
		Office visit		Mobile service	
	ei	bi	be	b	be
Discount offering	4	5	20	3	12
Lower price	5	4	20	2	10
Visit appeal	3	3	9	4	12
Visit loyalty	4	5	20	4	16
Privacy of visit	4	5	20	3	12
Overall assessment			89		62

Interpretation of results

1. Evaluation(ei) is the average response on the evaluative components by the 150 respondents on the evaluation criteria.
2. Belief(bi) is the average response on the behavior belief components by the 150 respondents on the strength of belief
3. "be" is the behavioral belief multiplied by the evaluative component.
4. The higher the score, the more positive the attitude toward the behavior.
5. Office visit received the best scores of 89. This shows the attributes that make X-ray users react more favorable to the in-office service.

Implications of results

1. Quality Mobile X-rays should apply money saving strategies to the customers.
2. Quality Mobile X-rays should apply a more private approach in their service offering.

Calculation steps

1. Identify the major attributes of the behavior.
2. Measure the strength of customers' evaluative and belief components on the behavior attributes.
3. Add up the response for each question for the 150 respondents.
4. Calculate the evaluative(ei) by dividing the total for each question in the evaluative component by 150.
5. Calculate the belief (b) by dividing the total for each question in the belief component by 150.
6. Calculate behavior belief and evaluative component (be) by multiplying #4 by #5.

PART THREE

MARKETING RATIOS

Rowland Chidomere

CHAPTER 7

MARKET ACTIVITY RATIO

Accounts Receivable Turnover

What is an accounts receivable turnover?

It is a measure of the average times it takes for a business to receive the money for the sales it made on credit.

Why does a marketer need to know the accounts receivable turnover?

1. To know how many times the business will collect on the sales made on credit during the year.

How does a marketer find the accounts receivable turnover?

Come & "C" Used Appliances Inc. is a reseller of used refrigerators, freezers, electric ranges, and washers, and dryers that started in 1990 in Oaks, AZ. Because Come & "C" Used Appliances had a policy of cash and carry, and did not sell on credit, it was very profitable during the first eight years. However, in the ninth year two competitors entered the market with a variation of credit offerings and paid delivery strategies. In order to retain existing customers and attract new ones, Come & "C" had to reciprocate.

Photo 14: Priority One

However, they were not sure how the estimated $247,000 credit sales for the following year was to affect the cash flow. The intention was to start the year with about $86,000 sales or transactions on credit, and end with about $50,000 in uncollected credit balance. Come & "C" needed to know how much time to allow for the collection on each credit sale without a cash flow disruption. In other words, they needed to know the maximum time a credit should be collected on during the year. They did the following.

Table 7-1
Come and "C" Used Appliances
Account Receivable Turnover

$$Accounts\ Receivable\ Turnover = \frac{Annual\ credit\ sales}{Average\ Accounts\ receivable}$$
$$(Beginning\ Receivable + Ending\ Receivable)/2$$

$$\frac{\$247,000}{(\$86,000 + \$50,000)/2} = \frac{\$247,000}{\$68,000} = 3.6\ times$$

Interpretation of the results.

1. The average time that Come and "C" Used Appliances Inc. collected on the total for each credit account during the year 2000 was 3.6 times.

Implication of the results.

1. Come and "C" must assure that each credit sale is collected 3.6 times during the year.

Calculation steps.

1. Estimate the credit sales for the year.
2. Determine the average accounts receivable by adding the preferred amount of credit sales at the beginning of the year to

the desired amount of credit sales balance at the end of the year, and divide by two.

3. Divide the credit sales for the year by the average accounts receivable.

Average Collection Period

What is an average collection period?

It is the average length of time a business could wait after making a credit sale before it receives the payment without having a cash shortage.

Why does a marketer need to know the average collection period?

1. To know the maximum number of days that the business can wait after making a credit sale before it receives payment without a cash flow disruption.

How does a marketer find the average collection period?

Wesley & Wise Law Office Inc. is a debt relief and bankruptcy assistance law office owned by Miss Shemika Wesley and Mr. Olu

Wise. The law office was started in 1971 to take advantage of the rising bankruptcy and debt problems during that period. Wesley & Wise catered to both individuals and the government. The income in the year 2000 was $3.9 million,

Photo 15: Barron & Berry L.L.P.

and the anticipated income in 2001 was $4.6m or an average daily income of $12,603. While the individuals paid for the service at the time of the service or soon after, the government took too much time to pay.

The law firm anticipated credit sales of $452,000 in 2001, with a beginning balance of $100,000 and an ending balance of $73,000. In order to maintain an adequate cash flow in 2001, Wesley and Wise needed to decide the average time it could wait before collecting a credit sale, and so it did the following.

Table 7-2
Wesley & Wise Law Office Inc.
Average Receivable Turnover

$$\text{Collection Period} = \frac{\textit{Days in the year}}{\textit{Accounts Receivable Turnover}} = \frac{365}{5.2 \text{ times}} = 70 \text{ days}$$
$$\$452,000/\{(100,000 + 73,000)/2\}$$

$$\textit{Av Collection Period} = \frac{\textit{Accounts receivable}}{\text{Total sales}/365} = \frac{\$452,000}{\$4.6m/365} = \frac{\$452,000}{\$12,603}$$

$$= 35.9 \text{ days}$$

$$or \qquad \frac{\textit{Accounts receivable}}{\textit{Average daily sales}} = \frac{\$452,000}{\$12,603} = 35.9 \text{ days}$$

Interpretation of the results.

1. Wesley and Wise had an account receivable period of 5.2 times. This means that it has a 70-day period to collect each credit account for 5.2 times each year.
2. The average collection period is 35.9 days.

Implication of the results.

1. Wesley and Wise will have difficulties accumulating funds for operation due to the extraordinary long collection period.

Calculation steps.

1. To find the collection period: (a) determine the accounts receivable turnover by dividing the total credit sales by the average accounts receivable, and (b) divide the number of days in the year (365 days) by the accounts receivable turnover.
2. To find the average collection period, divide the accounts receivable by the average daily sales.

Fixed Assets Turnover

What is a fixed asset turnover?

It is a measure of sales productivity of assets or how efficient a business utilizes its plants and equipment in selling.

Why does a marketer need to know the fixed asset turnover?

1. To know the amount of sales revenue generated with each dollar of fixed assets owned by the business.

How does a marketer find the fixed assets turnover?

Shields Glues and Adhesives Inc. was started in 1983 by Ms. Shields to make and sell glues and adhesives. Mrs. Shields was a supervisor in a glue manufacturing plant. When she lost her job in 1982 due to company downsizing, she took a loan of $1m and began making and distributing glues and adhesives out of an abandoned family dairy plant. A majority of the loan was invested in production machines and equipment. Shields Glues and Adhesives had very impressive profit margin during the first five years. In 1989, Ms. Shields decided to make the business more efficient, and therefore invested to upgrade the machines and equipment. The value of the fixed assets increased to $2.8m and $3.1m in 1999 and 2000 respectively. Sales also increased to $4.9m and $5.1m in 1999 and 2000 respectively. The company needed to know how productive or how well it has utilized the fixed assets, and so it did the following.

Table 7-3
Shields Glue and Adhesives Inc.
Fixed Assets Turnover

$$\text{Fixed Assets Turnover} = \frac{Sales}{Fixed\ Assets}.$$

1999	=	$\frac{\$4.9m}{\$2.8m}$	= $1.75
2000	=	$\frac{\$5.1m}{\$3.1m}$	= $1.65

Interpretation of the results.

1. In 1999, each dollar of fixed assets generated $1.75 in sales.
2. In 2000, each dollar of fixed assets generated $1.65 in sales.
3. Although sales increased in 2000, the assets were less productive.

Implication of the results.

1. Shields Glues and Adhesives Inc. should adopt marketing strategies that utilize less assets to produce more sales.

Calculation steps.

1. Determine the net sales.

2. Determine the fixed assets.
3. Divide #1 by #2.

Total Assets Turnover

What is a total asset turnover?

It is the overall measure of how effectively a company's assets are used during a period of time.

Why does a marketer need to know the total assets turnover?

1. To know the amount of sales revenue generated with each dollar of assets owned by the business.
2. To know how effectively the marketing mixes are used to generate sales.

Photo 16: BEDBATH & BEYOND

How does a marketer find the total assets turnover?

A-Comfort-World Inc. sells beds, mattresses, bedspreads, pillow cases, and other bedding materials in Dashmi, Conn. In 1998, A-Comfort-World embarked on a modest expansion of the display space in its sales floor. It also purchased some equipment and machines to load items into customers' vehicles. At the end of the year the assets increased from $2m to $3m. Sales for the year increased from $4.4m to $5.6m. A-Comfort-World needed to know the amount of sales revenue generated with each additional dollar of the asset and by the total asset. It did the following.

81

Table 7-4
A-Comfort-World Inc.
Total Assets Turnover

$$Additional\ Assets\ Turnover = \frac{Additional\ Sales\ Increase}{Addition\ to\ Assets}$$

$5.6m-$4.4m = $\frac{\$1,200,000}{\$1,000,000}$ = 1.2 times
$3m - $2m =

$$Total\ Assets\ Turnover = \frac{Sales}{Total\ assets}$$

$\frac{\$5,600,000}{\$3,000,000}$ 1.89 times

Interpretation of results

1. Each additional $1 that A-Comfort-World spent on the expansion generated an additional $1.20 in sales.
2. Each dollar of the total asset generated $1.89 in sales during the year.

Implications of results

1. The additional assets turnover was lower than the total assets turnover. Therefore, the expansion was not very profitable.
2. A-Comfort-World should endeavor to increase the sales by making better use of new equipment and the assets.

Calculation steps

1. Divide the additional net sales by the additional investment.
2. Divide the total net sale by the total asset.

Cashflow Per Share

What is a cash flow per share?

It is a measure of the discretionary funds over and above the business expenses that are available for the business to use as it wants.

Why does a marketer need to know the cash flow per share?

1. To determine the amount of funds available for expenses.
2. To know how effective the marketing strategies have been in increasing the cash income.

How does a marketer find the cash flow per share?

Goodlife Christian Bookstore Inc. sells bibles, hymnals, and other Christian books. Because it is the largest bookstore in the area, Goodlife sells a lot of merchandise to both in-store and on the web-site customers. The 1998 sales was $5m. Half of the sales was utilized to cover the cost of the goods and operations. Twenty percent of the remaining income went to paying taxes. The depreciation during the year was $310,000. Because Goodlife went

Photo 17: Special Occasions

public in 1977, there were 200,000 outstanding shares. The firm needed to know the amount of discretionary funds or money left for spending for every share outstanding, and it did the following.

Table 7-5
Goodlife Christian Bookstore
Cashflow Per Share

Cash flow per Share = $\dfrac{\textit{Aftertax profits} + \textit{Depreciation}}{\textit{Number of common shares outstanding}}$

Sales	$5,000,000
Cost of goods sold & Operations	$2,500,000
Taxes	$500,000
After Tax Profit	$2,000,000

Cash flow per share = $\dfrac{\$2,000,000 + 310,000}{200,000}$ = $\dfrac{\$2,310,000}{200,000}$ = $11.55

Interpretation of the results

1. Goodlife Christian Bookstore Inc. made a cash flow of $11.55 for every outstanding share.

Implication of the results

1. Goodlife Christain Bookstore Inc. had enough money for discretionary spending, including marketing.

Calculation steps

1. Subtract the sum of the cost of goods sold, cost of operation, and taxes from the net sales to get the after tax profit.
2. Divide the after tax profit by the number of shares outstanding.

CHAPTER 8

MARKET LEVERAGE RATIO

Fixed-Charge Coverage

What is a fixed-charge coverage?

It is a technique that is used to measure the ability of a business to meet all of its fixed-charge obligations.

Why does a marketer need to know the fixed charge coverage?

1. By knowing the fixed cost coverage, the marketer should be able to determine the amount of money that is left for the variable marketing expenses.
2. The marketer could know when the fixed charge is too much.

How does a marketer find the fixed charge coverage?

Serv-Em-Up Inc. is a popular soul food restaurant located in Feel Good, Al. Serv-Em-Up cooks and sells traditional African-American dishes that include fried and baked chicken, green beans, corn, baked and cooked ham, soup and corn bread. The restaurant is known for

Photo 18: Skip's Hot Dogs

its fresh and tasty food that is sold in an all you can eat buffet style. In 2001, Serv-Em-Up had a sales of $910,040. The operation cost and the cost of goods sold were $582,425.60 or sixty-four percent of sales. The remaining $327,614.40 was the profit before taxes and interests.

In 2001, the total bank interest charge on the loan to Serv-Em-Up Inc. was $17,472.77. Fifteen percent of the cost of operations or $87,363.84 was used to pay the annual lease for thc building. The other fixed charges including business security and insurance accounted for five percent or $29,121.28 of the operation cost. In setting up the budget for 2002, Serv-Em-Up needed to know how much ability it had to cover the fixed cost in that year. It did the following.

Table 8-1
Serv-Em-Up Inc.
Fixed-Charge Coverage

Sales (2001)		$910,040
Cost of goods sold & cost of operations:		
(a). Fixed Cost:		
Lease obligations	$87,363.84	
Security & Insurance	$29,121.28	
Total fixed cost		$116,485.12
(b). Total Variable costs		$465,940.48
Total cost		$582,425.60
Profit before taxes and interest		$327,614.40

Fixed-Charge Coverage

$$= \frac{\text{Profits before taxes and interest + Lease \& other fixed costs}}{\text{Total interest charges + Lease \&other fixed costs}}$$

$$= \frac{\$327,614.40 + \$116,485.12}{\$17,472.77 + \$116,485.12} = \frac{\$444,099.52}{\$133,957.89} = \$3.3$$

Interpretation of the results.

1. In 2001, Serv-Em-Up had $3.30 to cover each dollar of fixed charge.

Implication of the results.

1. Serv-Em-Up may use the same amount used in 2001.

Calculation steps

1. Determine the sales for the period or year.
2. Add up fixed and variable costs separately, and subtract their total from the sales to find the profit before taxes and interest.
3. Add the profit before taxes and interest to the fixed cost.
4. Add the total interest charges to the fixed cost.
5. Divide #3 by #4.

Debt-to-Assets Ratio

What is a debt-to-assets ratio?

It is a technique that measures the extent to which a marketer operates the activities with borrowed money.

Why does a marketer need to know the debt-to-assets ratio?

1. To determine the pricing strategy that could increase the contribution margin and provide more money to pay debts or bills.
2. To determine if and which marketing cost should be reduced or eliminated.

How does a marketer find the debt to assets ratio?

Had-I-Known Inc. is a tree cutting and trimming service started in 1974 in Boomstown, NM by Mr. Yu Kno. Mr. Kno lost his big mansion when fire raged through the town in 1973. Luckily, he was out on a vacation trip with his family. A month before, a friend advised Mr. Kno to cut down or trim some of the trees that were very close to the mansion. He did not heed to that. Therefore, the first words he shouted at the news of the fire was "had I known."

When he was settled, Mr. Kno bought a modest home with the insurance claims, and used the leftover of $59,000 to start Had-I-Known, a business to cut and trim trees around buildings. The first two years of the business were not profitable because not very many homes and businesses were eager to get rid of the greenery that hugged the roofs and walls. However, as events turned out, Boomstown had another massive fire in 1977. The residents were so frightened that they demanded for tree cutting and trimming services. In response to the heavy demand, Mr. Kno borrowed $289,000 and expanded the marketing and services. By December 1998, Had-I-Known was the largest cutting and trimming business in the area.

In 1999, the business still owed $50,987 on the original loan, and had an asset of $10m, excluding the $100,000 it invested in stocks and bonds. In January 1999, Had I Known wanted to take a loan of $4.4m to expand into the two neighboring states. Mr. Kno needed to know the extent to which the business operation in 1999 would be funded with borrowed money, so he calculated the ratio.

Table 8-2
Had-I-Known Inc.
Debt-to-Assets Ratio

$$\text{Debts-to Assets ratio} = \frac{\text{Total debt}}{\text{Total assets}} \times 100 = \frac{\$4,450,987}{\$10,100,000} \times 100$$

$$= 44.1\%$$

Interpretation of the results.

1. In 1999, forty-four percent of Had-I-known Inc's business was operated with borrowed money.

Implication of the results.

1. The debts-to-assets ratio is high, and Had-I-known Inc. should not be encouraged to go any higher.

Calculation steps

1. Add all debts (short-term and long-term) to find the total debts.
2. Add all assets (current and long-term) to find the total assets.
3. Divide #1 by #2.

Debt-to-Equity Ratio

What is a debt-to-equity ratio?

It is a technique that compares the amount of operating funds that is borrowed to the amount that is provided by the stockholders or owners.

Why does a marketer need to know the debt-to-equity ratio?

1. It is used to determine how to price a merchandise in order to raise enough money to pay the debts and the dividends.

How does a marketer find the debt-to-equity ratio?

Adults Pleasure Inc. sells exotic magazines, videos, CDs, and DVDs. When it started in 1991, the owner Mr. Jacob Jones did not have enough funds to embark on the type of elaborate full line stores that he had envisioned. He sold a piece of land that belonged to the family, and used the proceeds as a down payment for a $750,500 loan. With the loan, Mr. Jones built a massive adult sex retail store. By 1996, Adults Pleasure was the largest store of its kind in the city. The business was so successful that Mr. Jones thought of building two more stores in other cities. There was $250, 000 balance leftover from the 1991 loan which he had seven more years to pay off. The short-term debt was $59,000. Mr. Jones decided to raise the funds for the

expansion by offering some stocks to few investors. He raised $576,000 from the investors. When the expansion was completed in 1999, Mr. Jones became concerned on how much to price the merchandise and services in order to get enough income to pay the debts, and at the same time have the profit to share among the investors as

Photo 19: Harper's Cabaret

dividends. He wanted to know the ratio of the outstanding debts to the amount contributed by the investors. He did the following.

Table 8-3
Adults Pleasure Inc.
Debt-to-Equity Ratio

$Total\ Debt\text{-}to\text{-}Equity\ Ratio$ = $\dfrac{Total\ debt}{Total\ stockholders'\ Equity}$

= $\dfrac{\$309,000}{\$576,000}$ = .54

$Long\ Term\ Debt\text{-}to\ Equity\ Ratio$ = $\dfrac{Long\text{-}term\ debt}{Total\ stockholders'\ equity}$

= $\dfrac{\$250,000}{\$576,000}$ = .43

Interpretation of the results.

1. In 1999, the retailer's total debt ratio was .54, which meant that for every $1 available for the stockholders, Adults Pleasure owed 54 cents to the bank.
2. In 1999, the retailer's long-term debt ratio was .43, which meant that for every $1 for the stockholders, Adults Pleasure owed the bank 43 cents on a long-term basis.
3. Both the total debt-to-equity ratio and the long-term debt-to-equity ratio were moderately high.

Implication of the results.

1. Adults Pleasure Inc. should avoid borrowing additional funds, because lenders may be reluctant due to the moderately high debt ratio.

Calculation steps.

1. Determine the total of the outstanding debts.
2. Determine the total funds contributed by stockholders.
3. Divide #1 by #2.

Times-Interest Earned (or coverage) Ratio

What is a times-interest earned ratio?

It is a technique that measures how low a business' profits can decline and the business will be unable to pay annual interest cost.

Why does a marketer need to know the times-interest earned ratio?

1. Marketing costs affect the business income and profits.

2. The marketer could modify the prices of merchandise or increase sales to achieve a safe level of profit to pay the annual interest cost.

How does a marketer find out the times-interest earned ratio?

LuvNest Bridal Inc. rents and sells tuxedos, custom made wedding dresses, and wedding accessories. LuvNest Bridal started in 1980 in Los Armor, CA. The owner, Miss Lovett was successful in this venture. It was the only store of its kind in the city. Due to the low operating costs resulting from the low rental cost, the profit margins were more than sixty-percent during the first ten years. However, in 1991, three competitors expanded into Los Armor from the neighboring cities. The effect of the competition was very negative on LuvNest. The profit margin shrunk to forty-percent. Rather than a head-to-head competition, Miss Lovett adopted some flank defense marketing strategies to protect her market share. With a $1m loan in 1994, LuvNest expanded its business into the Internet by creating a web site called LuvNest-On-Net that has a reduced overnight delivery cost. It also provided discount wedding and honeymoon services. The total sales in 1996 was $2,100,000, and the profit before interest and taxes declined to $1,156,000. The total annual interest was $186,000. Miss Lovett was concerned, and wanted to know how low LuvNest's profit could decline without the business becoming unable to pay the annual interest cost. So she did the following.

Table 8-4
LuvNest Bridal Inc.
Times-Interest Earned (or coverage) ratio

Times-Interest Earned = *Profits before interest and taxes*
(or coverage) Ratio   *Total interest charges*

$$= \frac{\$1,156,000}{\$186,000} = 6.2 \text{ times}$$

Interpretation of the results.

1. In 1996 LuvNest's income covered its interest 6.2 times.
2. LuvNest Bridal Inc. paid $1 for every $6.20 it made.

Implication of the results.

1. LuvNest should not worry about not being able to pay the annual interest cost at the present.

Calculation steps.

1. Determine the profit before taxes and interest by subtracting the costs and expenses from sales.
2. Determine the total interest charge.
3. Divide #1 by #2.

CHAPTER 9

MARKET LIQUIDITY RATIO

Current Ratio

What is a current ratio?

It is the amount of cash or near cash assets that a business has to pay short-term bills as they are due.

Why does a marketer need to know the current ratio?

1. In setting up a marketing plan, a marketer needs to have an idea of the money available to pay for on going product, pricing, promotion and distribution activities.

How does a marketer find the current ratio?

Woods Pro Inc. is a retail and wholesale lumberyard that sells different forms of woods to businesses, individual homebuilders and contractors. Woods Pro sought a competitive advantage by stocking woods from various regions of the world. This often gives buyers a broad choice of stocks that suit their preferences. Also, the company encouraged constant and dependable supply by assuring that all suppliers are paid upon delivery. Each month three truck loads of wood each costing $40,000 were delivered. Also, Woods Pro Inc. spent $12,000 monthly

Photo 20: Burchette & Burchettte Hardwood Floor

94

on operations. The average sale for the months was $130,000. The company had invested $60,000 in Certificate of deposit in case of a shortfall in sales. At the end of August, Woods Pro Inc. needed to know the ratio of the monthly bills to the monthly income. It did the following.

Table 9-1
Woods Pro Inc.
Current Ratio

Current Ratio = Current Assets
                Current Liabilities

Current assets:	
Monthly sales	$130,000
Certificate of deposit	$ 60,000
Total current assets	**$190,000**
Current liabilities:	
Monthly supplies ($40,000x3)	$120,000
Monthly operation cost	$12,000
Total current liabilities	**$132,000**

$$\text{Current Ratio} = \frac{\$190,000}{\$132,000} = 1.44$$

Interpretation of results

1. Woods Pro Inc. had $1.44 to cover every $1 of immediate debt.

Implications of results

1. Woods Pro Inc. has a very high debt ratio. It will not have enough money to operate after paying its immediate bills. It will be left with 44 cents for every dollar it pays out.
2. Woods Pro Inc. needs to reduce the current liabilities. It cannot survive on 44 cents per dollar in debt.

Calculation of results

1. Add all the cash coming in to all the short-term investments to get the total current assets.
2. Add all the immediate expenses including operation costs and supplies to get the total current liabilitics.
3. Divide the total current assets by the total current liabilities.

Inventory to Net Working Capital Ratio

What is an inventory to net working capital?

It is a technique that measures the extent to which a company's working capital or operation funds are tied up in the inventory.

Why does a marketer need to know the inventory to net working capital ratio?

1. To know how urgent cash is needed for marketing operations, and how urgent a company has to liquidate the inventory.
2. To know how much fund is available for marketing operations.

How does a marketer find out the inventory to net working capital ratio?

Advanced Home Security Inc. was started in 1993 in Tomsboro, MS. by two brothers that discovered a method that used global positioning satellite and a surveillance camera system to picture homes anywhere in the world. The system was connected to the police computers' alarm networks. Because of the complexity, Advanced Home Security had to invest a large sum of money in this operation. It decided to offer franchises of the system to interested parties. A franchise package included the supplies of homes and business security features, contracts with the local police or security companies for responses to the alarms, and the apprehension of culprits. Each franchise package costs $80,000 to prepare, and it sold for $450,000. In anticipation for further expansion in 2001, Advanced Home Security prepared another 10,000 franchise packages. In August 2001, one hundred franchise packages were sold to customers in Asia. Advanced Home Security maintained a checking account of $15,000,000 for operations. It paid the government a monthly fee of $2,000 for access to the satellite, and the other monthly cost of operation was $1,109,000. At the end of August 2001, the company needed to know the ratio of its working capital or operation funds that was tied up in inventory, and it did the following.

Table 9-2
Advanced Home Security Inc.
Inventory to Net Working Capital Ratio

$$\text{Ratio of inventory to net working capital} = \frac{\text{Inventory}}{\text{Current assets} - \text{Current liabilities}}$$

Inventory (9,900 packages x $80,000)		**= $792,000,000**
Current assets		
Sales (100 x $450,000)	= $45,000,000	
Checking Account	= $15,000,000	
Total current assets		**= $60,000,000**
Current liabilities		
Monthly govt. fees	=$2,000	
Monthly operations	=$1,109,000	
Total current liabilities		**= $1,111,000**

$$\text{Ratio of inventory to net working capital} = \frac{\$792,000,000}{\$60,000,000 - \$1,111,000}$$

$$= \frac{\$792,000,000}{\$58,889,000} \quad 13.44$$

Interpretation of the results.

1. At the end of August 2001, Advanced Home Security had $13.44 of inventory for every dollar it had in the current asset.

Implications of the results.

1. A large amount of Advanced Home Security's working capital or operation funds is tied up in the inventory at the end of August 2001.
2. Advanced Home Security may have to go on sale, or borrow money, or use long-term assets for operations.

Calculation steps.

1. Add all the cash coming in to all short-term investments to get the total current assets
2. Add all the immediate expenses including operation costs and supplies to get the total current liabilities.
3. Determine the inventory by multiplying the number of packages by the cost of preparing each.
4. Divide the total current assets by the total current liabilities.

Quick Ratio (acid-test)

What is a quick ratio or acid test?

It is a technique that measures a business's ability to pay short-term bills in times of real crises without relying on the sales of inventory.

Why does a marketer need to know the quick ratio?

1. A marketer needs to know the short-term bills on the product, promotion and distribution, and how much sales dollars to reserve for this payment.

How does a marketer find the quick ratio?

NorthWest Discount Furniture Inc. is a furniture retail store that is located in the city of Johnson, Va. since 1985. Being the only store in the NW side of the city, NorthWest Discount Furniture was popular, and had a high customer loyalty. In 1999, the store had an average monthly sales of $160,910, including $41,000 in credit. It purchased $67,000 worth of inventory each month, and paid $45,600 in salaries and operations. In order to maintain an effective weekly management of the store, the owner, Mr. Cosby needed to know the ability of the store to pay its monthly expenses and he did the following.

Table 9-3
NorthWest Discount Furniture
Quick Ratio (acid test)

$$Quick\ Ratio\ (acid\ test) = \frac{Current\ assets - Inventory}{Current\ Liabilities}$$

$$= \frac{\$160,910 - \$67,000}{\$45,600} = \frac{\$93,910}{\$45,600} = \$2.1$$

Interpretation of the results.

1. NorthWest Discount Furniture's quick ratio is 1 to 2.1, which meant that the store had $2.1 of currents assets for every $1 of current liabilities that it had.

Implication of the results.

1. The company is in a good financial standing to take care of immediate or short-term bills

Calculation steps

1. Determine the current assets, the inventory, and the current liabilities.
2. Subtract the inventory from the current assets.
3. Divide the sum in #2 by the current liabilities.

CHAPTER 10

Market Profitability/Productivity

Cost-Volume Profit Analysis

What is a cost-volume profit analysis?

It is a technique that is used to determine how the cost and the profit of a product or service will change as the volume of sales changes.

Why does a marketer need a cost-volume profit analysis?

1. It enables a marketer to obtain a cost advantage by showing the change that has to be made in the cost and profit estimate when the sales volume differs from the estimate.
2. It is used to determine the price that will result in maximum sales and profit.

How does a marketer use a cost –volume profit analysis?

LizTex Check Printing Services Inc. was started in 1981 by Ms. Lisa Textile to print checks for local banks. Due to the high cost to design, code, and print the checks, Ms. Textile realized that to be profitable LizTex had to secure accounts with medium and large banks in the city, and take the advantage of the large volume. Ms. Textile wanted to know how the cost of producing the checks could change with the volume. At that time, the unit variable cost of a checkbook was 45cents and the fixed cost was $75,000. LizTex sold each check to the banks for $2.35, which was a profit of 65cents per checkbook. LizTex considered marketing the checkbooks to three banks, and needed to know how the volume of the checks to the banks might affect the production cost. Below are the considerations.

Table 10-1
LizTex Check Printing Services Inc.
Cost -Volume Profit Analysis of Checkbook Production

	Bank #1	Bank #2	Bank #3
Volume demanded	60,000 units	100,000 units	150,000 units
Variable unit cost	45cents	45cents	45cents
Total Variable cost	$27,000	$45,000	$67,500
Total direct,traceable fixed cost	$75,000	$75,000	$75,000
Total cost	$102,000	$120,000	$142,500
Cost per checkbook (volume/cost)	$1.70	$1.20	$.95
Total sales	$141,000	$235,000	$352,500
Profit (Sales-Cost)	$39,000	$115,000	$210,000

Interpretation of the results.

1. It costs less to produce more checkbooks.
2. Profit increased as the number of checkbooks sold increased.

Implications of the results.

1. Due to the cost advantage, LizTex should consider serving the high volume banks.
2. LizTex should know that the production cost will increase as the volume increases. However, the unit cost decreases.

Calculation steps

1. Multiply the number of check books demanded by the variable cost.
2. Add the direct and fixed cost to the total variable cost to get the total cost.
3. Divide the total cost by the number of units to find the cost per checkbook.
4. Subtract the cost from the sales to get the profit.

Dividend Yield On Common Stock or Equity

What is a dividend yield on common stock?

It is a pro rated distribution of money or additional shares of stock to common share holders.

Why does a marketer need to know the dividend yield on common stock?

It is used to determine if the prices should be raised to increase or leverage the yield of the common stocks.

How does a marketer find the dividend yield on common stock?

Sit-In-Comfort Inc. was started in 1976 by Mr. and Mrs. Eagles to manufacture and distribute recliners, sofas, and chairs. Upon graduating from a business college in 1974, John Eagles got married to Jean, his college sweetheart who majored in accounting. After working in the corporations for two years, they decided to quit and start their own business. In 1976, the Eagles sold shares to family and friends, and raised a sum of $2m at $1,000 per share. The venture was a success, and Sit-In-Comfort soon became one of the reputable furniture maker/wholesaler in the city of High Point, NC. In order to maximize the return or dividend to the stockholders, Sit-In-Comfort decided to increase the yield of each share. They set three levels of annual yields per share - $120, $145, and $160, and wanted to know what percentage each level was to the original worth of the stock. They did the following.

Table 10-2
Sit-In-Comfort
Dividend Yield On Common Stock or Equity

Dividend Yield on Common Stock(%) =*Annual dividends per share*
$\qquad\qquad\qquad\qquad\qquad\qquad\qquad\qquad$ *Current market price per share*

Level #1 $\quad \dfrac{\$120}{\$1,000} \times 100 = 12\%$

Level #2 $\quad \dfrac{\$145}{\$1,000} \times 100 = 14.5\%$

Level #3 $\quad \dfrac{\$160}{\$1,000} \times 100 = 16\%$

Interpretation of the results.

1. The $120 annual yield was 12% of the stock value.
2. The $145 annual yield was 14.5% of the stock value.
3. The $160 annual yield was 16% of the stock value.

Implication of the results.

1. Sit-In-Comfort should avoid paying a high dividend if this capital is needed for operations.

Calculation steps.

1. Decide the amount to pay off as dividend.
2. Find out the current market price per share.
3. Divide #1 by #2.

Dividend Pay Out to Preferred Stock or Equity

What is a dividend pay out to preferred stock?

It is the percentage of the profit that is paid out as dividends to preferred stockholders.

Why does a marketer need to know the dividend pay out to preferred stockholders?

1. To know how much of the profit to retain and use for marketing.
2. To see if and how the promise of a high dividend pay out to preferred stocks could be applied in the marketing strategy to entice investors.

How does a marketer find the dividend pay out ratio?

Whuman Genetics Inc. is a medium-sized S-corporation that analyzes human genes to determine human relationship in genes. When Mr. Randy Boss started the business in 1990, little did he know that ten years later the government will require every citizen to have a DNA classification code to be stored at the local police departments for a quicker investigation of crimes. In response to the increase market demand, Mr. Boss decided to raise the capital to increase the size and capability of Whuman Genetics. Rather than getting a loan from the bank, the company decided to use the advantage of the high demand to solicit individuals and businesses to invest in Whuman Genetics, by buying the stocks. The initial stock offering raised $1.8m with 360,000 shares sold to friends and relatives at a $5 par value. At the end of 2000, the company made an after tax profit of $210,000. It decided to pay out a third of the profit as dividend. Mr. Boss was concerned to know what ratio of the profit this was, and the amount that will be left for reinvestment, so he did the following.

Table 10-3
Whuman Genetics Inc.
Dividend Pay Out to Preferred Stock or Equity

Dividend Pay-out Ratio = *Annual dividends per share*
*Aftertax earning per share*

Dividend Pay-out Ratio
= (payout/outstanding shares) $\quad$ = $\quad$ \$70,000 / 360,000 = \$.19
(After tax profit/outstanding shares) \$210,000/360,000 $\quad\quad$ \$.58
 = .33

Interpretation of the results.

1. Each share had an after-tax value of 58 cents.
2. Each share had an annual dividend value of 19 cents.
3. The dividend pay-out ratio is 1 to .33, which means that Whuman genetics can payout 33 cents from every \$1 it made.
4. The sum of \$140,700 is available for reinvestment.

Implication of the results.

1. Whuman Genetics should use the high pay-out rate to entice more investors.

Calculation steps.

1. Determine the annual dividend per share by dividing the pay-out amount by the outstanding shares.
2. Determine the aftertax earning per share by dividing the aftertax profit by the outstanding shares.
3. Divide #1 by #2.

Earning per share

What is an earning per share?

It is the amount of the earnings available to the owner of each share of the common stock in the business.

Why does a marketer need to know the earning per share?

1. It helps a marketer to know how profitable the venture is to the owners.
2. It enables the marketer to decide price flexibility or how to adjust the price in order to maximize profit.
3. It guides the marketer to decide the proportion of the profit to reinvest in the products, promotion and distribution.

How does a marketer find out the earning per share?

MeriAnn Chinaware Inc. manufactures china and crystal silver plates, and wholesales them to department stores and specialty stores. In 1995, Mrs. Mary Annitty, the owner, raised $700,000 from ten relatives to modernize and update the production and distribution facilities. Three people bought 10,000 preferred stocks at $20 per share (30% of $700,000), and seven people bought 100,000 common shares at $5 per share (70% of $700,000). In 2000, MeriAnn Chinaware made an after tax profit of $1.9m. The profit from the common stocks was $1,349,000 (70% of $1.9m), and that from the preferred stock was $551,000 (30% of $1.9m). In order to decide whether to use the profit for the several costly marketing strategies proposed for the next year, Mrs. Annitty needed to find out the present earning per share. She did the following.

Table 10-4
MeriAnn Chinaware Inc.
Earning Per Share

Earning Per Share = *Profits after taxes – Preferred stock dividends*
  (common)   *Number of shares of common stock outstanding*

$$= \frac{\$1,900,000 - \$551,000}{100,000} = \$13.49$$

There is $13.49 that could be distributed as dividend for every one common stock outstanding.

Earning Per Share = *Profits after taxes - Common stock dividends*
  (preferred)   *Number of shares of preferred stock outstanding*

$$= \frac{\$1,900,000 - \$1,349,000}{10,000} = \$55.10$$

Interpretation of the results.

1. Each share of common stock earned $13.49 or 270%.
2. Each preferred stock earned $55.10 or 276%.

Implication of the results.

1. Both common and preferred stock are very profitable, and should provide enough funds for Mrs. Annity to invest on marketing strategies.

Calculation steps.

1. To determine the earning on the common stock, subtract the preferred stock dividends from the profit after tax and divide by the number of common stocks outstanding.
2. To determine the earning on the preferred stock, subtract the common stock dividends from the profit after tax and divide by the number of preferred stocks outstanding.

3. Subtract the preferred stock dividend from the profit after taxes.
4. Divide #3 by the number of shares of common stock outstanding.

Selling Price on Profit

What is the effect of selling price on profit?

It is a technique that is used to determine how a change in the selling price of a product would affect its profitability. It is also used to determine the unit sales required to earn the same total gross profit as before the price change.

Why does a marketer need to know the effect of selling price on profit?

1. The marketer needs to know how low to price a product without losing money.
2. The marketer needs to know how to integrate sales promotion and price markdowns.

How does a marketer find out the effect of selling price on profit?

Happy Homes Funeral Inc. is an eighty-year old funeral home that is located in Mojos, New Mexico. Its age, and the fact that there was no strong competition in the burial business in Mojos in the past years made Happy Homes the major funeral home in the area. However, in 1998, Pete's Funeral Home and Dave's Eternal Rests Inc. expanded into Mojos. As a response, Happy Homes decided to lower the prices of its services in order not to be priced out of the market. Usually, Happy Homes bought a burial package for $1,900 and sold it for $3,400. However, due to the competition it decided to reduce the selling price by 10 percent from the original selling price of $3,400 to $3060. This was a markdown of 6% from 44% ($3400-$1900)/$3,400 to 38% ($3060-$1900)/$3060. Because Happy Homes originally planned to sell 675 burial packages at $3,400, it was no longer sure

how many packages to sell at $3060 in order to maintain the originally estimated level of profit. Happy Homes wanted to find out the correct units to sell, so it did the following.

Photo 21: Community Funeral Home

Table 10-5
Happy Homes Funeral Inc.
Selling Price On Profit

Unit sales required to earn the same total gross profit with a price adjustment	=	*Original markdown (%)*	*Expected unit*
		Original markdown (%) x	*sales at original*
		+/- Price change (%)	*price*

$$\frac{44}{44-10} \times 675 = \frac{29,700}{34} = 874 \text{ burial packages}$$

Suppose that in 2000 Happy Homes decided to raise the price by 15% to $3,519. The new markup on selling price would be 46% ($3,519-$1,900)/$3,519 and the new units required to earn the same amount would be as follows.

Unit sales required to earn the same total gross profit with a price adjustment	=	*Original markup (%)*	*Expected unit*
		Original markup (%) x	*sales at original*
		+/- Price change (%)	*price*

$$= \frac{44 \times 675}{59 \,(44+15)} \qquad = 503 \text{ units}$$

Interpretation of the results.

1. If Happy Homes reduces the burial package price from $3400 to $3060, it would have to sell an additional 201 packages (876-675) to meet the original gross profit level.
2. If on the other hand Happy Homes increased the price of the burial package from $3,400 to $3,519, it would sell 503 packages or172 packages less to reach the desired profit level.

Implication of the results.

1. A marketer should be devoted to increase promotion to encourage purchases when the price of an item or service is lowered.

Calculation steps.

In case of a markdown:

1. Determine the cost of the burial packages.
2. Estimate how many packages the firm intends to sell.
3. Decide how much to reduce the selling price from the original price.
4. Determine how much this would decrease the markup on selling price.
5. Find out how many burial packages to sell at the reduced price in order to maintain the originally hoped level of profit.

In case of a Markup:

1. Determine the cost of the burial packages.
2. Estimate how many you intend to sell.
3. Decide how much to increase the selling price from the original price.
4. Determine how much this would increase the markup on selling price.
5. Find out how many burial packages you would have to sell at the increased price in order to maintain the originally hoped level of profit.

Gross Margin on Inventory Investment

What is a gross margin on inventory investment?

It is a technique that measures the profit return on the amount invested to buy an inventory.

Why does a marketer need to know the gross margin on inventory investment?

1. The marketer uses it to know how profitable the items are when sold.
2. Pricing decisions are enabled by the knowledge because it shows the return on sales at the various price ranges.

How does a marketer use the gross margin on inventory investment?

Dick's Fruit Baskets Inc. was started in 1978 by Mr. Dicky Jones, to supply fruit baskets that are used as presents on special occasions. The fruits included oranges, tangerines, pears, apples, bananas, plums, and grapes. In order to keep the fruits fresh, Mr. Jones bought fruits that were ready to ripe, stored them, and selected them for inclusion

A Handbook of Marketing Mathematics
with automatic spreadsheets for Quantitative Marketing solutions

in the baskets as they ripened. In 1996, Mr. Jones spent $13 to make a fruit basket, and he sold it for $45. He sold at least one hundred fruit baskets every week.

In 1997 through 1999, there were a series of adverse hot, dry, and cold weather conditions in the fruit growing regions, and this reduced the supply of fruits in the United States. By 1999, Dick's Fruit Baskets Inc. spent $16 to make a fruit basket, and sold it for $50. The inventory turnover was still one hundred fruits baskets per week. At the end of 1999, Mr. Jones wanted to know how Dick's Fruit Baskets' profit was affected by the changes in the inventory cost, and he calculated it as follows.

Table 10-6
Dick's Fruit Basket
Gross Margin On Inventory Investment-1996

Gross margin on inventory investment $=$ $\dfrac{\text{Gross margin x Inventory turnover rate}}{\text{Price of inventory}}$

a. Gross margin on Inventory investment per week $= \dfrac{(\$4,500 - \$1,300) \times 1}{\$13} = \dfrac{\$3,200}{\$13} = \$246$

b. Gross margin on inventory investment per month $= \dfrac{(\$4,500 - \$1,300) \times 4}{\$13} = \dfrac{\$12,800}{\$13} = \$984.60$

c. Gross margin on inventory investment per year $= \dfrac{(\$4,500-\$1,300) \times 52}{\$13} = \dfrac{\$166,400}{\$13} = \$12,800$

Table 10-7
Dick's Fruit Basket
Gross Margin On Inventory Investment-1999

a. Gross margin on $\quad=\quad \dfrac{(\$5,000 - \$1,600) \times 1}{\$16} = \dfrac{\$3,400}{\$16} = \$212.50$
   Inventory investment
   per week

b. Gross margin on $\quad=\quad \dfrac{(\$5,000 - \$1,600) \times 4}{\$16} = \dfrac{\$13,600}{\$16} = \$850$
   inventory investment
   per month

c. Gross margin on
   inventory investment $= \dfrac{(\$5,000-\$1,600) \times 52}{\$16} = \dfrac{\$176,800}{\$16} = \$11,050$
   per year

Interpretation of the results.

1. In 1996, Dick's Fruit Basket Inc. had profit return of $246 per week, $984 per month, and $12,800 per year on the amount invested in inventory.
2. In 1999, the profit return for Dick's Fruit Basket Inc. declined to $212.50 per week, $850 per week, and $11,050 per year.

Implication of the results.

1. Dick's Fruit Baskets should increase the selling price of the baskets to $56 in order to increase the gross margin or profit return to the 1996 level.

Calculation steps.

1. Find the weekly gross margin on inventory investment by subtracting the sales from the cost of the fruit baskets, and dividing by the price.
2. To find the monthly gross margin on inventory investment, subtract the sales from the cost of the fruit baskets, multiply this by four weeks, and divide by the price.

3. Find the yearly gross margin on inventory investment by subtracting the sales from the cost of the fruit baskets. Multiply this by fifty weeks, and divide by the price.

Gross Margin on Return Per Square Foot

What is a gross margin on return per square foot?

It is the gross profit margin percentage that is attributed to sales in each square foot of the selling space.

Why does a marketer need to know the gross margin on return per square foot?

1. It is important for the marketer to know how efficient the marketing activities are.
2. It is used to decide how much to spend in making, buying or selling the product or service.
3. It is used to determine the price to charge for the product or service.
4. It is used to determine how efficient the selling space is.

How does a marketer find the gross margin on return per square foot?

Little Heaven Retirement & Rehab Inc. is a unique retirement center that combined a regular apartment and a commercial center into a huge enclave for living, shopping, and physical activities for retirees in Sun Village, Florida. The owner Smith Properties Inc. built the place in the effort to expand into the southeast regional market as the management decided in the 2000 strategic plan. Research showed that most retirees moved to the region because of the warm and pleasant weather conditions. At the present, more than 50 million retired people live in the region, and this is predicted to grow at an annual rate of .05%.

The center was built in 1994 at the cost of $900m ($2,066.11 per square foot), and occupied approximately ten acres (43,560sqft. x 10) of land. It cost $50m per year during the first five years to operate the center. The annual sales in these five years were $218m, $310m, $378m, $417m, and $448m respectively. Smith Properties wanted to find out how good the center was doing by looking at how many dollars each square foot in the center made or returned during the first five years. It did the following.

Table 10-8
Little Heaven Retirement & Rehab Inc.
Return Per Footage

$$Return\ per\ footage = \frac{Sales}{Square\ feet\ of\ selling\ space}$$

a. 1995 $\dfrac{\$218m}{435,600sq.ft.}$ = $500.45 per sq. ft.

b. 1996 $\dfrac{\$310m}{435,600sq.ft}$ = $711.66 per sq. ft.

c. 1997 $\dfrac{\$378m}{435,600sq.ft}$ = $867.76 per sq. ft.

d. 1998 $\dfrac{\$417m}{435,600sq.ft.}$ = $957.30 per sq. ft.

e. 1999 $\dfrac{\$448m}{435,600sq.ft.}$ = $1028.46 per sq. ft.

Interpretation of the results.

1. The dollars per square foot of the center increased every year.
2. The cumulative sales per square foot since 1995 broke even with the cost of building the center in 1998.

Implication of the results.

1. Little Heaven should increase its hold on the retirement market in Sun City by offering additional unique services to cater to the expected increases in the migration of retirees to the region.

Calculation steps.

1. Determine the sales for the period.
2. Determine the square feet of selling space.
3. Divide the sales for the period by the square feet of selling space.
4. Determine the profit return per footage of the center.

Gross Profit Margin

What is a gross profit margin?

It is the margin (difference between the sales and cost of product or service) before deducting other operating expenses such as salaries, rent, and utilities.

Why does a marketer need to know the gross profit margin?

1. It shows the amount of money that is available to pay marketing and other expenses.
2. It guides the marketer to find out the correct price to charge for the product or service.

How does a marketer find the gross profit margin?

Kic-Jim-Kic Karate Inc. is a karate sports gym located in downtown Hot City, Nevada. The company was established in the 1970s when aerobics and kick boxing were introduced in the city with no competition for the sports in the area. In 1989, Kic-Jim-Kic had

18,480 regular members that paid $35 monthly fees. It costs $15 per month to put together and provide a service package (57% gross margin). By 1992 there were three karate gyms and other exercise outlets in Hot City, and Kic-Jim-Kic's regular customers have now increased by 3,610. Also, the average cost to develop a service had increased to $19 per month. While competitors charged between $46.99 and $49.99 per month, Kick-Jim-Kick charged a lower price thinking that it would entice more gym users to patronize it. It needed to know how choosing a price of $45.99 could affect its original gross profit margin assuming that they keep the present members. So it did the following.

Table 10-9
Kic-Jim-Kic Karate Inc.
Gross Profit Margin

Gross Profit Margin = $\dfrac{Sales\text{-}Cost\ of\ goods\ sold}{Sales}$

1989 $\quad = \quad \dfrac{\$646,800\text{-}\$277,200}{\$646,800} \quad = 57\%$

1992 $\quad = \dfrac{\$1,015,919.8 - \$419,710}{\$1,015,919} = \dfrac{\$596,209}{\$1,015,919} = 58.68\%$

Interpretation of the results.

1. At the new price of $45.99, Kic-Jim-Kic had a profit margin of 58.68%, which was 1.68% more than the previous profit margin.

Implications of the results.

1. Kic-Jim-kic made more money by charging the lowest price in the market.
2. Kic-Jim-Kic had the advantage of attracting more customers than the competitors by using a low penetration price.

Calculation steps.

1. Determine the net sales by adding all the sales.
2. Determine the cost of goods sold by adding the cost of the goods, transportation and storage.
3. Determine the gross profit margin by subtracting the cost of goods sold from the net sales.
4. Divide the gross profit margin by the net sales to determine the gross profit margin.

Gross Margin Ratio (%)

What is a gross margin ratio?

It is the proportion of the net sale that is allocated to operating expenses and net profit.

Why does a marketer need to know the gross margin ratio?

It shows the marketer the amount of dollars available for possible spending.

How does a marketer find the gross margin ratio?

A-Man & A-Pan Mobile Foods Inc. is a mobile food service business started in 1988 by Mr. Inman Applebee. It caters food to workers on the roads and in building construction sites in Kansas city and surrounding towns. The boom in road and building constructions in the 1980's and 1990's resulted in a huge increase in business for A-Man & A-Pan. Sales in 1999 amounted to $950,098. The cost of goods sold was $409,098, and the gross margin was $541,000 ($950,098-409,098). A-Man & A-Pan felt that it could have gotten more margin if not for the high cost of food. Prior to making any changes, the company needed to know the percentage of the net sales that went to the cost of the good sold, and the percentage that was the gross margin. It did the following.

Table 10-10
A-Man & A-Pan Mobile Foods
Gross Margin Ratio (%)

Gross Margin Ratio (%)

$$= \frac{\text{Gross Margin}}{\text{Net sales}} = \frac{\$541,000}{\$950,098} = .57 \text{ or } 57\% \text{ or } 1: .57$$

Interpretation of the results.

1. 57% or 57 cents out of every dollar sales was left as the gross margin.
2. 43% or 43 cents out of every dollar sales was used to pay for the cost of goods sold.

Implications of the results.

1. A-Man & A-Pan should maintain the present high gross margin.
2. A-Man & A-Pan should continuously explore ways to reduce the cost of goods sold.

Calculation steps.

1. Determine the net sales by adding all the sales.
2. Determine the cost of goods sold by adding the cost of goods, transportation, and storage.
3. Determine the gross margin by subtracting the cost of goods sold from the net sales.
4. Divide the gross margin by the net sales to determine the gross margin ratio.

Investment Turnover Ratio

What is an investment turnover ratio?

It is the dollar sales generated by each dollar invested in the business.

Why does a marketer need to know the investment turnover ratio?

1. It enables the marketer to determine how effective the marketing activities are.
2. It guides the marketer to estimate the future marketing budget.

How does a marketer find out the investment turnover ratio?

Advanced Vinyl Sidings Inc. is an S-corporation started in 1981 by Mr. Nomwell to provide business and home vinyl services. Mr. Nomwell raised the beginning capital of $800,000 from friends and relatives by selling stocks. The average sale in the first five years was $2,879,500. Due to a sustained growth in home and office buildings in the 1980s and 1990s Advanced Vinyl Siding expanded the product lines to include seamless gutters and replacement windows. In 2000 Mr. Nomwell invested $1, 371,000 in the business, and sales rose to $4,234,200. Advanced Vinyl Sidings is considering an expansion into two neighboring states in 2004. It intends to borrow $5,000,000 from the bank, however, it needed to know the amount of the sales dollars that resulted from past investments, and it did the following.

Table 10-11
Advanced Vinyl Sidings Inc.
Investment Turnover Ratio

Investment Turnover Ratio	=	Net sales.
		Investment

$$1981\text{-}86 \qquad = \quad \frac{\$2,879,500}{\$800,000} = \$3.59$$

$$2000 \qquad = \quad \frac{\$4,234,200}{\$1,371,000} = \$3.08$$

Interpretation of the results.

1. Between 1981 and 1986, each dollar invested by Advanced Vinyl Siding Inc. yielded $3.59 in sales.
2. In 2000, each dollar invested by Advanced Vinyl Siding Inc. yielded $3.08 in sales.
3. The investment turnover for Advanced Vinyl Siding decreased by 58 cents between 1986 and 2000.

Implication of the results.

1. Advanced Vinyl Siding Inc. should have to reverse the downwards trend in the investment turnover ratio through: (1) reduced cost of operations; and (2) increased sales.

Calculation steps.

1. Determine the amount of total sales during the period by adding all the sales.
2. Determine the amount of total investment during the period by adding all the investments.
3. Divide the total sales by the total investment to find out the ratio of sales to investment.

Net Profit Margin or Net Return on Sales(%)

What is a net profit margin or net return on sales?

It is the portion of each sales dollar that is left as profit after the taxes and interests are deducted.

Why does a marketer need to know the net profit margin or net return on sales?

1. It acts as a guide to determine how much to increase or reduce the price of items in order to produce a higher profit margin.

How does a marketer find the net profit margin or net return on sales?

American Koast-to-Koast Inc. is an independent trucking firm with twenty trucks that hauled a variety of products to producers, wholesalers, and retail stores anywhere in the United States, Canada, and Mexico. The business was started in 1997 by Mr. Bright Face to take advantage of the high demand and the high price that existed in the hauling business in that period. The company proved to be lucrative. Sales in 1997, 1998, and 1999 were $1,990,000, $5,887,000, and $8,918,070 respectively. Thirty percent of the sales covered the cost of the trucks and operations, and the average tax during the period was 33%.

In 2000, American Koast-to-Koast decided to extend into warehousing to store, sort, and ship to general and specialty retail outlets. It borrowed half of the $10m needed for the project from the bank at an interest rate of 15%, with the intention of paying it with sales dollars and existing profit. It estimated to make $55m on sales between 2001 and 2005 as follows 2001- $10,000,000; 2002- $9,100,000; 2003 - $10,100,000; 2004 - $10,300,000; and 2005 - $10,500,000. The cost of sales to cover transportation and operations was 31% of the sales. The city of Chizmos where the company is located had just increased the municipal tax by two percent, this raised the business tax to 35%. Therefore, American Koast- to-Koast wanted to know the percentage of profit or the amount of money that would be left on each dollar of sales after paying the taxes and interests between 2001 and 2005, and how that would compare to the amount left between 1997 and 1999. It did as follows.

Table 10-12
American Koast-to-Koast
Net Profit Margin or Net Return on Sales

Net Profit Margin (net return on sales) $\dfrac{\textit{Profit after taxes} \times 100}{\textit{Sales}}$

Average for:

1997-1999   = $\dfrac{\$7,876,887.83 \times 100}{\$16,795,070}$ =   47% (47 cents per dollar)

2001-2005   = $\dfrac{\$22,424,994.36 \times 100}{\$50,000,000}$ =   45% (45 cents per dollar)

Interpretation of the results.

1. American Koast-to-Koast made 47% or 47 cents from every dollar that it invested between 1997 and 1999.
2. American Koast-to-Koast will make 45% or 45 cents from every dollar that it invests between 2001 and 2005.

Implication of the results.

1. In order to reach or surpass the original profit margin, American Koast-to-Koast should either have to raise prices or reduce cost or attract more customers to increase sales by at least $3m between 2001 and 2005.

Calculation steps.

1. Determine the total sales for the period involved.
2. Determine the profit for the period by subtracting the cost of the trucks and operations, and the taxes (or interest) from sales. For 1997-1999: ($16,795,070 – $5,038,521- $5,542,373) x 100. For 2001-2005: ($55,000,000-$17,050,000-$19,250,000-$750,000) x 100.

Percentage Variable Contribution Margin (PVCM).

What is the percentage variable contribution margin?

It is a technique that measures the percentage of each sales dollar that is available to cover fixed costs, and make profit.

Why does a marketer need to know the percentage variable contribution margin?

1. It indicates the operating funds available to cover the marketing fixed costs.

How does a marketer find out the percentage variable contribution margin?

Amity Termites Kontrol Inc. was started in 1978 by Mr. John Pesty in response to the increased termites and pests in Amity City due to the unusual weather patterns in the northeast United States. Amity Termites Kontrol maintained a constant growth in sales. In 2000 the company treated 20,000 homes and offices five times at a charge of $45 per treatment for a total sales of $4,500,000. The variable cost per treatment was $10 (or $1,000,000 total variable cost), and the variable contribution margin (VCM) was $3,500,000 ($4,500,000-$1,000,000). At this time, Amity Termites Kontrol was planning for 2001 and needed to know the percentage of 2002 to 2006 sales, and the percentage of 2001 sales dollars available to cover the fixed costs and profit in 2002. It did the following.

Table 10-13
Amity Termites Kontrol Inc.
Percentage Value Contribution Margin (PVCM)

$$PVCM = \underline{\textbf{Variable Contribution Margin(VCM)}} \qquad \textbf{(1)}$$
$$\textbf{Dollar sales}$$

$$PVCM = \underline{\$3,500,000} \times 100 = 77.8\%$$
$$\$4,500,000$$

Or

$$PVCM = \underline{\textbf{Unit price – Unit variable Cost}} \qquad \textbf{(2)}$$
$$\textbf{Unit price}$$

$$PVCM = \underline{\$45 - \$10} \times 100 = 77.8\%$$
$$\$45$$

Or

$$PVCM = \underline{\textbf{Sales – Variable Cost}} \qquad \textbf{(3)}$$
$$\textbf{Sales}$$

$$PVCM = \underline{\$4,500,000 - \$1,000,000} \times 100 = 77.8\%$$
$$\$4,500,000$$

Interpretation of the results.

1. Amity Termites Kontrol had 77.8% of the sales or 77.8cents of every one dollar sale in 2001 available to cover fixed costs and profit in 2002.

Implication of the results

1. Amity Termites Kontrol had a high percentage variable contribution margin (PVCM) in 2001, and that should provide adequate funds for 2002.

Calculation steps

1. Find the VCM by subtracting the total variable cost from the total sales.
2. In method #1, divide the variable contribution margin by the total sales, and multiply by 100.
3. In method #2, subtract the unit variable cost from the unit price, divide by the unit price, and multiply by 100.
4. In method #3, subtract the total variable cost from the total sales, divide by the total sales, and multiply by 100.

Price-Earnings Ratio

What is a price-earning ratio?

It is a technique that compares a company's market price per share to the earning per share.

Why does a marketer need to know the price-earning ratio?

1. It is used to show a company's growth potential.
2. It is used to show a company's earning stability.
3. It is used to show a company's management capability.
4. It indicates the financial ability of the marketer when borrowing from a bank

How does a marketer find the price-earning ratio?

JR Robotics Inc. was started in 1994 by Jane and Rico Buzzword to make and distribute artificial intelligent toys. The toys include different animals and human features that mimiced real life actions. Jane and Rico raised the $300,000 start-up capital by selling 8,451 shares to themselves, friends and relatives at $35.50 per share. The total sale in 1994 was $1,250,000. The after tax profit was $390,000 ($1,250,000 x .312). Fifty percent of this profit or $195,000 was distributed to preferred stockholders, and that left an earning per common share of $23.07. In 2001 the price of the shares went up to $84 per share. The total sales that year was $3,890,910, and the after tax profit was $1,245,091. Fifty percent of the profit or $622,545 or $74 earning per share was distributed. When Jane was preparing the 2002 strategic marketing plan for presentation at the 2001 annual meeting, and she needed to know how strong the company's earning from sales had been. She decided to compare the price-earning ratio in 1994 to that of 2001 as follows.

Table 10-14
JR Robotics
Price-Earning Ratio

Price-Earnings Ratio = Current market price per share
Aftertax earnings per share

1994 $\dfrac{\$35.5}{\$23.07} = 1.54$

2001 = $\dfrac{\$84}{\$74} = 1.14$

Interpretation of the results.

1. In 1994, each share earned 1.54 times its worth. Every one dollar share earned one dollar and fifty-four cents.
2. In 2001, each share earned 1.14 times its worth. Every one dollar share earned one dollar and fourteen cents.

Implication of the results.

1. JR Robotics Inc's. shares lost some of its earning power in 2001, and may not attract as many investors as they did in 1994.

Calculation steps.

1. Determine the market price per share.
2. Determine the earning per share by subtracting the preferred dividends from sales or income, and dividing it by the common shares.
3. Compute the price-earnings ratio by dividing the market price per share (#1) by the earning per share (#2).

Return on Total Assets

What is a return on total asset?

It is a technique that measures how productive a company's assets are.

Why does a marketer need to know about the return on total asset?

1. To measure how well the marketing activities are managed.

How does a marketer find the return on total assets?

A World of Pets Inc. was started in 1979 in Buffalo, New York by Mrs. Edna Jones to import animals from all over the world and resell to wholesalers. This idea occurred to her while in college in 1974. A biology major, Edna learned a lot about animals and how they live. She loved pets, and kept a Labrador dog and a variety of exotic fish in her apartment. She loved to discuss foreign pets with her foreign student friends. Edna's business intention was to supply the American pet market with unique animals from all over the world.

In 1979 Edna borrowed $500,000 from a bank at eighteen percent interest to set up the necessary facilities needed to import and distribute animals to various pets stores all over the Unites States. She imported one thousand animals of twenty different kinds from four countries. The demand was overwhelming, and it has since been that way. In 2001, A World of Pets Inc. earned $535,185 or 15% expansion with a $3,567,900 loan from the bank. The total asset increased to $6,984,000, including a five acres electronic storage facility, a health care facility, an automated feeding facility, and the facility for marketing and operations. The total sales in 2001 was $15,785,234, the profit after taxes was $8,185,614 and the interest income was $535,185. The company wanted to know how productive its assets were in 2001, so it calculated the return on assets below.

Table 10-15
A World of Pets
Return on Total Assets

$$Return\ on\ total\ assets = \frac{Profits\ after\ taxes + Interest\ Income}{Total\ assets}$$

$$\frac{\$8,185,614 + 535,185}{\$6,984,000} = \frac{\$8,720,799}{\$6,984,000} = 1.25\ cents$$

Interpretation of the results.

1. Each dollar that A World of Pets Inc. spent in asset produced 1.25 cents.

Implications of the results.

1. The relatively low productivity of the assets could be due to the low profit.
2. A World of Pets Inc. should have to maintain the sales level of the pets, and at the same time, hold down the cost of operations.
3. A World of Pets Inc. should use more of the profit to pay off some of the outstanding loan.

Calculation steps.

1. To determine the profit after tax, subtract the cost of goods sold, the fixed cost, the variable costs, and tax from sales.
2. Add the profit to any interest the company gets from all of its investments.
3. Add together all the assets owned by the company.
4. Divide #2 by #3.

Return on Investment (%)

What is a return on investment?

It is the percentage of the dollar profit generated by each dollar invested in the business.

Why does a marketer need to know the return on investment?

1. It is used to measure the productivity of new market areas, new accounts, or market investment, by looking at the sales output and the cost of sales.
2. It is used to measure how efficient the salespeople are.

How does a marketer find the return on investment?

American Toilet Supplies Inc. makes porcelain toilet bowls and seats, and porcelain toilet paper holders. The company is located in Freetown, NC. It sells to wholesalers who resell to retailers. In 1997, American Toilet Supplies invested $9,400,000 to build two additional production plants in Michigan and California. In 2000, sales from the two plants totaled $3,151,211, and the gross profit before tax was $1,473,169.2. As usual, the company wanted to know the return on the investment for the year in order to decide whether to continue the expansion. So American Toilet Supplies did as follows.

Table 10-16
American Toilet Supplies Inc.
Return on Investment(%)

Return on Investment (%) = $\dfrac{\text{Gross profit before taxes}}{\text{Investment}} \times 100$

$$= \frac{\$1,473,169}{\$9,400,000} \times 100 = 15.67\%$$

Interpretation of the results.

1. American Toilet Supplies Inc. had a 15.67% return on investment in 1999.
2. American Toilet Supplies made approximately 15.67 cents profit for every $1 sales it made in 1999.

Implication of the results.

1. The 15.67 return on investment is lower than the industry average.

Calculation steps.

1. Add up the total sales and the total expenses.
2. Find the net profit before taxes by subtracting the total expenses from the total sales.
3. Divide the gross profit before taxes by the total investment.
4. Multiply by 100.

Return on Investment model

What is a return on investment model?

It is a model that finds out the percentage of profit that a business makes for the owners by using the information from the balance sheet and income statement.

Why does a marketer need to know the return on investment model?

1. It is used to make pricing decision to achieve a target rate of profitability.

How does a marketer develop a return on investment model?

Gunminos Handguns Inc. was started in 1972 by Mr. Bobby Striker to make and sell handguns, long guns, ammunitions, and accessories. Because of the popularity of gun ownership and gun politics in the 1970s and 1980s, the demand for guns was very high. This was a boom period for Gunminos Inc., and the demand was so much that it opened another plant in the midwest. However, as the incidents of gun suicides and school shootings escalated in the 1990s, the demand for guns shifted to new guns that could be locked electronically or physically to prevent a non-owner usage. Gunminos was faced with a huge inventory of guns that do not lock when sales fell dramatically in the late 1990s. In 2000, Gunminos asked a bank for a $495m loan to retool one plant and make guns that lock with electronics. The bank demanded that Gunminos prepare a return on investment model that should guide them to assess the company's marketing efficiency and the rate of sales return. Gunminos presented some pertinent balance sheets and income statements information shown below in Figure 10-1, and used the model on Table 10-17 to find the return on the net worth.

Figure 10-17
Gunminos Handguns Inc.
Return on Investment Model

1. Sales   = $327.28m
2. Cost of Goods sold = $126m
3. Other fixcd costs   = $134m
4. Other variable costs = $20m
5. Inventory   = $154m
6. Accts. Receivable   = $29.45
7. Cash   = $360m
8. Fixed Asset   = $65.5m

9. Accts. Payable   = $39.3m
10. Notes Payable   = $3.3m
11. Other current liab. = $3.3m
12. Total current liab.   = $45.6m
13. Long-term liab.   = $16m
14. Total Asset   = $609m

Table 10-17
Guminos Handguns Inc.
Return On Investment Model

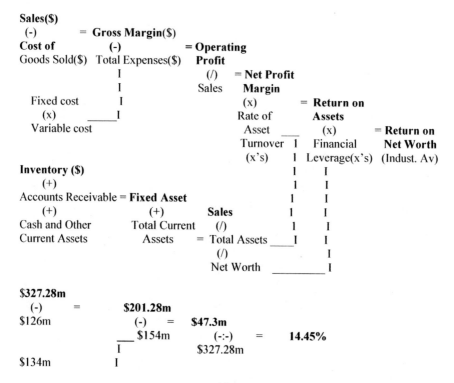

(+) _____ I   x   = 7.8%
$20m   (14.45 x .54)

                                    $327.28m   x   = 8.58%
$154m $65.5m   (-:-) _____ = .54xs
(+)   (+)   = $609m
$29.45m = $543.5m   (-:-) _____   = 1.1x
(+) $547.1m
$360m

Interpretation of the results.

1. In 1999, the return on net worth for Gunminos Inc. was 8.58%, the return on asset was 7.8%, the net profit margin was 14.45%, the operating profit was $47.3m, and the gross margin was $201.28m.
2. The 7.8% net worth meant that Gunmino Inc. got back only 7.8 cents for the stock holders for every dollar that it spent in 1999.

Implications of the results.

1. Gunminos had a lower return on net worth than the industry average and may not get the loan.
2. Gunminos should reduce both the cost of goods sold and the other expenses.

Calculation steps

Part 1
1. Subtract the cost of goods sold from sales to get the gross margin (S-CGS=GM).
2. Subtract the total expense from the gross margin to get the operating profit (GM-TE=OP).
3. Divide the operating profit by sales to get the net profit margin (OP/S = NPM) .

4. Multiply the net profit margin by the rate of asset turnover to get the return on assets (NPM x RAT =ROA).

Part 2
1. Add inventory to accounts receivable and cash and other assets to get the fixed asset (I+AR+CASH=FA).
2. Add the fixed asset to the current asset to get the total asset (FA+CA=TA).
3. Divide the sales by the total asset to get the rate of asset turnover (S/TA=RAT).
4. Divide the total asset by the net worth to get the financial leverage (TA/NW=FL).

Part 3
1. Multiply the return on assets by the financial leverage to get the **return of net worth.**

Variable Contribution Margin (VCM)

What is a variable contribution margin?

It is the sum or percentage remaining from sales after a business deducts all the variable costs such as sales commissions, material, labor, and packaging.

Why does a marketer need to know the variable contribution margin?

1. It gives the marketer an idea on the appropriate price to charge in order to increase profit.
2. It gives the marketer the knowledge of the level of price to charge in order to attain a desired profit level.

How does a marketer find the variable contribution margin?

Pave It-4-U Inc. is a medium sized contract company located in Greensboro, North Carolina. The firm builds and repairs driveways and parking lots, and does other types of seal coatings and patchworks. Some of the

Photo 22: Central Carolina Home Improvement

company's costs include management salary and sales force salary. Variable costs like labor and materials are the most expensive aspects of the cost. Pave It-4-U was always very concerned about the seasonal impacts of the variable costs on the amount left for the fixed costs and profit after deducting the variable costs. In 2000, the income was $1,560,000 from 1,000 contracts. The company spent $680,000 on labor and materials, and $29,000 on other variable costs. It was concerned that the variable cost was taking most of the income, and so it needed to know the percentage of income left after the variable costs are deducted. It did as follows

Table 10-18
Pave-It-4-U
Variation Contribution Margin

VCM = Sales – Variable cost of goods sold (labor, materials, packaging) – Variable
$$\frac{\text{selling cost(sales commission)}}{\text{Unit sold}}.$$

Sales (Income)	$1,560,000 or 1,000 jobs
Variable Cost of Goods Sold	-$ 680,000
Gross Margin	$880,000
Other variable costs	-$ 29,000
Variable Contribution Margin (VCM)	$851,000 or 54.5%

a. Var. Cost Per Job = $\underline{\text{Var. Cost of Goods Sold} + \text{other variable costs}}$

$$= \frac{\$680{,}000 + 29{,}000}{1{,}000} = \frac{\# \text{ of jobs}}{\frac{\$709{,}000}{1{,}000}} = \$709$$

b. Average Income Per Job = $\dfrac{\text{Sales (income)}}{\# \text{ of jobs}}$
(VCM income per job)

$$= \frac{\$1{,}560{,}000}{1{,}000} = \$1{,}560$$

c. Gross Profit Per Job = Average Income Per Job-Variable Cost Per

job (VCM per job) = $1,560-$709 = $851

Interpretation of the results.

1. The variable contribution margin or the sum left from sales after all variable costs were deducted was $851,000 or 54.5%.

2. The variable costs used up 45.5% of the sales income.
3. The average variable cost like labor and materials for each job completed by Pave-It-4-U was $709.
4. On the average, Pave-It-4-U charged $1,560 per job.
5. The gross profit from each job is $851.

Implications of the results.

1. Pave-It-4-U should not be very concerned because it has a high profit.
2. Pave-It-4-U could increase the gross profit to a desired level by setting the VCM to a higher percentage.

Calculation steps.

1. To find the total sales or income, add all the charges or prices for the jobs.
2. To find the total variable costs, add all the labor, materials, packaging, and variable selling cost such as sales commission.
3. To find the VCM, subtract the variable cost of goods sold from the sales or income.
4. To find the Variable Cost Per Job, add the variable cost of goods sold and the other variable costs to the total number of jobs, and divide by the total number of jobs.
6. To find the Average Price Per Job (VCM Income), divide the total sales by the total number of jobs.
7. To find the Gross Profit Per Job (VCM per unit), subtract the variable cost per job from the average price or income per job.

Non-traceable Cost Contribution Margin

What is a non-traceable cost contribution margin?

1. It is how much each unit sold (or in the case of Pace-It-4-U above how each job) contributed to cover the costs of operating the company that are non-traceable to particular unit

or jobs, such as company security, or yard maintenance like lawn mowing.

Why does a marketer need to know the non-traceable cost contribution margin?

1. Such knowledge is needed to determine how much each sales unit contributes to cover the costs that cannot be assigned to one department.

How does a marketer find the non-traceable cost contribution margin?

Assume that Pave-It-4-U needed to find out how much each job contributed to those indirect cost that cannot be traced such as materials and company security. Assume that in 2000, the company spent $19,000 for company security and $5,819 for yard maintenance. Therefore, the non-traceable unit cost should be as follows.

Table 10-19
Pave-It-4-U
Non-Traceable Unit Cost

Non-Traceable Unit Cost

$$= \frac{\text{the indirect non-traceable cost of operation}}{\text{\# of units or jobs}}$$

$$= \frac{\$19,000 + \$5,819}{1000} = \$24.81$$

Interpretation of the results.

1. Each job or unit contributed $24.81 to cover the non-traceable indirect cost of operations like the company's security and yard maintenance.

Implication of the results.

1. Pave-It-4-U has a low non-traceable cost, and should try to keep it that way.

Calculation steps.

1. To find the non-traceable cost per unit or job, add all the total indirect non-traceable costs to the total number of units or jobs, and divide it by the total number of units or jobs.

Territory Performance Measure

What is a territory performance measure?

It is a technique that measures the performance of a sales territory by using the rate of return on assets to stockholders and creditors, asset turnover, and contribution to cost.

Why does a marketer need a territory performance measure?

1. It is used to determine the sales performance of sales territories.
2. It is used to decide how much to invest in a sales territory.

How does a marketer use the territory performance measure?

Whoz-UP Fashions Inc. is a retail store that sells stylish pants, shirts, and T-shirts that appeal to teenagers. Whoz-Up Fashions had two locations in two market areas. Mr. John Solomon, the owner, used associate managers to operate each store. The managers determined the product assortments based on the appeals and demand of the teenagers. Every year, Mr. Solomon needed to know how profitable each territory is so as to decide how much to invest in it.

This year he needs to know the return on the asset or the asset turnover in each territory, and he did as follows.

Table 10-20
Whoz-UP Fashions Inc.
Territory Performance Measure - Territory One

Sales		$3,000,000
Less Variable costs		$1,800,000
VCM		$1,200,000
Less Direct Costs:		
Salaries	$400,000	
Travel Expenses	$100,000	
Sales Materials	$ 60,000	
Shipment	$ 40,000	
	$600,000	
Contribution to		
Indirect cost and Profit		$600,000
Assets Managed in Territory One		
Accounts Rec.		$ 280,000
Warehouse Assets		$1,200,000
Finished-good Inventory		$ 320,000
Total Asset		$1,800,000

Asset Turnover $= \dfrac{\text{Sales}}{\text{Total Asset}}$ $= \dfrac{\$3,000,000}{\$1,800,000} = 1.66$ times

% Contribution of sales to cost

$= \dfrac{\text{Contrib. To Ind. Cost and Profit}}{\text{Net sales}} = \dfrac{\$600,000}{\$3,000,000} = 20\%$

Return on Asset Managed = Asset turnover x Contribution as a
in Territory One   percent of sales
          = 1.66 times x 20% = 33.2%

Interpretation of the results.

1. The asset turnover for Territory One is 1.66 times, or each one dollar will return $1.66.
2. The variable contribution margin as a percentage of sales is 20% or 20% of sales is left for indirect cost and profit.
3. Territory One returned 33.2% of each dollar invested in the area.

Implications of the results.

1. The return on asset is high and Whoz-UP Fashion could still achieve a higher yield.
2. Whoz-UP should try to reduce the variable cost from the current level of 60%.
3. Whoz-UP should increase sales in order to increase the asset turnover.
4. The company should maintain a low direct cost in order to have a higher variable contribution margin as a percent of sales.
5. A high asset turnover resulting from high sales, and a high contribution as a percent of sales result in a high return on asset managed.

Calculation

1. To determine the Asset Turnover, divide Sales by Total asset.
2. To determine the Contribution as a Percent of Sales, divide the Contrib. To Ind. Cost and Profit by Net sales.
3. To determine the Return on Asset Managed, multiply Asset turnover by Contribution as a Percent of Sales.

Rowland Chidomere

PART FOUR

MARKET ATTRACTIVENESS

Rowland Chidomere

CHAPTER 11

MARKET POTENTIAL

Market Potential – Consumer market.

What is an <u>absolute consumer</u> market potential?

It is a technique used to determine the number of possible users of products or services and their maximum rate of purchase.

Why does a marketer need to know the <u>absolute consumer</u> market potential?

1. A marketer uses the absolute consumers market potential to decide how much to invest in the marketing activities, particularly in the product and promotion.
2. A marketer uses the absolute consumer market potential to estimate sales and income.

How does a marketer find the <u>absolute consumer</u> market potential?

Perfect Shapes Inc. is a barber shop located in Home Grooves, New York. This city has a diverse make up, including three large universities and ten corporate headquarters. Perfect Shapes is popular for its clean and stylish cuts. Most of the time, it is overwhelmed by

customers of all ages, and sometimes this resulted in delays due to the lack of barbers. In order to have a better knowledge of the market demand for hair cut in the city, Mr. King did a consumer marketing research at the beginning of every year.

Photo 23: Krush Kutz

With that knowledge, Mr. King effectively decided on how many barbers to employ, and how much sales to expect during the year. Below is the result of the marketing research showing the categories of the target groups and their potential in 2001.

Table 11-1
Perfect Shapes Inc.
Consumer Market Potential.

Market Potential = Percentage Purchasing x Population

Age Groups	Percent Needing Hair cut (%)	x	Population in Home Grooves (000)	=	Consumer Market Potential for hair cut in Home Grooves (000)
18-24	86		640		551
25-34	64		410		262
35-44	30		376		112.8
45-54	20		301		60.2
55-64	9		210		18.9
65-74	10		185		18.5
75-84	5		61		3.1
Total					1, 027

Interpretation of the results.

1. The total consumer market potential for hair cuts in Home Grooves, New York in 2001 was 1,027,000.
2. People in the 18-24 years age group had the most market potential for hair cuts.

Implications of the results.

1. Barber shops should be aware that the customers and their hair cuts vary from age to age.

2. Home Grooves should invest in hiring more barbers for the 18-24 years age group.

Calculation steps.

1. Categorize the population by age groups.
2. Determine the number of each age group in the total population.
3. Determine the percentage that needs the service in each age group.
4. Multiply the percentage that needs hair cuts in each age group by the number of the age group in the total population.

Market Potential – Industrial Market

Bill & Sons Foods Inc. manufactures canned vegetables, frozen vegetables, and dried vegetables in two plants located in Rollings, NC, and in Downing, Virginia. Bill & Sons needed to determine the sales and the value of its production output in the three vegetable categories in the two production plants.

The total shipments or expected sales of the vegetable manufacturers in the two states are shown below in Table 11-2. From past records, and from Bill's opinion he concluded that the cost of making the goods comprised of 30% of the value of the shipment of each category of vegetable in each state. Bill & Sons Foods needed to know the total market estimate for the three vegetable categories, and the cost of making the goods, therefore it did the following.

Table 11-2
Bill & Sons
Market Potential (in millions of $)

Items	NC	VA	Total shipment
31101	$1,068	$245	$1,313
32541	$987	$289	$1,276
33114	$1,522	$129	$1,651

Total	**$3,577**	**$663**	**$4,240**

Cost of Goods Sold (30%)	$1,073.1	$198.9	$1,272
Estimated Potential	**$2,503.9**	**$464.1**	**$2,968**

Interpretation of results.

1. The total value of shipment in the 2 states for the entire can, frozen, and dried vegetable industry is $4,240m.
2. The total estimated market potential for Bill & Sons Food is $2,968m.

Implication of the results.

1. Bill & Sons Food should increase the value of its shipments in the two states.

Calculation steps.

1. Determine the total value of shipment in the industry for each product by adding all the total shipments in the states
2. Multiply the total estimated sales in each state by the estimated market potential (.001).

Relative Market Potential – Single Index Approach

What is a single index relative market potential?

It is the percentage of the market potential in the different types of market that a firm sells its products or services.

Why does a marketer need to know the single index relative market potential?

1. It enables the marketer to use a single factor to forecast sales.

How does a marketer find the relative single index market potential?

Quality Import Cars Inc. imports and distributes two high quality cars from the country of Guallam. The cars, Digeria and Magnata each retails for more than $350,000 in the United States. The owner of the car dealership, Ms. Legot compares her cars with such models as Jaguars and Ferrari, and competes against them. Quality Import Cars is located in the city of New Hope, a huge metropolitan town composed of four big cities (A, B, C, D) that grew into each other. Ms.Legot had problems in determining the number of cars the people in each section of the city would buy, and that resulted into major planning inaccuracies.

The total market potential for high class cars in the United States in 2000 was $710 million. Utah, the state in which Quality Import Cars is located had 8.8 percent of the high income car buyers in the U.S. The city of New Hope has 20 percent of the state's high income car buyers. This was distributed as follows: A 30 percent, B 28 percent, C 20 percent, and D 22 percent. Ms. Legot needed to know the market potential of the state, the city, and the four sections of the city based on the high income residents, so she did the following.

Table 11-3
Quality Import Cars
Relative Market Potential - Single Index Approach

Relative Market Potential(state)
= Total U.S. Potential x State Population
$710,000,000 x 8.8 percent = **$62,480,000**

Relative Market Potential (city)
= Total State Potential x City Population

$62,480,000 x 20 percent =**$12,496,000**

Relative Market Potential (city section)
= Total City Potential x City Section
Population

City Sections:
A = $12,496,000 x 30 percent = $3,748,800
B = $12,496,000 x 28 percent = $3,498,880
C = $12,496,000 x 20 percent = $2,499,200
D = $12,496,000 x 22 percent = $2,749,120

Interpretation of the results.

1. The total income of high priced car buyers in the state of Utah in 2000 was $62,480,000.
2. The total income of high priced car buyers in the city of New Hope in 2000 was $12.496, 000.
3. The total income of high priced car buyers in the city sections A, B, C, and D in 2000 were $3,748,800, $3,498,880, $2,499,200, and $2,749,120 respectively.

Implication of the results.

1. The state of Utah and the city of New Hope are suitable for the sale of high priced cars.

Calculation steps.

1. Calculate the relative market potential of the state by multiplying the total U.S. market potential by the total state population of high priced car buyers.
2. Calculate the relative market potential of the city by multiplying the total state potential by the city's population.
3. Calculate the relative market potential of each of the city sections by multiplying the total city potential by each city section's population.

Total Market Potential

What is a total market potential?

It is the sum of sales that is possible to come from a given market area.

Why does a marketer need to know the total market potential?

1. It helps the marketer to decide on the amount of marketing effort and expenditure to give to a market area.

How does a marketer find the total market potential?

Perfect Denture Inc. is a small manufacturer and wholesaler of dentures in Haylow, NY. It is a one- person operation that neither had the time for nor the idea of marketing research. The operation, although not formally planned, is smooth. Perfect Denture reacted to market needs as they occurred. In 2000, the population of Haylow and the areas around grew to 256,000. There was also an increase in the demand for dentures. Mr. Clinton, the owner of Perfect Denture felt that the business needed an estimate of the number of people that are likely to buy dentures in the area. In order to know this, Mr. Clinton had to find out the market potential of dentures for existing and possible denture buyers in the area. Below are the income, population, and demand for dentures in the city in 2000. Furthermore, the city anticipated increases in demand of 3 percent, 4 percent, and 5 percent in 2002 in the income brackets of $0-$15,000, $35,001-$55,000, over $55,000 respectively. Mr. Clinton did the following.

Table 11-4a
Perfect Dentures Inc.
2001 Market Potential for Dentures in Haylow, Georgia

Total Market = Population x % of likely buyers

Income	Population	x	% of likely dentures buyers	= Market Potential
$0 – 15,000	50,000		3	1,500
$15,001 – 25,000	60,000		6	3,600
$25,001 – 35,000	70,000		9	6,300
$35001 - 55,000	41,000		21	8,610
Over 55,000	35,000		35	12,250
Total Market Potential				**32,260**

Table 11-4b
Perfect Dentures Inc.
2002 Projected Market Potential for Dentures in Haylow, Georgia

Income	Population	x	% of likely dentures buyers	= Market Potential
$0 – 15,000	50,000		3 (+3%)	3,000
$15,001 – 25,000	60,000		6	3,600
$25,001 – 35,000	70,000		9	6,300
$35001 - 55,000	41,000		21 (+ 4%)	10,250
Over 55,000	35,000		35 (+ 5%)	14,000
Total Market Potential				**37,150**

Interpretation of the results.

1. The number of dentures that could be sold in 2001 was 32,260.

2. Most of the buyers were in the $55,00 or more income bracket.
3. The total market potential was expected to increase by 4,890 in 2002.

Implications of the results.

1. Perfect Denture should get ready to get a share of the market increase, and increase the marketing efforts and expenditures.
2. Perfect Denture should inform the retailers of the sales potential in the various income brackets.

Calculation steps.

1. From the city or the Internet, collect sales data on dentures by income levels.
2. Multiply the proportion of the population in each income level by the percentage of dentures that they bought.
3. For future year potentials, multiply the projected percentage increase or decrease in the demand for dentures in each income bracket by the population in the bracket.

Total Market Potential for Combined Markets

What is a total market potential for combined markets?

It is a technique that determines the total market potential by using the value of shipment or the value of the production output in the market area.

How does a marketer find the total market potential for combined markets?

Ms. Agat Njoku owns an appliance/hardware distributing company. The company, Jokey's Products wholesales refrigerators, ovens, and dishwashers to appliance stores, hardware stores, and discount stores in Georgia, Alabama, Louisiana, and Florida. Jokey's Products could not determine the right amount of money to allocate to merchandise in each state every year. This was because it did not know the market potential or the number of appliances the stores in the four states buy.

In 2001, Ms. Njoku found the total industry value of shipment for the three products in each market in the *Census of Retailing, U.S. Industrial Outlook.* These values of shipment are shown below. Based on sales history, Ms. Njoku concluded that the cost of buying the merchandise comprised of 40 percent of the value of shipment. As shown below, she wanted to use these values to find out the total value of shipments and the market potential in the four states.

Table 11-5
Jokey's Products Inc.
Value of Shipment for the Combined Markets in 2001
(000)

Product/SIC	Georgia	Alabama	Louisiana	Florida
Refrigerators/ 31112	$900	$350	$315	$415
Ovens/ 30020	$300	$515	$345	$700
Dishwashers/ 30021	$300	$400	$300	$
400				
Total	**$1,500**	**$1,265**	**$960**	**$1,515**

Estimated Market Potential = (Location1 +Location 2 + Location 3
+ Location 4) x .40
= ($1,500   +$1265   + $960   +$1,515) x .40= $2,096

Interpretation of the results.

1. Based on the cost of buying the appliances, the market potential by the value of shipment for the four states in 2001 was $2,096,000.
2. The state of Florida had the highest market potential, and it was followed closely by Georgia.

Implication of the results.

1. Jokey's Product should determine the amount to allocate to buy and distribute each appliance in 2001 by projecting the percentage of its value of shipments from the total industry value of shipments.

Calculation steps.

1. Add the dollar amount of the value of shipments for all the states to get the total value of shipments.
2. To determine the total market potential for the combined markets, multiply the total value of shipment by the percentage of the cost of buying the merchandise.

Category Development Index (CDI)

What is a category development index?

It is an index or figure that shows the gap that exists in the demand for one product category like an SUV in different geographic market territories.

Why does a marketer need to know the category development index?

1. A marketer could use the category development index to determine the market territory that has the largest demand for a product or service category.
2. A marketer could use the category development index as a mirror to choose the appropriate strategies to better serve the buyers of a product category.

How does a marketer find the category development index?

Serve "U" Fast Inc. is a drive through restaurant with branches in North Carolina and Virginia. Headquartered in Greensboro, NC.,

Serve "U" Fast served three categories of food dishes: the American Combos, the Chinese Combos, and the African Combos. In order to plan the supply for the geographic regions in the two states, Serve "U" Fast chose five main cities annually to determine if

Photo 24: Chicken & Honey

gaps exist in the demand for each category of the fast food. As usual, they started with the American Combos category. According to the sales records, in 2001 the stores in Charlotte served 750,000 units of American Combos to 21,000 households, the stores in Raleigh served 459,000 units of American Combos to 14,000 households, and the stores in Durham served 350,000 units of American Combos to 10,000 households. In Virginia, the stores in Richmond served 854,100 units of American Combos to 18,500 households, and the one in Martinsville served 471,600 American Combos to 8,400 households. A total of 2,884, 700 units of American Combos were sold, and Serve "U" Fast Inc. needed to know how each city lagged in the sales of the American dish, and which ones needed additional marketing assistance or development. He did the following.

CDI = <u>Sales per 1000 for a product category</u> x 100
        Sales per 1000 household total

Table 11-6
Serv "U" Fast Inc.
Category Development Index

	Annual Unit Sales American Combos	Thousands of -:- Households	Sales Per = 1000 Households	Index
Total	2,884,700	72	40.06	100
Charlotte	750,000	21	35.7	89.1
Raleigh	459,000	14	32.7	81.6
Durham	350,000	10	35	87.4
Richmond	854,100	18.5	46.2	115.3
Martinsville	471,600	8.4	56.1	140

Interpretation of the results.

1. A total of $2,884,700 units were sold to 72,000 households in all the markets. The average sales per household is 40.06 units which is equal to the 100 index.
2. The cities of Charlotte, Raleigh and Durham lagged behind in the sales of the American Combos. They need to develop more market for the American Combos.
3. The city of Martinsville had the best sales performance in the sales of the American Combos with 140 index, followed by Richmond with 115.3.

Implications of the results.

1. Although the few buyers in these cities are well served, the city of Martinsville is saturated in American Combos. Existing buyers should be served as usual and maintained, and new markets must be penetrated.
2. Serve "U" Fast Inc. should provide additional market development assistance to the stores in the cities of Raleigh and Durham to sell the American Combos.

Calculation steps.

1. Determine the total annual sales for the American Combos in all the geographic regions.
2. Determine the total number of the American combos sold in the three cities during the year.
3. Determine the number of households in each city.
4. Determine the sales of American combo per thousand people in each city by dividing #1 by #2.
5. Find the sales index by multiplying the sales per 1000 household in each territory by one hundred, and dividing it by the sales per 1000 household total.

Brand Development Index (BDI)

What is a brand development index?

It is an index or number that shows the gaps in the selective demand (demand for brands) of similar products in different geographic market territories. It is a regional based demand gap in the product brands.

Why does a marketer need to know the brand development index?

1. Marketers could use the brand development index to determine the market territory with the largest selective gap in the demand of a brand of a product e.g. Honda Prelude X4X.
2. Marketers could utilize the brand development index as the mirror to develop the appropriate sales strategies.

How does a marketer find the brand development index?

Tecks-Com. Wireless Inc. sells TCI wireless phones in stores in Mclain, Jumpup, and Downhill, Va. Since its inception in 1989, the stores have had problems deciding the quantity of TCI wireless phones to carry in the inventory every year. The company did not have a way to determine the actual demand in the three cities. According to sales record in 1999, the store in Mclain with 65,000 households sold 35,600 TCI wireless phones. The store in Jumpup with 75,000 households sold 46,000 TCI wireless phones and the store in Downhill with 25,000 households sold 17,500 TCI wireless phones. Tecks-Com Inc. wanted to know which of the three cities was low in sales of the wireless phone and may require additional market development. Table 11-7 shows brand development index for the three cities.

Table 11-7
Tecks-ComWireless Inc.
Brand Development Index for the Three Market Areas

$$\text{BDI} = \frac{\text{Sales per 1000 household in territory}}{\text{Sales per 1000 household total}} \times 100$$

Area	Annual Unit Sales (TCI wireless)	-:-	Thousands of Households	Sales Per =1000 Households	Index
Total	99,100	165	6	100	
Mclain	35,600	6.5	5.47	91.16	
Jumpup	46,000	7.5	6.13	102.16	
Downhill	17,500	2.5	7	116.66	

Interpretation of the results.

1. The city of Downhill has the highest index, and sold the highest number of phones per household.
2. The cities of Downhill and Jumpup had higher indexes than the index of 100, and the demand for wireless phones in them was above the market level.

3. Downhill had the highest TCI wireless phone demand, followed by Jumpup and Mclain.
4. The city of Mclain had the lowest sales, and there is .53 or 8.84% gap in the demand for TCI wireless phones.

Implications of the results.

1. There is little or no urgency for additional development for the wireless phone markets in the cities of Jumpup and Downhill due to existing high brand development indexes in them.
2. Tecks-Com Inc. should increase the distribution of TCI wireless phones in Mclain.

Calculation steps.

1. Determine the total number of different wireless phones sold in the three cities during the year, including TCI wireless.
2. Determine the number of households in each city.
3. Determine the sales per thousand for each city by dividing #1 by #2.
4. Find the total brand development index by dividing the total sales by the households in each territory.
5. Find each city's brand development index by dividing the total sales for the city by the number of households in the city. Find the percentage of the city BDI to the total BDI.

Buying Power Index

What is a buying power index?

It is a technique that is used to determine the potential sales opportunity of a trading area based on three factors: the effective buying index, the retail sales, and the area's population.

Why does a marketer need to know the buying power index?

1. The buying power index aids the marketer to make location decisions based on the ability of the customers to buy.
2. A marketer could use the buying power index to make product or service mix decisions by determining the brand and category that the market is able to buy.

How does a marketer find the buying power index?

American Nail Care and Tan Inc. has two locations in Roland and in Edmond, Oklahoma. Both cities have strong demand for manicures and indoor tanning. Mr. Jung, the owner, wanted to increase the number of location in each or both cities. However, he did not know which city was the most profitable. The city of Roland had .00043 percent of US effective buying income, .00072 percent of US retail sales, and .00023 percent of US population. The city of Edmond had .00053 percent of US effective buying income, .00067 percentage of US retail sales, and .00062 percent of United States population. One major question was which city would be the most profitable with more than one store? Mr. Jung did the following.

Table 11-8
American Nail Care and Tan
Buying Power Index

Buying Power Index (BPI) = 0.5 (area's % of U.S. effective buying
income) + 0.3 (area's % of U.S. retail
sales) + 0.2 (area's % of U.S. population)

Roland's BPI = 0.5 (.00043) + 0.3 (.00072) + 0.2 (.00023)
.00022 +   .00022   .000046   = .00049

Edmond's BPI = 0.5 (.00053) + 0.3 (.00067) + 0.2 (.00062)
.00027   .00020   .00012   = .00059

Interpretation of the results.

1. Edmond's residents have .00010% more potential than Roland's residents.

Implications of the results.

1. The city of Edmond had a better chance to accommodate additional stores.
2. Although small in percentage, the difference in the BPI between the two cities amounted to 280,000 potential sales opportunities.

Calculation steps

1. Determine the area's percentage of US effective buying index, and multiply it by 0.5.
2. Determine the area's percentage of US retail sales, and multiply it by 0.3.
3. Determine the area's percentage of US population, and multiply it by 0.2.
4. Add #1, #2, and #3 to obtain the buying power index.

Product Survival Rate

What is a product survival rate?

It is the rate at which products survive the wear and tear of customers' usage or obsolescence.

Why does a marketer have to know the product survival rate?

1. To determine the rate at which to replace the firm's products in the market.
2. To estimate the number of products the firm should produce or store in a period of time.

How does a marketer find the product survival rate?

KompuAmerica Inc. retails PCs, software, laptops, and accessories. Since its inception in 1992, KompuAmerica had encountered problems dealing with the rapid rate at which the computer market had changed. Buyers often updated or replaced the old models as soon as new models or computer technology became available. Therefore, computers and computer parts sellers were not always sure of when customers will replace their computers. In the middle of 2000, KompuAmerica decided to find out the number of the PC Z models to be replaced in the year 2001 by finding out the number of this model that survived or remained with the owners. From the sales history and a survey of buyers, KompuAmerica determined that 1 percent of PC Z models bought in 1997 was scrapped in 2001. In the same year, the scrapping of the models bought in 1996 was 5%, 10% for the models bought in 1995, 25% for the models bought in 1994, 50% for the models bought 1993, 80% for the models bought 1992, and 100% for the models bought in 1991. Kompu America Inc. calculated the survival rates as follows.

Table 11-9
KompuAmerica Inc.
Product Survival Rate

(a) Year Id.	(b) Total Units Sold	(c) Units Scrapped in 2001	(d) Annual Surv. rate	(e) Surv. rate at end of 2001	(f) Surv. units at the end of 2001
		(%)	(%)	(%)	(units)
1997	439,000	1	(4,390)	99 (100-1) 99	434,610
1996	450,000	5	(22,500)	95 (100-5) 94(.99 x .95)	427,500
1995	399,000	10	(39,900)	90 (100-10) 85(.94 x .90)	359,100
1994	377,899	25	(94,475)	75 (100-25) 63(.85 x .75)	283,424
1993	349,800	50	(174,900)	50 (100-50) 32(.63 x .63)	174,900
1992	398,000	80	(318,400)	20 (100-80) 6(.32 x .20)	79,600
1991	348,010	100	(348,010)	0 (100-100) 0	0
Total Units	**2,761,709**	**(1,002,575)**			**1,759,134**

Interpretation of the results.

1. None of the PC Z models bought between 1998 and 2001 had been scrapped.
2. The total number of the PC Z model scrapped between 1997 and 1991 was 1,002,575.
3. The total number of the PC Z model surviving or remaining in 2001 from PC Z models sold since 1991 was 1,759,134.

Implication of the results.

1. Although KompuAmerica could replace up to 1,002, 575 models of PC Z models, the company should note the differences in the years of the models to be replaced.

Calculation steps.

1. To find the number of units scrapped in a year, multiply the total units sold during the year by the percent of units scrapped.
2. To find the percentage of the annual survival rate, subtract the percent units scrapped from 100 percentage.
3. To find the survival rate for e.g. 'f' at the end of 2000, multiply the previous year 'e' survival rate at the end of 2000 by the year 'f' annual survival rate.
4. To find the surviving units at the end of 2000 for any year, subtract the total units scrapped that year from the total units sold in 2000.

Replacement Potential

What is a replacement potential?

It is a technique that enables manufacturers to estimate the quantity of a brand of a product to produce in a period of time, by studying customers' historical rate of scrapping or getting rid of the brand.

Why does a marketer need to know the replacement potential?

1. It is necessary to determine the rate at which to replace the inventory to meet the demand gap caused by obsolescence or wear.

How does a marketer find the replacement potential?

Quality Sealed Air Inc. located in Sit Down, Idaho manufactures reusable plastic air pads for cheerleading landings. The mat is a tender soft inflated pad, and it is used for protective landing to avoid injuries in cases of acrobatic mishaps and hard landings. The turgidity and good stitching of the so called QualiFloat air pads made them a favorite for high school and college gymnastic teams and other physical and recreational groups. Because of their high quality, the air pads lasted for several years before they wore off. Therefore, Ms. Weekly, the inventory manager for the company had some problem in determining the correct number of air pads to produce every year. In 2001, she needed to come up with a more accurate estimate of the number of air pads for the company to produce. Prior years' data showed the percentage of the air pads sold since 1994 that were left in 2001 and the annual scrapping rate in those years. These were used to determine the number of air pads to replace in 2001 as shown below.

Table 11-10
Quality Sealed Air Inc.
Replacement Potential for QualiFloat Air Pads.

(a) Year Product Was Sold	(b) Company x Sales (000)	(c) Percent Left at Start of = 2001 (%)	(d) Number Left at Start of x 2001 (000)	(e) Annual Scrapping Rate (%)	= (f) 2001 Replacement Potential (000)
2000	11,300	100	11,300	1	113
1999	11, 800	99	11,682	5	584
1998	8,941	94	8,405	10	841
1997	12,400	85	10,540	25	2,635
1996	11,500	63	7,245	50	3,623
1995	12,111	32	3, 876	80	3,101
1994	12,500	6	750	100	750

Interpretation of the results.

1. The products sold in 1996 had the highest potential for replacement in 2001, followed by 1995, and 1997.
2. The products sold in 2000 had the least potential for replacement.
3. The year 1994 had the least percentage of products left in 2001.

Implication of the results.

1. QualiFloat should devote more time to replace the units bought in 1995 through 1999.

Calculation steps.

1. Find how many units of the product that the company sold each year.
2. Find the percentage of the product left or unsold at the start of 2001.
3. Multiply #1 by #2 to find the number of units left at the start of 2001.
4. To find the replacement potential for each product in 2001, multiply #3 by the annual scrapping rate.

Required Total Dollar Sales

What is a required total dollar sales?

It is the amount of sales in dollars that is necessary to achieve the minimum dollar contribution to cover cost and make profit.

Why does a marketer need to know the required total dollar sales?

1. It helps the marketer to find the benchmark level of sales to achieve.

How does a marketer find the required total dollar sales?

Carolina Standard Bank Inc. is a residential and commercial bank located in Slippery Bay, North Carolina. When it was started in 1987, CSB was the only bank located in the eastside of the city. The bank was very valuable to individuals and businesses in the area as evidenced by CSB's high market share and a profit of $2,000,000 in 1994. However, in 1995, two new banks expanded into the eastside to compete against Carolina Standard Bank.

As the competition intensified in 2000, Carolina Standard Bank decided that its main market strategy was to challenge the other two banks by charging the lowest fees for checking accounts. In order to do this, CSB needed to know the total dollar fees required

Photo 25: Bank of America

to cover the cost to service the checking accounts and make profit in 2000. At that time there were 20,000 checking account customers at the CSB. It wanted to lower its monthly service fees for the checks from $3.50(or $70,000 per month) to $3.20(or $64,000 per month) in 2000, the lowest among the three banks. At a variable cost of 76cents to service each account in 1999, CSB had a monthly variable contribution margin VCM (the amount left after deducting variable cost) of $2.44 or ($3.20-76cents) per account, and a monthly percentage variable contribution margin PVCM (the percentage of each additional sales dollar that was available to help CSB cover its direct, traceable fixed costs and make profit) of 76.25 % or ($3.20-.76 x 100/$3.20). The direct fixed cost in 1999 was fifty-seven percent of the VCM or $1.39, and the total contribution was $1.05 or ($2.44-

$1.39). Armed with this information, CSB determined the total monthly dollar income from checking fees required and the target total contribution at the reduced service charge. This is shown below.

Table 11-11
Carolina Standard Bank Inc.
2000 Required Total Dollar Sales

Checking Accounts Service Fee (20,000 x $3.20 x 12)	$768,000
x PCVM	.7625
Variable contribution margin VCM	$585,600
Direct, traceable fixed cost (57% of VCM)	$333,792
Target Total Contribution	$251,808

Total dollar sales required from the checking account = target total
(in order to achieve $64,000 monthly)   contribution + total
                                              direct or traceable fixed cost
                                                      PVCM

Total dollar sales required = $585,600 = $768,000 annual fees
                                   .7625   or $64,000 monthly fees

Total unit sales required = $585,600   = 240,000 annual
                                                      transactions
                                  2.44   or   20,000   monthly
                                  transactions.

Interpretation of the results.

1. At the reduced monthly checking fee of $3.20 and 20,000 customers, Carolina Standard Bank will have to make a total annual amount of $770,518 or $64,210 monthly from the checking fees, in order to achieve the minimum dollar contribution to cover cost and make profit.
2. The total fees collected each month will have to be increased by $210.

Implication of the results.

1. CSB should increase the number of customers in order to make more money with the low service charge.

Calculation steps

1. To find the total annual policy fees, multiply the number of customers by the policy, and by 12 months.
2. To determine the PVCM, subtract the variable cost from the lower monthly service fees, multiply by 100, and divide by the lower monthly service fees.
3. Multiply #1 by #2 to find the VCM.
4. Find the direct traceable fixed cost by multiplying the VCM by the direct fixed cost percentage
5. To find the target total contribution, subtract #4 from number #3.
6. To find the total dollar sales required, divide the VCM by the PVCM or divide #3 by #2.
7. To find the total unit sales required, divide the total VCM by the monthly VCM or divide #3/(#3/customers/12 months).

Required Total Unit Sales

What is a required total unit sales?

It is the number of units required to be sold in order to achieve the minimum dollar contribution to cover cost and make profit.

Why does a marketer need to know the required total unit sales?

1. It enables the marketer to estimate when a benchmark level of sales could be achieved.

How does a marketer find the required total unit sales?

Hu-Nose Tomorrow Inc. was started in 1985 in Hu-Nose, North Carolina by Mr. John Nose, to insure homes against foreclosure due to bankruptcy, a rampant event in the decade. Because Hu-Nose Tomorrow was the only one of its kind in the state, it was heavily used by the people from all over the state. The income in 1990 was $2,600,000.

In 1995 two other home bankruptcy insurance companies started in Hu-Nose. As the competition intensified, Hu-Nose Tomorrow decided that the best way for it to compete was to challenge the other two insurers with a low premium policy. In order to do this, Hu-Nose Tomorrow needed to know the total units or policy holders to have at a low premium in order to cover its cost and make profit. At that time, 20,000 customers had policies with Hu-Nose Tomorrow, and the monthly fees per policy was $35. This was $8,400,000 in annual income. Each policy was serviced at a cost of $7.6. The monthly percentage variable contribution margin PVCM (the percentage of each additional sales dollar that was available to pay the direct, traceable fixed costs and make profit) was 78.28 % or ($35-7.6 /35 x 100). The VCM or the amount left after deducting the variable cost from the price was $27.4, the direct fixed cost was fifty-seven percent of the VCM or $15.61, and the total contribution was $11.79 or ($27.4-$15.61).

In 2001 Hu-Nose Tomorrow lowered the fees to $32 per policy/per month. The variable cost per premium decreased to $5. The monthly variable contribution margin VCM (the amount left after deducting the variable cost) lowered to $27 or ($32-$5) per policy. The monthly percentage variable contribution margin PVCM (the percentage of each additional sales dollar that was available to help pay the direct, traceable fixed costs and make profit) was 84.75 % or ($32-5 /32 x 100). The direct fixed cost decreased to forty-seven percent of the VCM or $12.6, and the total contribution lowered to $14.4 or ($27-$12.6). Armed with this information, Hu-Nose Tomorrow attempted to find the total transactions required in the budget to achieve the minimum dollar contribution to cover cost and make profit. The following shows the results.

Table 11-12
Hu-Nose Tomorrow
2000 Total Required Units and Sales

Annual Policy Fees (20,000 x $35.0 x 12)	$8,400,000
x PCVM	.7828
Variable contribution margin VCM	$6,575,520
Direct, traceable fixed cost (57% of VCM)	$3,748,046.4
Target Total Contribution	$2,827,473.6

Total number of transactions required = target total contribution
to make $64,000 per month   + total <u>direct or traceable fixed</u>
<u>cost</u>

PVCM per unit

$$\textbf{Total required} = \frac{\$2,827,473.6 + \$3,748,046.6}{\text{VCM (VCM/Total untis/12)}} = \frac{\$6,575,520.2}{\$27.4}$$

transactions

= 239,982 annual transactions or
20,000 monthly transactions

$$\textbf{Total dollar sales required} = \frac{\$2,827,473.6 + \$3,748,046.6}{.7828}$$

$$= \frac{6,575,520.2}{.7828} = \$8,400,000 \text{ annual}$$

or $700,000 monthly

Table 11-13
Hu-Nose Tomorrow
2001 Total Required Sales and Units

Annual Policy Fees (20,000 x $32.0 x 12)	$7,680,000
x PCVM	.8438
Variable contribution margin VCM	$6,480,000
Direct, traceable fixed cost (47% of VCM)	$3,045,000
Target Total Contribution	$3,434,400

Total number of policies required = target total contribution + total
to make $64,000 per month   direct or traceable fixed cost

PVCM per unit

Total required premiums = $6,508,800 = 240,000 annual
checking account transactions $27   or 20,000 monthly

transactions

Total dollar sales required = $6,508,800 = $7,680,000 annual fees
                                   .8475 $640,000 monthly fees

Interpretation of the results.

1. At a reduced premium of $32, Hu-Nose Tomorrow should
    have 241,066 annual or 20,089 monthly premiums holders in
    order to achieve the minimum dollar contribution to cover its
    cost and make profit.
2. The total number of premium holders should be increased by
    89 in order to achieve the required income.

Implications of the results.

1. In order to attract more customers, Hu-Nose Tomorrow should have to emphasize the advantages of its low premium in its advertisements.
2. It only took Hu-Nose Tomorrow 89 more policyholders to recover the lost revenue from premium reduction. This is only a .45% increase, and it implies that the company could easily recover from a high policy reduction if the need be.

Calculation steps.

1. To find the total annual policy fees, multiply the number of customers by the policy and by 12 months.
2. To determine the PVCM, subtract the variable cost from the lower monthly service fees, multiply by 100, and divide by the lower monthly service fees.
3. Multiply #1 by #2 to find the VCM.
4. Find the direct traceable fixed cost by multiplying the VCM by the direct fixed cost percentage.
5. To find the target total contribution, subtract #4 from number #3.
6. To find the total dollar sales required, divide the VCM by the PVCM or divide #3 by #2.
7. To find the total unit sales required, divide total VCM by monthly VCM or divide #3/(#3/customers/12 months).

Required Market Share (RMS)

What is the required market share?

It is the number of customers that a firm requires in order to reach a target contribution margin or to make enough money from an individual product or service to cover the indirect and fixed costs and make profit.

Why does a marketer need to know the required market share?

1. It is essential to determine the correct number of products to provide to the market.
2. It is essential to determine the extent of promotion to embark on in a market area.
3. It is essential to determine the level of price to use to entice the customers, and to choose the right profit margin.

How does a marketer find the required market share?

Body & Soul Inc. is an independent alcoholic beverage retailer located in Hytime, Kansas. In addition to traditional hot drink brands like gins, brandies, and whiskies, Mr. Onasky retails Feel Good, a good tasting, high alcoholic local blend of gins, brandy, whisky drink and fruit drinks that he invented in 1991. This unique and popular drink was test marketed at $17.99 per 12 ounces. This was a premium price or a very high price, but the buyers did not mind. Mr. Onasky wanted to invest to mass distribute and commercialize his new drink, however, he does not know if there are enough drinkers to warrant such an investment and the time commitment to distribute his so called Feel Good drink.

The industry sales forecast for innovated mixed high alcoholic drinks such as Feel Good for the state of Kansas in 1992 was 750,000 bottles. Mr. Onasky was told that at $95,000 in advertising and a target total contribution of $245,000 which he operated, Body & Soul had to make and sell at least 98,000 bottles of the Feel Good drink. He wanted to know what percentage of the retail market share that was, and he did the following.

Table 11-14
Body & Soul Inc.
Required Market Share (RMS)

Required Market Share = <u>Required Level of Sales</u>
Industry Sales forecast

Required share = <u>98,000</u> = 13%
750,000

Interpretation of the results.

1. Body & Soul Inc. required to have 13 percent of the mixed alcoholic drink market in order to meet the target contribution for Feel Good.

Implication of the results.

1. Body & Soul should spend the $95,000 in the budget for advertising Feel Good.

Calculation steps.

1. To determine the required level of sale that the firm will have in order to cover cost and make a profit, divide the total cost by the total units, and add a desired profit margin.
2. Divide #1 by the industry sales forecast.

CHAPTER 12

MARKET FORECAST

Sales Forecast – Exponential Smoothing

What is exponential smoothing?

It is a forecasting technique that uses a weighted average of past time series of sales values to forecast future sales.

Why does a marketer need to know the exponential smoothing?

1. Forecasting sales accurately is important for a business to survive.
2. A good marketing and capital utilization plan depends on knowing how much could be sold.
3. It is a better method to forecast the number of products to carry, because it considers the differential weights to the number of products sold in the various time periods.

How does a marketer use the exponential smoothing?

Good Views Inc. is a camera store located in Fun Beach, Fl. It

was started in 1982 by Ms. Seawell, to sell small binoculars, disposable cameras, and other innovative apparatus to tourists to help them view and record attractions better. Next door to Good Views is a popular in-door and out-door attraction center that hosts more than one hundred

Photo 26: Camera Corner

179

and ten popular and crowded events every year. The ever-high demand kept Good Views store very busy and very profitable. The store opened every day and night depending on the schedules of the near-by attraction centers. It tried as much as it could to maintain adequate inventory and wide assortments to meet the high demand. However, it was always impossible for the store to determine the correct number of items to carry at different periods during the year. Ms. Seawell needed a better way to obtain a stable sales forecast of the number of items to carry every week.

Ms. Seawell was advised to forecast the sales for 2001 by using an exponential smoothing of each week of the year. She decided to forecast the disposable cameras first because they were the highest in demand. Good Views sold 651,00 cameras in 2000. The average weekly sales of the cameras for the first twelve weeks is shown below in Table 12-1. These are the average sales in these weeks for the past six years. The projected sales for the first week was 2,900 units of cameras, or approximately 415 units per day. The average of the actual sales units for the 52 weeks is taken as the smoothed sales units for the first week. The store determined that the smoothing constant, a number between zero and one that showed the errors due to different size constant was .7. This was high because Good Views anticipated a dramatic change in sales due to the planned expansion of Disney World and Global Fun into Fun City in 2001. Table 12-2 shows the exponential smoothing.

Table 12-1
Good Views Inc.
Sales of Portable Cameras For Twelve Weeks in 2000
(000)

Week: 1 2 3 4 5 6 7 8 9 10 11 12 ----52nd.

Units Sold(000): 2.9 2.5 3.3 2.7 2.5 2.9 3.4 3.1 2.8 2.6 3.5 3.3 ---
166.4 units.

$S_{t+1} = \&(S_t) + (1-\&)(S_{t-1})$

or

S_{t+1} = sales forecasted for period t+1

& =smoothing constant
S_t =actual sales in period t
$(1-\&)$ =one minus the smoothing constant
(S_{t-1}) =smoothed forecasted sales for period t-1

Table 12-2.
Good Views Inc.
Exponential Smoothing of 2001 Sales*
For the Portable Cameras

(Smoothing Constant=0.7)

Weeks(t)	Actual Sales in 2000 (St) (000)	Expon. Smoothing (1-&)+(St-1)	Smoothed Forecast Value for 2001 (St+1)	Forecast Error (Yi-Fi) (000)
1.	2.9		3.2	
2.	2.5	0.7(2.9) + 0.3(3.2)	2.9	-0.4
3.	3.3	0.7(2.5) + 0.3(2.9)	2.6	0.7
4.	2.7	0.7(3.3) + 0.3(2.6)	3.1	-0.4
5.	2.5	0.7(2.7) + 0.3(3.1)	2.8	-0.3
6.	2.9	0.7(2.5) + 0.3(2.8)	2.6	0.3
7.	3.4	0.7(2.9) + 0.3(2.6)	2.8	0.6
8.	3.1	0.7(3.4) + 0.3(2.8)	3.2	-0.1
9.	2.8	0.7(3.1) + 0.3(3.2)	3.1	-0.3
10.	2.6	0.7(2.8) + 0.3(3.1)	2.9	-0.3
11.	3.5	0.7(2.6) + 0.3(2.9)	2.7	0.8
12.	3.3	0.7(3.5) + 0.3(2.7)	3.3	0
		0.7(3.3) + 0.3(3.3)	3.3	
|	|	|		
|	|	|		
52nd				
Total	**166.4**			

*MARKETMATICS includes a full year.

Interpretation of the results.

1. The optimum smoothing constant or the forecast that gave the least forecasting error occurred in the twelfth week, which had

a sales of $3,300 and a smoothed value of $3,300, and an error of zero.

2. In the other months, the forecast errors were high because a high constant was used due to the predicted dramatic change in sales for the next year due to the coming of Disney World and Global Fun. The 3rd and 11th weeks had the most errors.

Implications of the results.

1. Good Views should adjust the forecast every week based on the forecast errors.
2. The forecast errors for most of the weeks were high. Because there was a prediction of a dramatic change in the camera sales, Good View should measure the forecasting errors produced by different size constants.

Calculation steps.

1. Record the actual sales for each week during the past years.
2. Choose a number between zero and one as the smoothing constant (a higher number predicts a dramatic change in sales).
4. To determine the exponential smoothed sales forecast for month #3, multiply the actual sales for month #2 by one minus the constant, and find the smoothed forecasted sales for week #2 by multiplying exponential smoothed units of the last week by the remaining smoothing constant. Add the results of the two.
5. Determine the forecast error by subtracting the exponential smoothed from the actual sales.
6. Note that the first week did not have a smoothed forecast because it did not have a previous week's smoothing.

Sales Forecast –Moving Average

What is a moving average?

It is a technique that uses the average sales in a specific period in the past to predict the sales for a future period.

Why does a marketer need to know the moving average?

1. It assists to speculate the amount of sales at a future period.

How does a marketer use the moving average?

J&J Blueprints and Supplies Inc. does enlargements, reductions, blue prints, plottings, and scanning. J&J started in 1993 and had a high demand for the services. Unlike goods resellers that could readily increase the supplies and equipment as demand grows, service resellers like J&J had to provide all the equipment and supplies prior to sales. Therefore, J&J faced the problem of determining the amount of major equipment and supplies to buy on a long-term basis in order to benefit from the discounts offered by the sellers. One thing that the company wanted to do was to forecast its sales for three years at a time and use that as the guide for all product and marketing expenses. Shown below are the actual sales for J&J in 1999. It also showed the three-month forecast values by using the moving average forecast.

Table 12-3
J&J Blueprints and Supplies Inc.
Sales Forecast –Moving Average

Months	*Actual Sales* (000)	*3-Year Forecast*		
		Value (000)	*Error* (Actual – Forecasted)	
Jan.	16			
Feb.	22			
Mar.	17	18.33a	(16+22+17)/3	-1.33
Apr.	15	18b	(22+17+15)/3	-3
May.	16	16c	(17+15+16)/3	0

183

Jun.	17	16	(15+16+17)/3	1
Jul.	14	15.66	(16+17+14)/3	-1.66
Aug.	21	17.33	(17+14+21)/3	3.67
Sept.	18	17.67	(14+21+18)/3	1.67
Oct.	21	20	(21+18+21)/3	1
Nov.	19	19.33	(18+21+19)/3	.33
Dec.	17	19	(21+19+17)/3	-2

$$\text{Moving Average} = \frac{\text{(Past 3-months data values)}}{n}$$
$$n=3$$

Interpretation of the results

1. The forecast values are close to the actual sales.

Implication of the results.

1. The closeness of forecast and actual sales indicates that this forecast method is effective.

Calculation steps.

1. List the actual sales for each month in the previous year.
2. Beginning at the first month, add the first three months, divide the total by three and write the value as the forecasted sales for the third month. Continue the process for the rest of the months.

$a = (16+22+17)/3$, $b = (22+17+15)/3$, $c = (17+15+16)/3$ etc.

Merchandise Planning-Basic Stock Method

What is the basic stock method?

It is a process used by a retailer to determine the base (lowest) level of inventory investment or the unit of merchandise to carry regardless of the predicted sales volume every month in the year.

Why does a marketer need to know the basic stock method?

1. To understand the correct amount of inventory to carry at all times.
2. It helps the marketer to plan the quantity of brands and assortments to carry at all times.
3. The basic stock method gives a better estimate of the quantity of merchandise to maintain when the turnover rate is less than six.

How does a marketer use the basic stock method?

Cruise-For-Fun Inc. contracts with luxury shipping lines for spaces in ships that sail to various neighboring islands around the United States. Cruise-For-Fun resells the spots along with a complete vacation fun-filled package to potential American vacationers to the islands. Usually, Cruise-For-Fun bought spaces every six months. It costs $150 per space, and it is sold for $300. Due to several reasons, the second half of the year was always the busiest for the company. In 2000, the company

Photo 27: TRIAD MARINE

planned to sell $8million worth of vacation packages during the last six months of the season, with an inventory turnover rate of 6. In the past three years Cruise-For-Fun had underestimated the demand for vacation in the market area, and therefore has not had enough spaces for potential vacationers. The company wanted to avoid such embarrassments in the coming year, and therefore they needed to know the least number of spaces to make available at the beginning of every month (BOM) in 2000.

In order to find out the correct numbers of spaces for each month, Cruise-For-Fun had to determine the planned sales for each month and add the basic stock to it. The company did the following.

Table- 12-4
Cruise-For-Fun Inc.
Dollar Merchandise Planning For Cruise-For-Fun

Average monthly sales for the season
= *Total planned sales for the season/number of months in the season*
= $8,000,000/12=$1,333,333

Average stock turnover for the season
= *Total planned sales/ estimated inventory turnover*
rate for the season
= $8,000,000/6 =$2,666,667 or 17,778 cruise spaces every
two months

Basic Stock = average stock for the season – average monthly sales
for the season
=$266,667-$1,333,333 =$1,333,334 (or 4,444 cruises)
BOM (Beginning of Month merchandise) = Planned monthly sales + basic stock

July-Dec. 2001

	Planned Monthly Sales	Basic Stock	BOM ($)	BOM Units	Min Cost (BOM/$150)
BOM(July) =	$1,000,000 +	$1,333,334	$2,333,333	7,778	$1,166,700
BOM(Aug) =	$1,500,000 +	$1,333,334	$2,833,333	9,444	$1,416,600
BOM(Sept) =	$1,600,000 +	$1,333,334	$2,933,333	9,778	$1,466,700
BOM(Oct) =	$1,200,000 +	$1,333,334	$2,533,333	8,445	$1,266,750
BOM(Nov) =	$1,750,000 +	$1,333,334	$3,083,333	10,278	$1,541,700
BOM(Dec) =	$ 950,000 +	$1,333,334	$2,283,333	7,611	$1,141,650
	$8,000,000				

Interpretation of the results.

1. Cruise-For-Fun should have an average monthly sales of $1,333,333 in the next six months.
2. Cruise-For-Fun should maintain an average stock of $2,666,667 or 17,778 cruise spaces for every two months because it intended to turnover or sell-out that many 3 times during the six months. The average cost depends on the amount of the planned sales and the rate of turnovers.
3. Cruise-For-Fun should need a basic stock of $1,333,333 each month. The basic stock is the amount or number of cruise spaces that Cruise-For-Fun will draw from whenever cruisers' demand exceed the average stock.
4. Cruise-For-Fun should have at least $1,333,334 or 4,444 worth of spaces every month during the season, regardless of the monthly demand.
5. BOM which stands for the beginning of the month, is the number of cruises Cruise-For-Fun plans to sell each month plus the basic stock. For example, the BOM in October is $2,533,333 ($1,200,000 + $1,333,334). This is equivalent to 8,445 cruise spaces every month, and it costs $1,266,750.

Implication of the results.

1. Cruise For Fun should adhere to the present monthly sales average, monthly stock average, and the monthly basic number of spaces.

Calculation steps.

1. Calculate the average monthly sales for the season by dividing the total planned sales by the number of months in the season.
2. Calculate the average stock for the season by dividing the total planned sales by estimated inventory turnover rate for the season.
3. Calculate the basic stock by subtracting the average monthly sales for the season from the average stock for the season.

Merchandise Planning-Percentage Variation Method

What is a percentage variation method?

It is a technique that enables a marketer to determine the amount of inventory to carry to face fluctuations in sales without having a set or given level of inventory at all times. It assumes that the percentage fluctuations in monthly stock from average stock should be half as great as the percentage fluctuations in monthly sales from average sales.

Why does a marketer need to know the percentage variation method?

1. It enables the marketer to avoid having a low level of inventory available at all times.
2. It helps the marketer to face fluctuation in sales without keeping a given level of inventory available at all times.
3. The percentage variation method gives a more accurate estimate of the merchandise whenever the turnover rate exceeds six.

How does a marketer use the percentage variation method?

Jo-Jo Utensils wholesales cooking and eating utensils. The product line included pots and pans, eating and serving spoons and forks, enamel and breakable dishes, and drinking cups. In order to avoid inventory stock out, Jo-Jo utilizes the inventory reorder methods that allows her to maintain enough safety stock. Jo-Jo Utensils estimated to have a net sales of $1,900,500 from the Pots & Pans-Combos in 2002. The average cost of the 10-piece Pots & Pans-Combos from the producers is $12.50, and Jo-Jo Utensils wholesales them to retailers for $25. It anticipated an average monthly sales of $272,000. Jo-Jo Utensils wanted to know how much the quantity of the 10-piece Pots & Pans-Combos could vary, and still meet any fluctuations in demand between July and December. It expected to turnover 6 times during the seven months, and calculated the percentage variation as follows.

Table 12-5
Jo-Jo Utensils Inc
Percentage Variation Method

Average stock for the season
= *Total planned sales/ estimated inventory turnover*
rate for the season
= $1,900,500/6 =$316,750 or 12,670 units

Average monthly sales for the season
= *Total planned sales for the season/number of months in*
the season
= $1,900,500/7 =$271,500 or 10,860 units

PVM = Average stock for the season x ½ {1 + (Planned sales for the month/Average monthly sales)}

Percentage Variation Method Dollar Merchandise Planning For Jo-Jo Utensils
June-Dec. 2001

Av. Stock Planned Sales	Av. Monthly Sales	PVM ($)	BOM Units	BOM Cost
June= $316,750 x1/2(1+($250,000/ $271,500))		$304,208	12,168	$152,104
Jul. = $316,750 x1/2(1+ ($290,000/$271,500))		$327,542	13,102	$163,770
Aug=$316,750 x 1/2(1+($190,000/$271,500))		$269,208	10,768	$134,604
Sept. = $316,750x1/2(1+ ($210,500/$271,500))		$281,167	11,247	$140,583
Oct = $316,750 x1/2(1+ ($315,000/$271,500))		$342,125	13,685	$171,062
Nov.= $316,750 x1/2(1+ ($345,000/$271,500))		$359,625	14,385	$179,813
Dec.= $316,750 x1/2(1+ ($300,000/$271,500))		$333,375	13,335	$166,688

Interpretation of the results.

1. Jo-Jo Utensils should have an average monthly sales of $271,500 in the next seven months.
2. Jo-Jo Utensils should have an average stock of $316,750 or 12,670 ten piece Pots & Pans-Combos between June and December because it intends to turnover or sell-out that much 6 times during the seven months. The average cost depends on the amount of the planned sales and the rate of turnovers.
3. Jo-Jo Utensils should have at least $271,500 or 10,680 units of Pots & Pans-Combos for sale every month.

Implication of the results.

1. The BOM units for the months do not vary significantly. Jo-Jo Utensils should adhere to the monthly sales average, the monthly stock average, and the PVM.

Calculation steps.

1. Calculate the average monthly sales for the season by dividing the total planned sales by the number of months in the season.

2. Calculate the average stock for the season by dividing the total planned sales by the estimated inventory turnover rate for the season.

3. Calculate the PVM or percentage variation method by dividing the planned sales for the month by the average monthly sales, add one to the answer, and divide by two. Multiply the answer by the average stock for the season.

Merchandise Planning- Weekly Supply Method

What is a weekly inventory supply planning method?

It is a technique for planning the inventory on a weekly basis for retailers whose sales do not fluctuate substantially.

Why does a marketer need the weekly inventory supply planning method?

1. To set the inventory to a predetermined number of supply each week.

How does a marketer use the weekly inventory supply planning method?

Elm Street Antiques Inc. is a huge regional retailer that sells antiques, collectibles, and crafts. Elm Street Antiques estimated a sale

 of $2million in 2002 (52 weeks). It also estimated a stock turnover rate of 12 times during the period. The store needed to know three things: (1) the average weekly sales, (2) the number of weeks to be stocked, and (3) the amount of inventory to have in stock every week. It did the following.

Photo 28: GREENSBORO ANTIQUES

Table 12-6
Elm Street Antiques
Merchandise Planning-Weekly Supply Method

(1) Average weekly sales = estimated total sales for the period/the number of weeks in the period.

$$= \frac{\$2,000,000}{52} = \$38,461.54$$

(2) Number of weeks to be stocked at a time = the number of weeks in the period/stock turnover rate for the period.

$$= \frac{52 \text{ weeks}}{12 \text{ times}} = 4.33 \text{ weeks}$$

(3) Weekly stock supply or WSM = Average weekly sales divide by the number of weeks to be stocked at a time.

$$= \frac{\$38,461.54}{4.33} = \$8,882.57$$

BOM Stock = Average weekly sales x number of weeks to be stocked at a time.

$$= \$38,461.54 \times 4.33 = \$166,538.46$$

Interpretation of the results.

1. The average weekly sales is $38,461.54.
2. The inventory should be stocked or supplied for 4.3 weeks at a time.
3. $8,882.57 worth of inventory should be bought every week.

Implication of the results.

1. Elm Street Antiques Inc. should adhere to the average weekly sales and the beginning of the month stock.

Calculation steps

1. Calculate the average weekly sales.
2. Determine the number of weeks to be stocked at a time.

3. Calculate the weekly sales.
4. Calculate the BOM or the lowest number of inventory to make available at all times regardless of demand.

PART FIVE

MARKETING STRATEGY

CHAPTER 13

MARKETING RESEARCH

Analysis of variance (ANOVA)

What is the analysis of variance?

It is a technique that measures the difference between the means or average of two or more groups or activities.

Why does a marketer need to know the analysis of variance?

1. To determine how market segments differ in terms of the purchase activities so as to choose the right marketing strategies.
2. To determine how retailers, wholesalers and agents differ in the strategies they select to expose a firm's new products to the market.

How does a marketer find the analysis of variance?

Elegance Mall Inc., located in Elegance, SC. was opened in 1974. Because of the make-up of its seventy-stores and the pleasant mall atmosphere, the mall was well patronized by the locals and guests that stayed in the enclosed ten-story Elegance Hotel. The mall's elegant and attractive view from the nearby highway enticed travelers to stop and shop. In 1999, a second mall, the Millennium Mall, was built five miles away along the highway to compete with the Elegance Mall. The Millennium Mall is a high-class technology mall that is completely outfitted with e-commerce and in-house electronic dazzles that attracted all market segments and made shopping more fun and exciting.

In 2002, the Elegance Mall noticed a decrease in the mall's patronage or attendance. A survey of customers in the two malls' parking lots indicated that most customers preferred the Millennium mall's newness. Elegance Mall considered several marketing strategies to reverse or stabilize the situation. It embarked on a massive six months in-store and out-store sales promotion with coupons and gift certificates. The mall wanted to determine the effect of in-store promotion on sales and patronage for men, women, and teenagers in the area. Thirty-six stores were randomly selected to participate, and twelve stores were randomly assigned to accept coupons and gift certificates on all major items in the stores.

The mall kept records of the coupon and certificate redemptions by men, women, and teenager. At the end of six months, the sales or outputs of each store were measured and normalized according to the store size, traffic, prices, etc. The measures were converted into a 1-to-10 scale, one being the lowest, and ten is highest. Additionally, the loyalty of the customers to the mall was assessed through the cashiers' questions and observations, and ranked using a 1-to-10 scale. High numbers denoted more loyalty or attachment to the Elegance Mall. Table 13-1a shows the scores of the respondents on sales and patronage.

Table 13-1a
<u>Sales and Patron Ratings In Selected Stores For Men, Women, and Teenagers</u>

Stores	Sales			Patron Rating		
	Men	Women	Teenagers	Men	Women	Teenagers
1	10	7	6	10	10	8
2	9	8	6	9	9	9
3	9	8	6	9	4	8
4	10	6	5	10	8	8
5	10	7	6	10	7	5
6	10	9	3	10	2	7
7	8	7	1	8	3	9
8	9	6	4	9	7	10
9	7	9	6	7	9	5

	10	10	6	2	10	10	7
	11	8	7	3	8	7	3
	12	10	5	4	10	5	6
Total		110	85	52	110	81	85

To test the effect of the in-store promotion (X) on sales (Y) in the selected stores during the period, the Elegance Mall calculated the means and the sums of squares as follows:

A. Sales:

Column Totals   110   85   52

Category means $\overline{Y}_j$: $= \dfrac{110}{12}$ $\dfrac{85}{12}$ $\dfrac{52}{12}$

$$= 9.2 \quad 7.1 \qquad 4.3$$

Grand mean $\overline{Y}$: $= \dfrac{(110 + 85 + 52)}{36} = \dfrac{247}{36} = 6.861$

To test the null hypothesis (the assumption of no effect), the mall computed the various sums of squares for the men, women, and the teenagers as follows:

1. Men

$$SSy = (10-6.861)^2 + (9-6.861)^2 + (9-6.861)^2 + (10-6.861)^2 + (10-6.861)^2 + (10-6.861)^2 + (8-6.861)^2 + (9-6.861)^2 + (7-6.861)^2 + (10-6.861)^2 + (8-6.861)^2 + (10-6.861)^2$$

$$(3.139)^2 + (2.139)^2 + (2.139)^2 + (3.139)^2 + (3.139)^2 + (3.139)^2 +$$
$$(1.139)^2 + (2.139)^2 + (.139)^2 + (3.139)^2 + (1.139)^2 + (3.139)^2$$

(9.85) + (4.58) + (4.58) + (9.85) + (9.85) + (9.85) + (1.30) + (4.58) + $(.02)$ + (9.85) + (1.30) + (9.85)

$$=75.46$$

2. Women

$$SSY= (7-6.861)^2+(8-6.861)^2+(8-6.861)^2+ (6-6.861)^2+(7-6.861)^2+(9-6.861)^2+(7-6.861)^2+(6-6.861)^2+(9-6.861)^2+(6-6.861)^2+(7-6.861)^2+(5-6.861)^2$$

$$= (.139)^2 + (1.139)^2 + (1.139)^2 + (-.861)^2 + (.139)^2 + (2.139)^2 + (.139)^2 + (-.861)^2 + (2.139)^2 + (-.861)^2 + (.139)^2 + (-1.861)^2$$

$$= (.02) + (1.30) + (1.30) + (-.75) + (1.30) + (4.58) + (.02) + (-.75) + (4.58) + (-.75) + (.02) + (-3.46)$$

$$=18.27$$

3. Teenagers

$$SSy= (6-6.861)^2+(6-6.861)^2+(6-6.861)^2+(5-6.861)^2+(6-6.861)^2+(3-6.861)^2+(1-6.861)^2+(4-6.861)^2+(6-6.861)^2+(2-6.861)^2+(3-6.861)^2+(4-6.861)^2$$

$$= (-.861)^2 + (-.861)^2 + (-.861)^2 + (-1.861)^2 + (-.861)^2 + (-3.861)^2 + (-5.861)^2 + (-2.861)^2 + (-.861)^2 + (-4.861)^2 + (-3.861)^2 + (-2.861)^2$$

$$= (-.74) + (-.74) + (-.74) + (-3.46) + (-.74) + (-14.90) + (-34.35) + (-8.18) + (-.74) + (-23.62) + (-14.90) + (-8.18)$$

$$=111.29$$

Total = 205.02

$$SSx = 12(9.2-6.861)^2 + 12(7.1-6.861)^2 + 12(4.3-6.861)^2$$
$$= 12(2.34)^2 + 12(.239)^2 + 12(-2.561)^2$$
$$65.7 + \quad .685 + \quad 78.7$$

$$= 145$$

In order to verify if the sums of square are correct, the Elegance Mall tested the standard errors as follow:

1.   **SSerror=SSy-SSx**
                60.02=205.02-145

2.   SSy=SSx+SSerror
                205.02 = 145+60.02

The strength of the effects of in-store promotion on sales is determined by 145/205.02 = .707 or 70.7%. This means that 70.7% of the variation in sales for men, women, and teenagers at the Elegance mall during the period was attributed to the in-store promotion.

Part 1.

The Elegance Mall conducted a one-way analysis of variance in order to understand how purchases by each set of customers effected the sales in the period. The result of the analysis is shown below.

Table 13-1b
One-Way Analysis of Variance on Sales For Men, Women, and Teenagers

Anova: Single Factor   Sales For Men, Women, and Teenagers

SUMMARY

Groups	Count	Sum	Average	Variance
Column 1	12	110	9.166667	1.060606
Column 2	12	85	7.083333	1.537879
Column 3	12	52	4.333333	3.151515

ANOVA

Source of Variation	SS	df	MS	F	P-value	F crit
Between Groups	141.0556	2	70.52778	36.7971	3.96E-09	3.284924
Within Groups	63.25	33	1.916667			
Total	204.3056	35				

Interpretation of the results.

1. The strength of the effects of gift certificates on sales is: 145/205.02 = .70.7 or 70.7%. Although this does not indicate if or how much sales went up or down, however, 70.7% of any variation in sales at the Elegance mall during the period was attributed to the in-store promotion.

2. In Table 13-1b the SSx or the between-group sum of square is 141.06 at two degrees of freedom, and the SSerror or within-group sum of squares is 63.25.

3. The MSx or the between-group mean square is 141.06/2 or 70.53, and the MSerror or the within-group mean square is 63.25/33 or 1.917.

4. The value of F is 70.53/1.917 or 36.79 with 2 and 33 degrees of freedom, at a probability of 3.28.

5. Since the calculated value of F (36.79)is greater than the critical F (5.34) in the Statistical Appendix, the null hypothesis

of no difference in the effect of in-store promotion on sales was rejected.

6. The average sales to men and women during the period were higher and closer. Sales to teenagers were lower and more varied.

Part 2.

The Elegance Mall calculated a similar analysis to see how men, women, and teenagers felt on the in-store promotion by the stores. The result of the analysis is presented below.

Table 13-1c
One-Way Analysis of Variance on Mall Patronage For Men, Women, and Teenagers

Anova: Single Factor   Patron Ratings For Men, Women, and Teenagers

SUMMARY

Groups	Count	Sum	Average	Variance
Column 1	12	110	9.166667	1.060606
Column 2	12	81	6.75	7.295455
Column 3	12	85	7.083333	4.083333

ANOVA

Source of Variation	SS	df	MS	F	P-value	F crit
Between Groups	41.16667	2	20.58333	4.964068	0.013039	3.284924
Within Groups	136.8333	33	4.146465			
Total	178	35				

Interpretation of the results.

1. On Table 13-1c, the SSx or the between-group sum of square is 41.17 at 2 degrees of freedom, and the SSerror or within-group sum of squares is 136.88 at 33 degrees of freedom.
2. The MSx or the between-group mean square is 41.174/2 or 20.58, and the MSerror or the within-group mean square is 136.88/33 or 4.15.
3. The value of F is 20.58/4.15 or 4.96 with 2 and 33 degrees of freedom, at a probability of 3.28.
4. Since the calculated value of F (4.96)is less than the critical F (5.34) in the Statistical Appendix, the null hypothesis of no difference in the effect of in-store promotion on sales was accepted. There was no significant difference between the patronage or loyalty of the men or women or teenager to Elegance Mall.
5. The average patronage for men and women during the period did not vary significantly.

Implications of the results.

1. The teenagers may be more attracted to the new mall than men and women.
2. Elegance Mall should retain gift certificates as in-store promotion because it is attractive to some target markets.
3. Elegance Mall should consider in-store promotion as a viable strategic option to increase sales because older buyers' loyalty to both malls does not vary much.

Calculation steps.

1. Randomly select the thirty-six stores, and assign the three levels of gift certificates.
2. Find out the variation in means of sales by finding out the category means and the grand means.

3. To find the category means, separate the thirty-six stores into three, and categorize them by sales as high, medium, and low. Find the total of each column, and divide it by twelve.

4. To find the grand mean, add the three category means and divide by thirty-six.

5. Find the variation in the means of the sales by adding the square root of each sale after it is subtracted from the grand mean.

6. Find the variation in the means of the in-store promotion by adding the square root of each category mean minus the grand mean, and multiply by twelve.

7. Find the error in the variations by subtracting the total variation in the sales from the total variations in the gift certificates.

Cluster Analysis

What is a cluster analysis?

It is a technique that is used to divide or classify people or objects into homogeneous or similar groups based on selected variables.

Why does a marketer need a cluster analysis?

1. Cluster analysis can be used to segment or divide the market or customers in order to determine and apply the appropriate marketing strategy.

2. Cluster analysis can be used to group customers on habits such as the similarities in product or service choices, store patronage, and numerous other customer characteristics.

3. It can be used to determine the competitive sets within a market by grouping buyers by the brands of the products they buy.

4. It can be used to group customers according to the amount of utility or satisfaction they get from each function that a business performs.

How does a marketer perform cluster analysis?

Fresh For 'U' Inc. is an independent grocery store started in 1981 by Mrs. Dive in Lookout, NE. The philosophy of the store is to maintain a fresh image and nice atmosphere. Fresh For 'U' used different techniques to assure that the fruits, vegetables, meat and produce remain fresh as long as possible. All the items are regularly checked, and all items that are ready to expire are removed and placed in a large section in the back of the store called "Ready to Expire". Fresh For 'U' had daily sales for all the ready to expire items. This section was a big bargain and attracted different types of buyers. Both the fresh and ready to expire sections of Fresh For 'U' turned out to be successful. Interestingly, the customers' demand for the fresh goods was steady despite the high price.

In 1989 Fresh For 'U' noticed a dramatic drop in the sales of both the fresh and the ready to expire items. This trend continued for three years. In 1993 Fresh For 'U' decided to study the customers and come up with the strategies to reverse the trend. It grouped or clustered current buyers of fresh and ready to expire items according to their attitude towards shopping at Fresh For 'U'. Thirty customers including fifteen fresh buyers and fifteen ready to expire buyers were randomly selected and asked to agree or disagree with the eight attitudinal statements below on a five-point scale (1 = disagree, 5 = agree).

V_1: Fresh For 'U' carries fresher food than other stores.

V_2: Shopping at Fresh For 'U' is pleasing.

V_3: I feel that Fresh For 'U' cares for my health.

V_4: There is no difference between Fresh For 'U' and the other food stores.

V_5: I do not want Fresh For 'U' to go out of business.

V_6: I see a lot of benefits in buying from Fresh For 'U'.

V_7: I buy most of my grocery from Fresh For 'U'.

V_8: Fresh For 'U' is customer-oriented

Also, the respondents were asked to indicate their income, occupation, sex, zip code, but not their names. The ratings for the eight statements are presented below.

Table 13-2a
Fresh For "U"

ATTITUDINAL DATA FOR CLUSTERING
Fresh buyers

V_1	V_2	V_3	V_4	V_5	V_6	V_7	V_8
4.00	3.00	4.00	3.00	4.00	3.00	5.00	4.00
5.00	4.00	3.00	4.00	4.00	3.00	4.00	4.00
5.00	5.00	4.00	3.00	4.00	3.00	5.00	4.00
4.00	3.00	2.00	4.00	3.00	3.00	4.00	4.00
5.00	4.00	2.00	3.00	5.00	2.00	4.00	2.00
5.00	3.00	1.00	5.00	5.00	2.00	5.00	2.00
4.00	3.00	2.00	3.00	5.00	1.00	4.00	2.00
5.00	3.00	1.00	5.00	4.00	1.00	3.00	7.00
5.00	2.00	2.00	4.00	4.00	1.00	2.00	5.00
4.00	3.00	3.00	3.00	5.00	1.00	3.00	5.00
5.00	2.00	4.00	2.00	5.00	2.00	2.00	1.00
5.00	3.00	5.00	3.00	4.00	2.00	4.00	6.00
4.00	4.00	5.00	4.00	5.00	2.00	5.00	6.00
5.00	3.00	5.00	5.00	4.00	3.00	3.00	6.00
5.00	5.00	5.00	4.00	5.00	4.00	5.00	6.00
4.00	3.00	4.00	3.00	4.00	3.00	5.00	9.00
5.00	4.00	3.00	4.00	4.00	3.00	4.00	9.00
5.00	5.00	4.00	3.00	4.00	3.00	5.00	9.00
4.00	3.00	2.00	4.00	3.00	3.00	4.00	9.00
5.00	4.00	2.00	3.00	5.00	2.00	4.00	2.00
5.00	3.00	1.00	5.00	5.00	2.00	5.00	2.00
4.00	3.00	2.00	3.00	5.00	1.00	4.00	2.00
5.00	3.00	1.00	5.00	4.00	1.00	3.00	7.00
5.00	2.00	2.00	4.00	4.00	1.00	2.00	7.00
4.00	3.00	3.00	3.00	5.00	1.00	3.00	7.00
5.00	2.00	4.00	2.00	5.00	2.00	2.00	1.00

5.00	3.00	5.00	3.00	4.00	2.00	4.00	4.00
4.00	4.00	5.00	4.00	5.00	2.00	5.00	1.00
5.00	3.00	5.00	5.00	4.00	3.00	3.00	4.00
5.00	5.00	5.00	4.00	5.00	4.00	5.00	6.00

Case Processing Summary

Cases

Valid		Missing		Total	
N	Percent	N	Percent	N	Percent
30	100.0	0	.0	30	100.0

a Squared Euclidean Distance used
b Average Linkage (Between Groups)

Table 13-2b
Average Linkage(Between Groups)
Agglomeration Schedule

Stage	Cluster Combined Cluster 1	Cluster 2	Coefficients	Stage Cluster First Appears Cluster 1	Cluster 2	Next Stage
1	15	30	.000	0	0	16
2	11	26	.000	0	0	26
3	8	23	.000	0	0	11
4	7	22	.000	0	0	7
5	6	21	.000	0	0	20
6	5	20	.000	0	0	7
7	5	7	3.000	6	4	20
8	14	29	4.000	0	0	21
9	12	27	4.000	0	0	21
10	10	25	4.000	0	0	22
11	8	24	4.000	3	0	17
12	17	19	4.000	0	0	18
13	2	4	4.000	0	0	19

14	16	18	5.000	0	0	18
15	1	3	5.000	0	0	19
16	13	15	6.000	0	1	24
17	8	9	6.667	11	0	22
18	16	17	7.000	14	12	28
19	1	2	7.000	15	13	23
20	5	6	7.500	7	5	25
21	12	14	8.000	9	8	23
22	8	10	10.000	17	10	27
23	1	12	11.250	19	21	24
24	1	13	12.708	23	16	27
25	5	28	15.667	20	0	26
26	5	11	18.714	25	2	29
27	1	8	22.879	24	22	28
28	1	16	24.662	27	18	29
29	1	5	36.037	28	26	0

Interpretations:

1. The first line is the stage 1, and it has 29 clusters. As explained later, the analysis combined the last respondent 30 with another respondent 15 at the 1st stage of the "Cluster Combine," thus resulting in one short of the original total.
2. The column "Coefficient" indicates the squared euclidean distance or the square root of the sum of the squared differences in values for each item.
3. The "Stage Cluster First Appears" column indicated the stage at which a cluster is first formed. For example, the entry of 4 at stage 7 shows that respondent 7 was first grouped at stage 4. The entry of 1 at stage 16 indicates that respondent 16 was first grouped at stage one. The entry of 8 at stage 21means that respondent 21 was first grouped at stage 8.
4. The "Next Stage" column indicates the stage at which respondents combined. For example, the first line indicates that at stage 16, respondent 13 combined with 15 to form 30. Also 26 and 11 are grouped together in stage 2.

208

Table 13-2c
Cluster Membership

Case	3 Clusters
1	1
2	1
3	1
4	1
5	2
6	2
7	2
8	1
9	1
10	1
11	2
12	1
13	1
14	1
15	1
16	3
17	3
18	3
19	3
20	2
21	2
22	2
23	1
24	1
25	1
26	2
27	1
28	2
29	1
30	1

Interpretations:

1. The respondents are grouped into three clusters as follows: Cluster 1=17 respondents, Cluster 2 =8 respondents, and Cluster 3 = 4 respondents.

Table 13-2d
Vertical Icicle

Case Number of clusters	26	11	28	21	6	22	7	20	5	19	17	18	16	25	10	9	24	23	8	30	15	13	29	14	27	12	4	2	3	1
1	x	x	x	x	x	x	x	x	x	x	x	x	x	x	x	x	x	x	x	x	x	x	x	x	x	x	x	x	x	x
2	x	x	x	x	x	x	x	x	x	x	x	x	x	x	x	x	x	x	x	x	x	x	x	x	x	x	x	x	x	
3	x	x	x	x	x	x	x	x	x	x	x	x	x	x	x	x	x	x	x	x	x	x	x	x	x	x	x	x		
4	x	x	x	x	x	x	x	x	x	x	x	x	x	x	x	x	x	x	x	x	x	x	x	x	x	x	x			
5	x	x	x	x	x	x	x	x	x	x	x	x	x	x	x	x	x	x	x	x	x	x	x	x	x	x				
6	x	x	x	x	x	x	x	x	x	x	x	x	x	x	x	x	x	x	x	x	x	x	x	x	x					
7	x	x	x	x	x	x	x	x	x	x	x	x	x	x	x	x	x	x	x	x	x	x	x	x						
8	x	x	x	x	x	x	x	x	x	x	x	x	x	x	x	x	x	x	x	x	x	x	x							
9	x	x	x	x	x	x	x	x	x	x	x	x	x	x	x	x	x	x	x	x	x	x								
10	x	x	x	x	x	x	x	x	x	x	x	x	x	x	x	x	x	x	x	x	x									
11	x	x	x	x	x	x	x	x	x	x	x	x	x	x	x	x	x	x	x	x										
12	x	x	x	x	x	x	x	x	x	x	x	x	x	x	x	x	x	x	x											
13	x	x	x	x	x	x	x	x	x	x	x	x	x	x	x	x	x	x												
14	x	x	x	x	x	x	x	x	x	x	x	x	x	x	x	x	x													
15	x	x	x	x	x	x	x	x	x	x	x	x	x	x	x	x														
16	x	x	x	x	x	x	x	x	x	x	x	x	x	x	x															
17	x	x	x	x	x	x	x	x	x	x	x	x	x	x																
18	x	x	x	x	x	x	x	x	x	x	x	x	x																	
19	x	x	x	x	x	x	x	x	x	x	x	x																		
20	x	x	x	x	x	x	x	x	x	x	x																			
21	x	x	x	x	x	x	x	x	x	x																				
22	x	x	x	x	x	x	x	x	x																					
23	x	x	x	x	x	x	x	x																						
24	x	x	x	x	x	x	x																							
25	x	x	x	x	x	x																								
26	x	x	x	x	x																									
27	x	x	x	x																										
28	x	x	x																											
29	x	x																												

Interpretation

1. The columns indicate the objects being clustered.
2. The rows correspond to the number of clusters.
3. The analysis combined the 30th respondent and the 15th respondent thus resulting in 29 clusters.

Table 13-2e
Dendrogram

******HIERARCHICAL CLUSTER ANALYSIS******
Dendrogram using Average Linkage (Between Groups)
Rescaled Distance Cluster Combine

```
Case    0       5          10      15   .20      25
Label#--+---------+-----------+------+----+-------+
 24---I
 30---I------I
 17---I      I
            I-----------I
 23---I      I          I
 29---I------I          I
 16---I                 I
                       I---------------I
 22---I                 I               I
 28---I-----------I      I               I
 15---I           I      I               I
                 I------I                I
 21---I           I                      I
 27---I-----------I                      I
 14---I                                  I
                                        I-----I
 3--------I-------I                      I     I
 6--------I         I------I             I     I
 7----------------I  I      I            I     I
 5----I---I          I------I            I     I
 9----I   I-----------I I    I           I     I
 1--------I          I-I     I           I     I
 2------I-----------I I      I-------I    I
 4------I          I-I       I           I     I
 10---------------I          I           I     I
 8----------------------------I          I     I
                                         I
 11---I----------------------------I     I     I
 18---I                            I     I     I
                                  I--------I
 20---I                            I
 26---I-----------I                I
 13---I           I---------------I
                 I
 19---I           I
 25---I-----------I
 12---I
```

212

Interpretation:

1. The dendrogram or the graphic illustration of the clusters and respondent combinations is read from left to right. The vertical lines indicate how the clusters are joined together, while the position of the line on the scale shows the distance at which the clusters are joined.
2. Cluster 1 combines more respondents than the other two clusters.

Table 13-2f
Final Cluster Centers

	Cluster		
	1	2	3
VAR00001	4.77	4.50	4.67
VAR00002	3.85	2.75	3.11
VAR00003	4.38	2.00	2.56
VAR00004	3.69	4.00	3.33
VAR00005	4.23	4.00	5.00
VAR00006	2.92	1.50	1.78
VAR00007	4.38	3.00	3.89
VAR00008	5.92	6.38	1.67

Interpretation

1. Cluster 1 has high values on V1(Fresh For 'U' carries fresher food than other stores), V3(I feel that Fresh For 'U' cares for my health), V5(I do not want Fresh For 'U' to go out of business), V7(I buy most of my grocery from Fresh For 'U'), and V8(Fresh For 'U' is customer-oriented). Therefore, Cluster 1 is loyal to Fresh For 'U'.
2. Cluster 2 has high values on V1(Fresh For 'U' carries fresher food than other stores), V4(There is no difference between Fresh For 'U' and other food stores), and V8(Fresh For 'U' is customer-oriented). These indicated that Cluster 2 commends

213

the food at Fresh For 'U', but they are not as loyal to them as Cluster one.

3. Cluster 3 has high values on V1(Fresh For 'U' carries fresher food than other stores) and V5 (I do not want Fresh For 'U' to go out of business). Cluster three commends and cares for Fresh For 'U', but they are not loyal customers.
4. All the respondents recognized Fresh For 'U' as a quality food carrier.

Table 13-2g
ATTITUDINAL DATA FOR CLUSTERING-Ready to Expire

V1	V2	V3	V4	V5	V6	V7	V8
5.00	3.00	3.00	5.00	4.00	3.00	5.00	4.00
5.00	4.00	4.00	4.00	4.00	2.00	5.00	4.00
4.00	5.00	4.00	5.00	4.00	3.00	5.00	4.00
5.00	4.00	3.00	3.00	4.00	2.00	5.00	4.00
4.00	3.00	2.00	4.00	4.00	3.00	5.00	4.00
3.00	4.00	3.00	5.00	4.00	2.00	5.00	4.00
2.00	5.00	4.00	4.00	4.00	3.00	5.00	4.00
3.00	2.00	5.00	3.00	4.00	2.00	5.00	4.00
4.00	3.00	2.00	4.00	3.00	3.00	5.00	4.00
5.00	4.00	3.00	5.00	3.00	2.00	5.00	5.00
1.00	5.00	4.00	4.00	3.00	3.00	2.00	3.00
2.00	2.00	3.00	3.00	3.00	4.00	2.00	5.00
3.00	3.00	4.00	4.00	3.00	3.00	3.00	5.00
4.00	4.00	5.00	3.00	5.00	4.00	3.00	5.00
5.00	5.00	4.00	4.00	5.00	5.00	3.00	5.00
4.00	4.00	5.00	5.00	5.00	4.00	3.00	3.00
5.00	5.00	4.00	5.00	5.00	5.00	3.00	3.00
1.00	5.00	4.00	4.00	3.00	3.00	2.00	3.00
2.00	2.00	3.00	3.00	3.00	4.00	2.00	5.00
3.00	3.00	4.00	4.00	3.00	3.00	3.00	5.00
4.00	4.00	5.00	3.00	5.00	4.00	3.00	5.00
5.00	5.00	4.00	4.00	5.00	5.00	3.00	5.00
4.00	4.00	5.00	5.00	5.00	4.00	3.00	3.00

5.00	5.00	4.00	5.00	5.00	5.00	3.00	3.00
2.00	2.00	3.00	3.00	3.00	4.00	2.00	5.00
3.00	3.00	4.00	4.00	3.00	3.00	3.00	5.00
4.00	4.00	5.00	3.00	5.00	4.00	3.00	5.00
5.00	5.00	4.00	4.00	5.00	5.00	3.00	5.00
4.00	4.00	5.00	5.00	5.00	4.00	3.00	3.00
5.00	5.00	4.00	5.00	5.00	5.00	3.00	3.00

Table 13-2h
Case Processing Summary

Cases

Valid		Missing		Total	
N	Percent	N	Percent	N	Percent
30	100.0	0	.0	30	100.0

a Squared Euclidean Distance used
b Average Linkage (Between Groups)

Table 13-2i
Average Linkage(Between Groups)
Agglomeration Schedule

	Cluster Combined		Coefficients	Stage Cluster First Appears		Next Stage
Stage	Cluster 1	Cluster 2		Cluster 1	Cluster 2	
1	24	30	.000	0	0	7
2	23	29	.000	0	0	8
3	22	28	.000	0	0	9
4	21	27	.000	0	0	10
5	20	26	.000	0	0	11
6	19	25	.000	0	0	12
7	17	24	.000	0	1	17
8	16	23	.000	0	2	17

9	15	22	.000	0	3	19
10	14	21	.000	0	4	19
11	13	20	.000	0	5	23
12	12	19	.000	0	6	23
13	11	18	.000	0	0	27
14	5	9	1.000	0	0	16
15	2	4	2.000	0	0	20
16	1	5	3.500	0	14	22
17	16	17	4.000	8	7	24
18	3	6	4.000	0	0	21
19	14	15	5.000	10	9	24
20	2	10	5.000	15	0	22
21	3	7	5.000	18	0	25
22	1	2	5.889	16	20	25
23	12	13	6.000	12	11	27
24	14	16	8.500	19	17	28
25	1	3	8.833	22	21	26
26	1	8	13.556	25	0	28
27	11	12	15.000	13	23	29
28	1	14	18.150	26	24	29
29	1	11	20.545	28	27	0

Interpretation:

1.   The first line is the stage 1, and it has 29 clusters. As shown later, the analysis combines the last respondent 30, with another respondent 24 at the 1st stage of the "Cluster Combine" to result in one short of the original total.

2.   The column "Coefficient" indicates the squared euclidean distance or the square root of the sum of the squared differences in values for each item.

3.   The "Stage Cluster First Appears" column indicates the stage at which a cluster is first formed. For example, the entry of 7 at stage 1 indicates that respondent 7 was first grouped at stage 1. The entry of 8 at stage 2 indicates that respondent 8 was first grouped at stage 2,

and the entry of 17 at stage 7 means that respondent 7 was first grouped at stage 17.

4. The "Next Stage" column indicates the stage at which the respondents combined. For example, the first line indicates that at stage 7, respondent 17 combined with 24, and 23 and 29 are grouped together at stage 2.

Table 13-2j
Cluster Membership

Case	3 Clusters
1	1
2	1
3	1
4	1
5	1
6	1
7	1
8	1
9	1
10	1
11	2
12	2
13	2
14	3
15	3
16	3
17	3
18	2
19	2
20	2
21	3
22	3
23	3
24	3
25	2

26	2
27	3
28	3
29	3
30	3

Interpretation:

1. The respondents are grouped into three clusters as follows: Cluster 1=10 respondents, Cluster 2=8 respondents, and Cluster 3 = 12 respondents. These clusters are closer in size than the Fresh buyers.'

Table 13-2k
Vertical Icicle

Case

Number of clusters	26	20	13	25	19	12	18	11	30	24	17	29	23	16	28	22	15	27	21	14	8	7	6	3	10	4	2	9	5	1
1	x	x	x	x	x	x	x	x	x	x	x	x	x	x	x	x	x	x	x	x	x	x	x	x	x	x	x	x	x	x
2	x	x	x	x	x	x	x	x	x	x	x	x	x	x	x	x	x	x	x	x	x	x	x	x	x	x	x	x	x	x
3	x	x	x	x	x	x	x	x	x	x	x	x	x	x	x	x	x	x	x	x	x	x	x	x	x	x	x	x	x	x
4	x	x	x	x	x	x	x	x	x	x	x	x	x	x	x	x	x	x	x	x	x	x	x	x	x	x	x	x	x	x
5	x	x	x	x	x	x	x	x	x	x	x	x	x	x	x	x	x	x	x	x	x	x	x	x	x	x	x	x	x	x
6	x	x	x	x	x	x	x	x	x	x	x	x	x	x	x	x	x	x	x	x	x	x	x	x	x	x	x	x	x	x
7	x	x	x	x	x	x	x	x	x	x	x	x	x	x	x	x	x	x	x	x	x	x	x	x	x	x	x	x	x	x
8	x	x	x	x	x	x	x	x	x	x	x	x	x	x	x	x	x	x	x	x	x	x	x	x	x	x	x	x	x	x
9	x	x	x	x	x	x	x	x	x	x	x	x	x	x	x	x	x	x	x	x	x	x	x	x	x	x	x	x	x	x
10	x	x	x	x	x	x	x	x	x	x	x	x	x	x	x	x	x	x	x	x	x	x	x	x	x	x	x	x	x	x
11	x	x	x	x	x	x	x	x	x	x	x	x	x	x	x	x	x	x	x	x	x	x	x	x	x	x	x	x	x	x
12	x	x	x	x	x	x	x	x	x	x	x	x	x	x	x	x	x	x	x	x	x	x	x	x	x	x	x	x	x	x
13	x	x	x	x	x	x	x	x	x	x	x	x	x	x	x	x	x	x	x	x	x	x	x	x	x	x	x	x	x	x
14	x	x	x	x	x	x	x	x	x	x	x	x	x	x	x	x	x	x	x	x	x	x	x	x	x	x	x	x	x	x
15	x	x	x	x	x	x	x	x	x	x	x	x	x	x	x	x	x	x	x	x	x	x	x	x	x	x	x	x	x	x
16	x	x	x	x	x	x	x	x	x	x	x	x	x	x	x	x	x	x	x	x	x	x	x	x	x	x	x	x	x	x
17	x	x	x	x	x	x	x	x	x	x	x	x	x	x	x	x	x	x	x	x	x	x	x	x	x	x	x	x	x	x
18	x	x	x	x	x	x	x	x	x	x	x	x	x	x	x	x	x	x	x	x	x	x	x	x	x	x	x	x	x	x
19	x	x	x	x	x	x	x	x	x	x	x	x	x	x	x	x	x	x	x	x	x	x	x	x	x	x	x	x	x	x
20	x	x	x	x	x	x	x	x	x	x	x	x	x	x	x	x	x	x	x	x	x	x	x	x	x	x	x	x	x	x
21	x	x	x	x	x	x	x	x	x	x	x	x	x	x	x	x	x	x	x	x	x	x	x	x	x	x	x	x	x	x
22	x	x	x	x	x	x	x	x	x	x	x	x	x	x	x	x	x	x	x	x	x	x	x	x	x	x	x	x	x	x
23	x	x	x	x	x	x	x	x	x	x	x	x	x	x	x	x	x	x	x	x	x	x	x	x	x	x	x	x	x	x
24	x	x	x	x	x	x	x	x	x	x	x	x	x	x	x	x	x	x	x	x	x	x	x	x	x	x	x	x	x	x
25	x	x	x	x	x	x	x	x	x	x	x	x	x	x	x	x	x	x	x	x	x	x	x	x	x	x	x	x	x	x
26	x	x	x	x	x	x	x	x	x	x	x	x	x	x	x	x	x	x	x	x	x	x	x	x	x	x	x	x	x	x
27	x	x	x	x	x	x	x	x	x	x	x	x	x	x	x	x	x	x	x	x	x	x	x	x	x	x	x	x	x	x
28	x	x	x	x	x	x	x	x	x	x	x	x	x	x	x	x	x	x	x	x	x	x	x	x	x	x	x	x	x	x
29	x	x	x	x	x	x	x	x	x	x	x	x	x	x	x	x	x	x	x	x	x	x	x	x	x	x	x	x	x	x

Interpretation

1. The columns indicate the objects being clustered.
2. The rows correspond to the number of clusters.
3. The analysis combined the 30th respondent and the 24th respondent thus resulting in 29 clusters.

Table 13-2L
Dendrogram

******HIERARCHICAL CLUSTER ANALYSIS******
Dendrogram using Average Linkage (Between Groups)
Rescaled Distance Cluster Combine

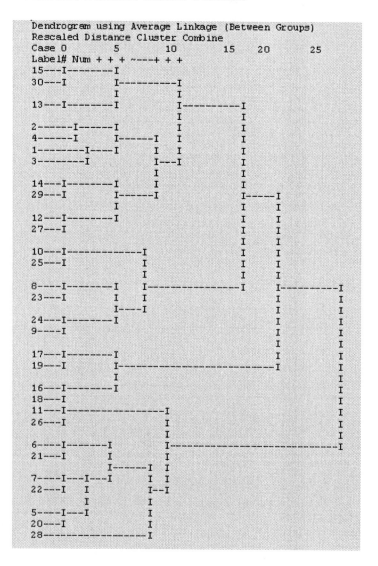

Interpretation:

1. The dendrogram or the graphic illustration of the clusters and respondent combinations is read from left to right. The vertical lines indicate how the clusters are joined together, while the position of the line on the scale shows the distance at which the clusters are joined.
2. The clusters are almost equally distributed.

Table 13-2m
Final Cluster Centers

	Cluster		
	1	2	3
VAR00001	4.00	4.50	2.13
VAR00002	3.70	4.50	3.13
VAR00003	3.30	4.50	3.63
VAR00004	4.20	4.25	3.63
VAR00005	3.80	5.00	3.00
VAR00006	2.50	4.50	3.38
VAR00007	5.00	3.00	2.38
VAR00008	4.10	4.00	4.50

Interpretation

1. Cluster 1 has high values on V1(Fresh For 'U' carries fresher food than other stores), V4(There is no difference between Fresh For 'U' and other food stores), V7(I buy most of my grocery from Fresh For 'U'), and V8(Fresh For 'U' is customer-oriented). The respondents may not be very loyal to Fresh For 'U' because they find no difference between it and the other stores.
2. Cluster 2 has high values on all the variables except V7(I buy most of my grocery from Fresh For 'U'). This indicates that they are not a loyal group to the store.
3. Cluster 3 has a high value on V8 only (Fresh For 'U' is customer- oriented).

Rowland Chidomere

4. All the respondents recognized Fresh For 'U' as a quality food carrier.

Calculation methods

1. The agglomerate clustering method develops a hierarchy or tree-like structure.
2. The square euclidean distances is the square root of the sum of the squared differences in values of each variable
3. The Ward's procedure is used to compute the means of all the variables, the squared euclidean distances to the cluster means for each object, and the sum of all the objects.
4. The Centroid procedure is a variance method in which the distance between two clusters is the distance between the means for all the variables (centroids)

Conjoint analysis

What is a conjoint analysis?

It is a technique that is used to determine the relative importance the consumers attach to the service a company offers and the level of utilities they get from them.

Why does a marketer need a conjoint analysis?
1. To find out which attributes are important in the consumers' choice process for a product or service.
2. To determine the market shares or number of buyers of brands that differ in attributes.
3. To determine the make-up or features of the brands the buyers preferred the most.
4. To divide the market or buyers according to the similarity of the features they prefer.

222

How does a marketer perform a conjoint analysis?

TCI Agric. Inc. sells fertilizers, herbicides, and utensils to farmers in Hardwork, KS. The farmers always needed information on equipment availability, price, and delivery before the planting season. During the planting period, the farmers needed training on the product usage, crop testing, and crop safety, and during the harvesting period, the farmers needed information on the market, including buyers, storage, and transportation.

In order to provide better services, TCI Agric. needed to know the attributes in the services they provided that are the most important to the farmers in each of the three periods - pre-, during-, and post-seasons. It conducted a personal interview of 500 farmers that had at least 150 acres of land dedicated to corn and wheat. It asked the farmers to rate each attribute in the three sets of attributes according to their importance to them. In order to find out the relative importance of each set and type of attribute to the farmers, TCI Agric. decided to use the conjoint analysis model below. The results are shown on Tables 13-3a, 3b, 3c, and 3d.

$$U(X) = \sum_{i=j}^{m} \sum_{j-I}^{kj} aijxij$$

$U(X)$ = overall utility of an alternative
aij = the part-worth contribution or utility associated with the jth level $(j, j – 1, 2 \ldots ki)$
of the *i*th attribute $(i, i = 1,2,\ldots m)$
$ki.$ = number of levels of attribute *i.*
m = number of attributes
xy = 1 of the *i*th level of the *i*th attribute is present
= 0 otherwise

As shown on Table 13-3a, each service attribute- pre-use, during-use, and post-use was defined into three types, and these were designated as levels 1, 2, and 3.

Table 13-3a
TCI Agric. Inc
Service Attributes and Levels

Attributes	Levels	Description
a. Pre-use	3	Information on equipment availability
	2	" on price
	1	" on delivery
b. During-use	3	Training on product usage
	2	" on crop testing
	1	" on crop safety
c. Post-use	3	Market info on buyers
	2	" " on storage
	1	" " on transportation

Using a pair-wise method (*two-factor evaluation*) to evaluate two attributes at a time, all the possible pairs of pre-use, during-use, and post-use attributes on Table 13-3a were evaluated. Three pair-wise charts were made as shown on Table 13-3b. Each side presented the three levels, and level 3 is the base level.

Table 13-3b

Pair-wise Approach
Pre-use attributes
(A,B)

A Pre-use

		Info on equipment	Info on Price	Info on Delivery
	Training on product use			
During use B	Training on crop testing			
	Training on crop safety			

224

During-use attributes
(A,C)

A Pre-use

		Info on equipment	Info on Price	Info on Delivery
	Info. On buyer			
Post-use C	Info. On storage			
	Info. On transportation			

Post-use attributes
(C,B)

C Post-use

		Info on buyers	Info on storage	Info on transportation
	Training on product Use			
During use B	Training on crop testing			
	Training on crop safety			

The farmers were asked to rank all the cells of each matrix in terms of their desirability. The farmers were required to provide preference rating for services described by the nine profiles in the estimation set. The ratings were obtained using a nine-point Likert scale (1 = not preferred, 9 = greatly preferred). The ratings were analyzed and placed in cells. A total of 3 x 3 x 3 =27 profiles were constructed as shown on Table 13-3c. In order to reduce the respondent evaluation task, a fractional design was employed, and a set of nine profiles was constructed to constitute the estimation stimuli set.

Table 13-3c

SERVICE PROFILE AND THEIR RATINGS

Profile Number	Pre-	Attribute Levels Preference During-	Post-	Rating
1	1	1	1	8
2	1	2	2	9
3	1	3	3	6
4	2	1	2	7
5	2	2	3	5
6	2	3	1	6
7	3	1	3	8
8	3	2	1	9
9	3	3	2	5

In order to estimate the basic model, the numbers on Table 13-3c were analyzed using ordinary least squares (OLS) regression dummy variables. As shown on Table 13-3d, there were two dummy variables for each attribute, for a total of six dummy variables. These are called predictors or independent variables and were obtained by subtracting one from the total attributes. The dependent variables are the preference ratings which in this case are the dummy or predictor variables that represent the differences in the attribute levels of the services to the farmers (K3-1). The X_1 and X_2 were the dummy variables that represent the pre-use attributes; X_3 and X_4 were the dummy variables that represent the during-use attributes, and X_5 and X_6 were the dummy variables that represent the post-use attributes. The preference ratings were the independent variables.

Table 13-3d

SERVICE DATA CODED FOR DUMMY VARIABLE REGRESSION

Preference				Attributes		
Ratings		Pre-		During-		Post
Y	X_1	X_2	X_3	X_4	X_5	X_6
8	1	0	1	0	1	0
9	1	0	0	1	0	1
6	1	0	0	0	0	0
7	0	1	1	0	0	1
5	0	1	0	1	0	0
6	0	1	0	0	1	0
8	0	0	1	0	0	0
9	0	0	0	1	1	0
5	0	0	0	0	0	1

The dummy variables were created by alternating 1's and 0's three times in occurrence as in the case of the real data. Table 13-3e showed the data from a single farmer. In this example only an individual-level analysis was conducted. In order to find out the worth or utility and the relative importance of the attributes, the model below was used.

$$U = d_0 + d_1X_1 + d_2X_2 + d_3X_3 + d_4X_4 + d_5X_5 + d_6X_6$$

The parameters were estimated as follows:

$d_0 = 5.33$	$d_4 = 4.1$	$d_8 = .9$
$d_1 = 2.4$	$d_5 = 5.7$	$d_9 = 5.6$
$d_2 = .4$	$d_6 = 3.1$	

$$d3 = 2.8 \qquad d7 = 2.8$$

Each dummy variable coefficient represents the difference in the part-worth for the level minus the part-worth for the base level or level 3. For the pre-use, the results are as follows:

$$a1-a3 = b1$$
$$a2-a3 = b2$$

Original constraint;

$$a1+a2+a3 = 0$$

$$\text{Therefore, } a1-a3 = -.444$$
$$a2-a3 = -2.44$$

Pre-use Services:

$$a1 = 2.4$$
$$a2 = .4$$
$$a3 = -2.8$$

Interpretation:

1. As seen from the result above, most farmers preferred having information on delivery, followed by information on price, and the least preferred is information on equipment availability.

During-use Services

$$b1 = -5.7$$
$$b2 = -4.1$$
$$b3 = -9.8$$

Interpretation:

1. As seen from the result above, most farmers did not prefer during-use services.

Post-use Services:

$c_1 = -3.7$
$c_2 = -1$
$c_3 = 4.7$

Interpretation:

1. As seen from the result above, most farmers preferred having market information on buyers.

Table 13-3e
RESULTS OF CONJOINT ANALYSIS

Attribute	Number	Description	Utility	Importance
Pre-use	3	Equipment availability	-0.44	
	2	Price	-2.44	
	1	Delivery	2.48	0.387
During-use	3	Crop usage	-5.71	
	1	Crop testing	-4.1	
	1	Crop safety	-9.8	-.980
Post-use	3	Buyers	-3.7	
	1	Storage	-1	
	1	Transportation	4.7	0.757

Each dummy variable coefficient represents the difference in the part-worth for that level minus the part-worth for the base level.

Implication of the results.

1. Since the information on transportation is high for this farmer, he or she could be labeled distribution-oriented.

Calculation steps.

1. Define the most important or salient attributes in the pre- during- and post- service stages.
2. Define each salient attribute in three levels (levels 1, 2,and 3)
3. Use a pair-wise approach (*two-factor evaluation*) to evaluate two attributes at a time, until all the possible pairs of attributes are evaluated.

Correlation Analysis-Product Moment

What is a correlation analysis?

It is a technique that is used to measure the strength of association or relationship between two variables. It is used to show the degree to which the variation in one variable X is related to the variation in another variable Y.

Why does a marketer need a correlation analysis?

1. To measure how strongly one marketing mix relates to the total market result. For example, how sales increase relates to increase in advertising.
2. To measure how strongly one marketing mix associates with the marketing result. For example, how market share relates to the size of the sales force.
3. To find how customers' perception of a product attribute relates to their purchase response. For example, how product quality relates to customers' perception on price.

How does a marketer perform a correlation analysis?

I Hear 'U' Inc. is a complete hearing test and hearing aids mini-store located inside Global Foods, a huge food chain store with locations in fifteen eastern US states. As agreed in the contract, Global Foods provided the introductory promotion necessary to inform and expose the buyers to I Hear 'U'. Global Foods also agreed to include I Hear 'U' in the regular store promotions for a quarterly fee of $4,000.

In 2001 I Hear 'U' wanted to cancel the promotion contracts with Global Foods stores in North Carolina because the latter insisted on increasing the promotion fees. Because I Hear 'U' was going through a budgetary constraint, the management wanted to cancel the promotion contract in the twenty stores in North Carolina. They felt that I Hear 'U' was now well established and therefore did not need much promotion. Also its location in a food store assured it a good exposure. However, I Hear 'U' felt that before it made the final decision it should find out the relationship between their sales and the promotion by Global Foods in the state of North Carolina.

Table 13-4a presents the ranking of twenty I Hear 'U' stores in terms of their sales, advertisement, and the customers' ratings of the value of their location in each grocery store. The sales were ranked on a 20-point scale, 1 represented the lowest and 20 represented the highest. The advertisement was ranked on a 20-points scale, 1 represented the lowest ad expense and 20 represented the highest. Customers' perception of the importance of the location of I Hear 'U' in a grocery store was measured on a 20-points scale, with 20 as extremely valuable and 1 as extremely useless.

Table 13-4a
CUSTOMERS' RATING OF I HEAR "U"

Stores	Sales	Advertisement	Location
1	20	14	15
2	12	13	13
3	12	15	12
4	13	16	15
5	15	20	6
6	16	13	8
7	13	7	9
8	15	9	16
9	16	7	18
10	20	16	20
12	13	12	20
13	4	7	13
14	5	5	6
15	7	14	8
16	12	9	17
17	13	7	9
18	4	12	12
19	6	13	4
20	5	7	6
Total	221	216	227

$$R = \frac{\sum_{i=1}^{n} (X_i - \bar{X})(Y_i - \bar{Y})}{\sum_{i=1}^{n}(X_i - \bar{X})^2 \; \sum_{i=1}^{n}(Y_i - \bar{Y})^2}$$

Division of the numerator and denominator by (n-1) gives

$$r = \sum_{I=1}^{n} \frac{(X_i - \bar{X})(Y_i - \bar{Y})}{n-1}$$

$$= \frac{COV_{xy}}{S_x S_y}$$

Explanations:

1. $\bar{X}$ is the sample mean for advertisement ranking

2. $\bar{Y}$ is the sample mean for sales ranking
3. S_x and S_y are the standard deviation
4. COV_{xy} is the covariance between X and Y, and measure the extent to which X and Y are related.

Mean of Advertisement

$$\bar{X} = \frac{(1+10+7+7+9+5+8+4+6+1+2+2+6+9+10+5+8+3+4+10)}{20} = \frac{117}{20}$$
$$= 5.85$$

Mean of Sales

$$\bar{Y} = \frac{(9+15+12+6+17+10+7+2+20+11+3+1+4+16+19+5+8+13+14+18)}{20} =$$
$$= \frac{210}{20} = 10.5$$

Sum of Means of Advertisement and Sales

$$\sum_{i=1}^{n} (X_i - \bar{X})(Y_i - \bar{Y})$$

$$= (1-5.85)(9-10.5)+(10-5.85)(15-10.5)+(7-5.85)(12-10.5)$$
$$+(7-5.85)(6-10.5)+(9-5.85)(17-10.5)+(5-5.85)(10-10.5)$$
$$+(8-5.85)(7-10.5)+(4-5.85)(2-10.5)+(6-5.85)(20-10.5)$$
$$+(1-5.85)(11-10.5)+(2-5.85)(3-10.5)+(2-5.85)(1-10.5)$$
$$+(6-5.85)(4-10.5)+(9-5.85)(16-10.5)+(10-5.85)(19-10.5)$$
$$+(5-5.85)(5-10.5)+(8-5.85)(8-10.5)+(3-5.85)(13-10.5)$$
$$+(4-5.85)(14-10.85)+(10-5.85)(18-10.5)$$

$$= 7.275 +18.675 + 1.725 -6.39 + 20.475 + .425 -7.525$$
$$+ 15.725 + 1.425 - 2.425 + 28.875 + 36.575 - .975$$
$$+ 17.325 + 35.275 + 4.675 - 5.375 -7.125 -5.827 + 31.125$$
$$= 183.933$$

Sum of the mean of ad.

$$\sum_{i-1}^{n} (X_i - \bar{X})^2 = (1-5.85)^2+(10-5.85)^2+(7-5.85)^2+(7-5.85)^2+(9-5.85)^2+(5-5.85)^2+(8-5.85)^2$$

$$+(4-5.85)^2+(6-5.85)^2+(1-5.85)^2+(2-5.85)^2+(2-5.85)^2+(6-5.85)^2 +(9-5.58)^2$$

$$+(10-5.85)^2+(5-5.85)^2+(8-5.85)^2+(3-5.85)^2+(4-5.85)^2+(10-5.85)^2$$

$$= 23.5225 + 17.2225 + 1.3225 + 1.3225 + 9.9225 + .7225 + 4.6225$$
$$+ 3.4225 + .0225 \quad + 23.5225+ 14.8225+ 14.8225 + .0225 + 9.9225$$
$$+ 17.2225 + .7225 \quad + 4.6225 + 8.1225 \quad +3.4225 \quad + 17.2225$$
$$=176.55$$

Sum of the mean of sales

$$\sum_{i-1}^{n} (Y_i - \overline{Y})^2$$

$$= (9-10.5)^2 + (15-10.5)^2 + (12-10.5)^2 + (6-10-5)^2 + (17-10.5)^2 + (10-10.5)^2$$

$$+ (7-10.5)^2$$

$$+ (2-10.5)^2 + (20-10.5)^2 + (11-10.5)^2 + (3-10.5)^2 + (1-10.5)^2 + (4-10.5)^2 +$$

$$(16-10.5)^2$$

$$+ (19-10.5)^2 + (5-10.5)^2 + (8-10.5)^2 + (13-10.5)^2 + (14-10.5)^2 + (18-10.5)^2$$

$$= 2.25 + 20.25 + 2.25 + 20.25 + 42.25 + .25 + 12.25 + 72.25 + 90.25$$
$$+ .25 + 56.25 + 90.25 + 42.25 + 30.25 + 72.25 + 30.25 + 6.25 + 6.25$$
$$+ 12.25 + 56.25$$
$$= 665$$

$$r = \frac{183.933}{\sqrt{(176.55)(665)}} = \frac{183.933}{324.594} = .5666$$

Table 13-4b
Correlation Matrix

Relationship Between Sales, Advertisement, and Location

	Sales	Advertisement	Location
Sales	1		
Advertisement	0.386234	1	
Location	0.52265	0.061044	1

Interpretation of the results.

1. The r is positive, and that implies a positive relationship r = .566, a value just above half of 1.0 means that sales at I Hear 'U' is not strongly associated with advertisement at Global Foods.
2. The correlation matrix shows the coefficient of correlation between each pair of variables.
3. Although the relationship between the elements is not high, there is a slight significant relationship between sales and location.

Implications of the results.

1. I Hear 'U' could discontinue the promotion fees and survive on its own. There is almost a fifty-fifty chance that it will survive.
2. I Hear 'U' could use a generic promotion without mentioning specific stores or locations.

Calculation steps.

1. Create a four-column table showing the store numbers, sales, advertisement, and the importance of location to the customers.
2. To find the correlation coefficient:
   (a) Find the mean or average ranking for advertisement (add up the ranking and divide by 20).
   (b) Find the mean or average ranking for sales (add up the ranking and divide by 20).
   (c) Find the sum of the means of advertisement and sales by subtracting the ratings of the ad and sales from their means, and adding them together.
   (d) Find the sum of the means of advertisement by adding the square of the ratings, and subtracting them from the means.

(e) Find the sum of the means of the sales by adding the square of each rating, and subtracting them from the means.

(f) Find the correlation by adding the sum of the squares of the ad and sales, and dividing by the square root of the sum of sales times the sum of ad.

Discriminant Analysis

What is a discriminant analysis?

It is a technique that is used to classify customers or objects into two or more categories in order to find out the variables responsible for success or failure in the different categories.

Why does a marketer need a discriminant analysis?

1. To find out how customers with high store loyalty differ from those that do not.
2. To find out how heavy users of one product differ in terms of the use of a different product.
3. To find out how one group of consumers differs in product consumption from another group of consumers.
4. To find out the demographic and psychographic distinguishing characteristics of a store's customers that differ in lifestyle.
5. To find out the distinguishing characteristics of profitable and non-profitable businesses.

How does a marketer perform a discriminant analysis?

In 1987, Mr. Young started two nightclubs in Tonka County, OH. Club Jam 'O' Jam Inc. was located in Fresh Valley city, a large metropolitan area with a

Photo 29: Lost Dimension

237

diverse population makeup and an active nightlife. The other club, Club Kool was located in Westover city, also a large and attractive city about 40 miles away from Fresh Valley. Both clubs performed well during the first two years of operation and had profit margins of 30% and 35% respectively.

Since the past four years, only Club Jam 'O' Jam has been profitable. Mr. Young noticed a drop in the patronage of Club Kool and was worried. He wanted to find out the factors or reasons for the low performance of Club Kool. A survey of the club patrons was taken to determine the correlates of club patronage. The predictor variables Mr. Young chose to examine were five factors related to club going, including attitude toward club attendance, drinking habits, dating habits, income, and sex. The dependent variable was the patrons' proneness to go to Club Kool. Respondents were placed in three frequency categories as follows: Non-active goers which were those people that came to the club once in a year. The second group was the light goers which were those people that came to the club only during the holidays and special occasions. The third group was the frequent goers, which were the people that came to the club at least once a week.

Mr. Young decided to take a monthly survey of thirty-three patrons in each category and to use a multiple discriminant analysis method to find out the salient or outstanding characteristics of the three groups of patrons. Completed questionnaires were divided into two. Table 13-5a presents the data from the first twenty respondents. This group is called the analysis sample.

The characteristics explored were the patrons' opinion or attitude toward switching to another club, the drinking habit, dating habit, income, and sex. The attitude toward switching to other clubs was measured on a seven-point scale (1 = May be, 7 = Unlikely). The drinking habit was measured on a three-point scale (1 = light, 2 = medium, 3 = heavy). The dating habit was measured on a three-point scale (1 = light, 2 = medium, and 3 = heavy). The income was measured in thousands. Males were coded as 2, and females were coded as 1. Table 13-5a presents the estimate of the analysis sample.

Due to its complexity, the discriminant analysis is solved here using computerized SPSS DISCRIMINANT procedure.

Table 13-5a
INFORMATION ON CLUB PATRONAGE
Estimation or Analysis Sample

FCA	OP	ATS	DH	DTH	I	S
1.00	3.00	4.00	1.00	3.00	76.00	2.00
2.00	3.00	3.00	1.00	3.00	56.00	1.00
2.00	3.00	5.00	3.00	3.00	71.00	1.00
1.00	1.00	5.00	3.00	2.00	57.00	1.00
2.00	1.00	7.00	3.00	1.00	66.00	1.00
1.00	1.00	7.00	3.00	2.00	35.00	2.00
2.00	2.00	7.00	3.00	2.00	90.00	2.00
1.00	2.00	7.00	1.00	3.00	36.00	2.00
2.00	3.00	7.00	2.00	1.00	76.00	2.00
1.00	2.00	7.00	3.00	3.00	45.00	2.00
2.00	3.00	7.00	3.00	1.00	98.00	2.00
1.00	2.00	5.00	3.00	3.00	38.00	1.00
2.00	2.00	5.00	3.00	2.00	76.00	1.00
1.00	2.00	5.00	3.00	1.00	89.00	1.00
2.00	3.00	5.00	3.00	2.00	38.00	2.00
1.00	3.00	6.00	3.00	2.00	97.00	2.00
2.00	3.00	5.00	1.00	3.00	65.00	1.00
2.00	3.00	6.00	2.00	1.00	98.00	1.00
2.00	2.00	1.00	3.00	3.00	60.00	2.00
1.00	1.00	4.00	3.00	1.00	53.00	1.00
2.00	1.00	7.00	3.00	2.00	49.00	2.00
1.00	3.00	4.00	3.00	1.00	66.00	2.00
2.00	1.00	5.00	3.00	4.00	55.00	2.00
1.00	2.00	7.00	3.00	5.00	66.00	1.00

Frequency of Club Attendance (FCA)	Opinion of Patron(OP)	Attitude Toward Switching (ATS)	Drinking Habit(DH)	Dating Habit(DTH)	Income(I)	Sex(S)

The discriminant function coefficients were found using a stepwise discriminant analysis that entered the predictor variables sequentially, based on their ability to discriminate among groups.

Table 13-5b
Analysis Case Processing Summary

Unweighted Cases		N	Percent
Valid		24	100.0
Excluded	Missing or out-of-range group codes	0	.0
	At least one missing discriminating variable	0	.0
	Both missing or out-of-range group codes and at least one missing discriminating variable	0	.0
	Total	0	.0
Total		24	100.0

Table 13-5c
Group Statistics

		Mean	Std. Deviation	Valid N (listwise)	
				Unweighted	Weighted
VAR00007					
1.00	VAR00001	1.5455	.5222	11	11.000
	VAR00002	2.0909	.8312	11	11.000
	VAR00003	5.1818	1.1677	11	11.000
	VAR00004	2.5455	.8202	11	11.000
	VAR00005	2.2727	1.2721	11	11.000

	VAR00006	66.8182	16.7500	11	11.000
2.00	VAR00001	1.5385	.5189	13	13.000
	VAR00002	2.2308	.8321	13	13.000
	VAR00003	5.6923	1.8432	13	13.000
	VAR00004	2.6154	.7679	13	13.000
	VAR00005	2.2308	.9268	13	13.000
	VAR00006	63.1538	22.7077	13	13.000
Total	VAR00001	1.5417	.5090	24	24.000
	VAR00002	2.1667	.8165	24	24.000
	VAR00003	5.4583	1.5598	24	24.000
	VAR00004	2.5833	.7755	24	24.000
	VAR00005	2.2500	1.0734	24	24.000
	VAR00006	64.8333	19.8618	24	24.000

Interpretation:

1. The between group mean difference is small. Also the standard deviation between the groups is insignificant.

Table 13-5d
Pooled Within-Groups Matrices

		VAR00001	VAR00002	VAR00003	VAR00004	VAR00005	VAR00006
Correlation	VAR00001	1.000	.193	-.052	-.064	-.100	.238
	VAR00002	.193	1.000	-.183	-.441	-.048	.459
	VAR00003	-.052	-.183	1.000	.123	-.122	.097
	VAR00004	-.064	-.441	.123	1.000	-.182	.028
	VAR00005	-.100	-.048	-.122	-.182	1.000	-.371
	VAR00006	.238	.459	.097	.028	-.371	1.000

Interpretation:

1. There is a low correlation between the variables.

Table 13-5e
Eigenvalues

Function	Eigenvalue	% of Variance	Cumulative %	Canonical Correlation
1	.029	100.0	100.0	.167

Interpretation:

1. Only one discriminant function is estimated because there are two groups.
2. The eigenvalue of .029, accounts for 100% of the variance. This function is associated with a canonical correlation of .167.
3. The square of this correlation or $(.167)^2 = .028$ indicates that only 2.8% of the dependent variables is explained by this model.

Table 13-5f
Wilks' Lambda

Test of Function(s)	Wilk's Lambda	Chi-square	df	Sig.
1	.972	.535	6	.997

Interpretation:

1. The Wilks' Lambda statistics associated with the function is .972, at a chi-square of .535 at 6df. This is insignificant at the .05 level.

Table 13-5g
Standardized Canonical Discriminant Function Coefficients

	Function 1
VAR00001	.052
VAR00002	1.028
VAR00003	.718
VAR00004	.505
VAR00005	-.169
VAR00006	-.921

Table 13-5h
Prior Probabilities for Groups

	Prior	Cases Used in Analysis	
VAR00007		Unweighted	Weighted
1.00	.500	11	11.000
2.00	.500	13	13.000
Total	1.000	24	24.000

Table 13-5i
Classification Results

			Predicted Group Membership		Total
		VAR00007	1.00	2.00	
Original	Count	1.00	8	3	11
		2.00	4	9	13
	%	1.00	72.7	27.3	100.0
		2.00	30.8	69.2	100.0

Factor Analysis

What is a factor analysis?

It is an interdependent technique that is used to reduce a large number of variables into a manageable level by examining the relationships among the sets of variables and representing them by a few underlying factors.

Why does a marketer need a factor analysis?

1. It can be used to determine how marketing factors act together to produce a big result. For example, a business may lower price and increase advertising in an effort to increase sales during a sales period, and at the end it wants to know how much lower price or advertising contributed to the total sales
2. It can be used to find out the brand attributes that influence consumer choices
3. It can be used to determine the media consumption of a consumer segment.
4. It can be used to find out the underlying characteristics of a consumer segment.

How does a marketer perform a factor analysis?

Until 1979, Body & Soul Recreational Inc. was the only recreation center that offered aerobics, racquetball and outdoor swimming in Crosover, NC. In the summer of that year, a second center Good Fit Inc. opened on the other part of the city. In addition to the regular recreational line, Good Fit provided a playroom for babies, with full time baby caretakers. There was a noticeable decrease in the nursing parents' category at Body & Soul. Some nursing parents that patronized Body & Soul switched to Good Fit to avoid babysitting while exercising.

In an effort to bring back the lost customers, Body & Soul responded with an intensive promotion and price-cutting. It offered redeemable discount coupons to frequent users and nursing parents. It also increased the radio advertisement on the center as the best recreational center in the town. After the first three weeks of advertising, Body & Soul noticed a 20% increase in the patronage by both nursing parents and the customers that used the center the most often. Sales increased by 15% during the period. The company was very pleased and it wanted to know how either advertising or lower price contributed to the sales increase.

Body & Soul decided to use a factor analysis to find out the underlying factors. A sample of thirty patrons was interviewed in the center using a store-intercept interviewing method. They were asked to indicate their degree of agreement to six statements; three for advertising, and three for lower price, using a ten-point scale (1= strongly disagree, 10= strongly agree). The ratings are shown on Table 13-6a.

V_1: I depend mostly on advertising for my choice of a recreation center.

V_2: Advertising exposes a recreation center's benefits.

V_3: I prefer a recreation center that advertises.

V_4: I patronize recreation centers that make life easy for nursing parents

V_5: Lower price always entices me to use a recreation center.

V_6: I tend to switch to recreation centers with lower price.

Factor Analysis $(X_i) = A_{i1}F_1 + A_{i2}F_2 + A_{i3}F_3 + \ldots A_{im}F_m + V_iU_i$
where:

X_i = ith standardized variable

A_{ij} = standardized multiple regression coefficient of variable i on common factor i.

F = common factor

V_i = standardized regression coefficient of variable i on unique factor j

U_i = the unique factor for variable I

M = number of common factors

Table 13-6a
ENTER ATTRIBUTE RATINGS

V_1	V_2	V_3	V_4	V_5	V_6
5.00	7.00	8.00	6.00	8.00	5.00
6.00	7.00	5.00	6.00	9.00	8.00
10.00	7.00	6.00	1.00	9.00	4.00
9.00	4.00	7.00	5.00	8.00	10.00
5.00	4.00	6.00	9.00	1.00	2.00
3.00	9.00	5.00	6.00	10.00	8.00
7.00	4.00	8.00	7.00	9.00	6.00
8.00	10.00	9.00	10.00	7.00	5.00
2.00	8.00	10.00	8.00	8.00	9.00
6.00	9.00	7.00	9.00	4.00	2.00
8.00	8.00	5.00	9.00	1.00	8.00
1.00	1.00	1.00	3.00	6.00	10.00
10.00	7.00	6.00	1.00	9.00	4.00
9.00	4.00	5.00	5.00	8.00	10.00
5.00	6.00	8.00	9.00	1.00	2.00
3.00	9.00	9.00	6.00	10.00	8.00
7.00	4.00	10.00	7.00	9.00	6.00
8.00	10.00	7.00	10.00	7.00	5.00
2.00	8.00	5.00	8.00	8.00	9.00
6.00	9.00	1.00	9.00	4.00	2.00
8.00	8.00	6.00	9.00	1.00	8.00
1.00	1.00	7.00	3.00	6.00	10.00
10.00	7.00	6.00	1.00	9.00	2.00
9.00	4.00	5.00	5.00	8.00	8.00
5.00	6.00	8.00	9.00	1.00	6.00
3.00	9.00	9.00	6.00	10.00	5.00
7.00	4.00	10.00	7.00	9.00	9.00
8.00	10.00	7.00	10.00	7.00	2.00
2.00	8.00	5.00	8.00	8.00	8.00
6.00	9.00	1.00	9.00	4.00	10.00
8.00	8.00	5.00	9.00	1.00	8.00

| 1.00 | 1.00 | 1.00 | 3.00 | 6.00 | 5.00 |

Table 13-6b
Correlation Matrix

	VAR00001	VAR00002	VAR00003	VAR00004	VAR00005	VAR00006
Correlation VAR00001	1.000	.208	.130	-.030	-.043	-.287
VAR00002	.208	1.000	.153	.553	-.067	-.351
VAR00003	.130	.153	1.000	.174	.268	-.113
VAR00004	-.030	.553	.174	1.000	-.493	-.050
VAR00005	-.043	-.067	.268	-.493	1.000	.078
VAR00006	-.287	-.351	-.113	-.050	.078	1.000
Sig. (1- VAR00001 tailed)		.131	.243	.436	.410	.059
VAR00002	.131		.205	.001	.359	.026
VAR00003	.243	.205		.175	.073	.272
VAR00004	.436	.001	.175		.002	.395
VAR00005	.410	.359	.073	.002		.337
VAR00006	.059	.026	.272	.395	.337	

Interpretation:

1. There is relatively more correlation between V2(Advertising exposes a recreation center's benefits) and V4(I patronize recreation centers that make life easy for nursing parents).

Table 13-6c
Communalities

	Initial
VAR00001	1.000
VAR00002	1.000
VAR00003	1.000
VAR00004	1.000
VAR00005	1.000
VAR00006	1.000

Extraction Method: Principal Component Analysis.

Interpretation:

1. The initial commonalities representing the units inserted in the diagonal of the correlation matrix is 1.00.

Table 13-6d
Total Variance Explained

Component	Initial Eigenvalues			Rotation Sums of Squared Loadings		
	Total	% of Variance	Cumulative %	Total	% of Variance	Cumulative %
1	1.940	32.340	32.340	1.759	29.317	29.317
2	1.421	23.677	56.016	1.406	23.436	52.753
3	1.082	18.032	74.048	1.278	21.295	74.048
4	.745	12.418	86.466			
5	.626	10.435	96.901			
6	.186	3.099	100.000			

Extraction Method: Principal Component Analysis.

Interpretation:

1. As shown in Table13-6d, the eigenvalues or the total variance attributed to each component or variable decreased in the order of magnitude as the total variance explained moved from component 1 to component 6.

2. The eigenvalue is greater than one for three variables, resulting in their being extracted. A look at the cumulative percentage of variance showed that three variables accounted for 74.05% of the variance.

3. Variable 1 accounted for a variance of 1.940 or 32.3% of the total variance. Variable 2 accounted for a variance of 1.42 or 23.67% of the total variance. Variable 3 accounted for 18.03%

of the total variance. Variable 4 accounted for .745 or 12.41% of the total variance. Variable 5 accounted for .626 or 10.43% of the total variance, and Variable 6 accounted for .186 or 3.09% of the total variance.

Table 13-6e
Rotated Component Matrix

	Component		
	1	2	3
VAR00001	-3.587E-02	.798	2.080E-02
VAR00002	.713	.382	.192
VAR00003	.263	6.420E-02	.833
VAR00004	.948	-8.535E-02	-7.140E-02
VAR00005	-.508	-2.620E-02	.736
VAR00006	-.151	-.782	-1.909E-02

Extraction Method: Principal Component Analysis. Rotation Method: Varimax with Kaiser Normalization.
a Rotation converged in 5 iterations.

Interpretation:

1. V2(Advertising exposes a recreation center's benefits) and V4(I patronize a recreation center that makes life easy for nursing parents) correlated highly with the factor 1. This factor may be labeled as "easy life promotion."
2. Only V1 correlated highly with factor 2. This factor may be labeled "benefit advertisement."
3. Only V3 correlated highly with factor three. This factor may be labeled "advertise recreation."

Table 13-6f
Component Score Coefficient Matrix

	Component		
	1	2	3
VAR00001	-.130	.602	-.061
VAR00002	.383	.171	.156
VAR00003	.193	-.066	.672
VAR00004	.572	-.188	.003
VAR00005	-.259	-.019	.561
VAR00006	.016	-.565	.050

Extraction Method: Principal Component Analysis. Rotation Method: Varimax with Kaiser Normalization.

Table 13-6g
Component Score Covariance Matrix

Component	1	2	3
1	1.000	.000	.000
2	.000	1.000	.000
3	.000	.000	1.000

Extraction Method: Principal Component Analysis. Rotation Method: Varimax with Kaiser Normalization.

Multidimensional Scaling

What is a multidimensional scaling?

It is a class of techniques for representing perceptions and preferences of buyers in spaces by using visual displays.

Why does a marketer need a multidimensional scaling?

1. It is used to produce a perceptual map of how the customers perceive a firm's products compared to the competitors.
2. It is used to compare customers' and non-customers' perceptions of a firm and how the firm perceives itself.
3. It is used to identify and group customers into homogeneous perception of a firm's brands and those of the competitors.
5. It is used to evaluate a new concept on an existing brand to determine how the consumers perceive it.
6. It is used to determine whether advertising has been successful in achieving the desired brand positioning.

How does a marketer develop the multidimensional scaling?

Fresh Choice Juice Inc. began in 1971 to bottle and distribute Top Fresh orange juice. This brand originally competed against two other brand of orange juice in America. However, by 1997 the number of competing brands had increased to eleven. As a result, the market share for Top Fresh decreased from 50% to 33.7%. In an effort to identify the reason for the drop in sales, Fresh Choice decided to utilize a direct approach multidimensional scaling to assess how similar or dissimilar the customers perceived Top Fresh to competing brands. They also used a derived approach to find out how customers rated Top Fresh brand against the other eleven competing brands in terms of freshness, flavor, and price attributes. One hundred respondents were asked to rate the similarity of Top Fresh to the other brands using the 5-point Likert scale below.

Table 13-7a
A Similarity & Dissimilarity Scale

	Very Dissimilar			Very Similar	
1. Top Fresh Vs Brand 1	1	2	3	4	5
2. Top Fresh Vs Brand 2	1	2	3	4	5
3. Brand 3 Vs. Top Fresh	1	2	3	4	5

4. Band 4 Vs Top Fresh	1	2	3	4	5
5. Top Fresh Vs Brand 6	1	2	3	4	5
6. Top Fresh Vs Brand 7	1	2	3	4	5
7. Brand 8 Vs Top Fresh	1	2	3	4	5
8. Brand 9 Vs. Top Fresh	1	2	3	4	5
9. Top Fresh Vs Brand 10	1	2	3	4	5
10. Top Fresh Vs Brand 11	1	2	3	4	5
11. Brand 12 Vs Top Fresh	1	2	3	4	5
.					
.					
.					
66. Brand 12 Vs. Top Fresh	1	2	3	4	5

Data Record:

Very Dissimilar			Very Similar	
4.00	3.00	5.00	4.00	5.00
3.00	2.00	4.00	3.00	3.00
4.00	4.00	3.00	2.00	4.00
3.00	5.00	5.00	4.00	3.00
4.00	2.00	2.00	5.00	4.00
4.00	4.00	4.00	4.00	2.00
3.00	5.00	4.00	5.00	4.00
4.00	4.00	3.00	3.00	2.00
2.00	5.00	5.00	5.00	4.00
5.00	4.00	4.00	3.00	2.00
4.00	3.00	5.00	4.00	3.00
5.00	2.00	4.00	3.00	1.00
4.00	4.00	3.00	4.00	3.00
5.00	5.00	2.00	3.00	2.00
4.00	3.00	4.00	4.00	3.00
4.00	3.00	1.00	5.00	4.00

The number of pairs to be evaluated is $n(n-1)/2$. In this example, that is $12(12-1)/2$ or $(12 \times 11/2)$ or 66. The data obtained from the survey were treated as rank-ordered and scales using a nonmetric procedure. Below are the mean ratings of the similarity of the pairs.

Table 13-7b
SIMILARITY RATINGS OF ORANGE JUICE BRANDS

Top Fresh	B2	B3	B4	B5	B6	B7	B8	B9	B10	B11
Top Fresh										
B2	4									
B3	2	3								
B4	5	4	2							
B5	3	5	5	1						
B6	4	2	4	2	3					
B7	4	3	1	4	2	2				
B8	2	3	4	5	1	3	2			
B9	5	4	3	1	2	4	4	3		
B10	5	1	2	3	5	3	2	3	4	
B11	1	2	4	2	4	3	2	5	5	3

The data above was used to construct the spatial map below. The map plots the stress versus the dimensionality of the data.

Table 13-7c
PLOT OF STRESS VERSUS DIMENSIONALITY

Derived Stimulus Configuration

Euclidean distance model

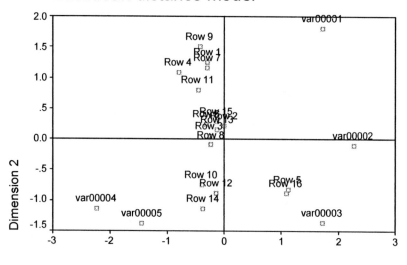

Interpretation:

1. Variables 1, 2, and 3 have high positive values or are more similar to each other.
2. Variables 4 and 5 are low in dimensions and could be termed poor or dissimilar to the other brands.

Table 13-7d

Scatterplot of Nonlinear Fit

Euclidean distance model

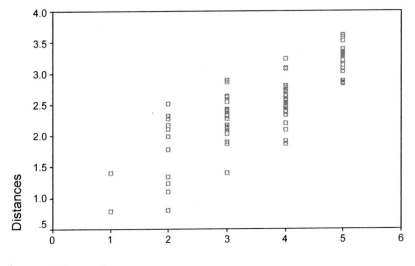

Observations

Scatterplot of Linear Fit

Euclidean distance model

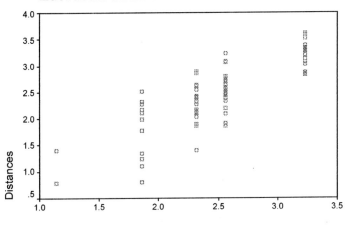

Disparities

255

Table 13-7e

Transformation Scatterplot

Euclidean distance model

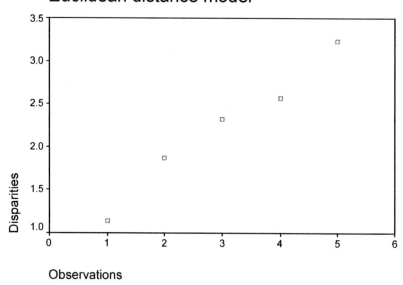

Observations

Multiple Regression

What is a multiple regression analysis?

It is a technique that is used to determine if there is any relationship or association between two or more independent variables or occurrences and an interval-scaled dependent variable.

Why does a marketer need a multiple regression analysis?

1. Multiple regression enables a business to find out how much one occurrence in the business could be associated or related to two or more activities. For example, how recent increases in

sales relate to or associate with the increased frequency of advertising, recent markdowns, and better quality brands?

How does a marketer develop a multiple regression analysis?

Mama-Me Foods Inc. is a Caribbean take-out restaurant located in Middle Road, Florida. During the 2001 Thanksgiving season, Mama-Me intended to increase customer patronage to the restaurant, and to  increase sales by at least 15%. It stocked new and better brands of menus and added some special seasonings. It marked down the prices of some of the regular menus like goat stews, fried plantains, ox tails, and steamed rice. It offered twenty

Photo 30: MAYFLOWER

minutes order waiting time or half price for all combination plates. It also doubled the frequency of its advertising during the Thanksgiving season.

By the end of the Thanksgiving season, Mama-Me noticed that the number of orders doubled compared to the previous years' Thanksgiving. It also noticed a triple in the amount of sales compared to the same period in the prior years. Mama-Me wanted to know which of the four actions: better quality food and seasoning, price markdown, quicker service, or increased frequency of advertising was most responsible for the increased patronage and sales. It decided to find out by conducting two multiple regression analyses. It conducted the first on Table 13-8a by using patronage as the dependent variable, and the three actions as the independent variables. In the second analysis on Table 13-8c, it used sales as the dependent variable, and the three actions as the independent variables.

$$Y \text{ (patronage)} = a + b_1X_1 + b_2X_2 + b_3X_3 + b_4X_4$$
$$Y \text{ (sales)} = a + b_1X_1 + b_2X_2 + b_3X_3 + b_4X_4$$

Mama-Mc conducted a random survey of twenty customers after the Thanksgiving period. The first part of the questionnaire asked the respondents to indicate on a five-point Likert scale (1 = not likely, 5 = extremely likely) if it was the price markdown, quicker service, or increased frequency of advertising that made them to increase their frequency to the restaurant during the Thanksgiving period. The second part of the questionnaire asked the respondents to indicate if it was the price markdown, quicker service, or increased frequency of advertising that made them to increase their purchases of the food.

Table 13-8a
STORE PATRONAGE AND STORE STRATEGIES

Respondents	Store Patronage	Quicker Service	Price Markdown	Advertising Frequency
1	5	4	4	5
2	4	5	3	3
3	5	4	5	4
4	3	5	3	3
5	4	4	5	2
6	5	5	3	3
7	4	3	5	4
8	2	4	3	5
9	3	5	5	3
10	1	4	3	4
11	4	5	5	2
12	5	3	3	4

13	3	4	5	5
14	4	5	3	3
15	5	3	2	4
16	2	4	3	2
17	3	5	5	3
18	4	4	4	4
19	2	5	3	5
20	3	5	5	4

Y   (c10:c29)
X   (d10:d29):(e10:e29):(f10:f29)

Y (patronage) = $a + b_1X_1 + b_2X_2 + b_3X_3 + b_4X_4$

Table 13-8b
<u>Store Patronage and Store Strategies</u>

SUMMARY OUTPUT

Regression Statistics	
Multiple R	0.322063
R Square	0.103725
Adjusted R Square	-0.06433
Standard Error	1.228684
Observations	20

ANOVA

	df	SS	MS	F	Significance F
Regression	3	2.795377	0.931792	0.617218	0.613849
Residual	16	24.15462	1.509664		
Total	19	26.95			

	Coefficients	Standard Error	t Stat	P-value	Lower 95%	Upper 95%	Lower 95.0%	Upper 95.0%
Intercept	6.158022	2.549308	2.415566	0.028036	0.753732	11.56231	0.753732	11.56231
X Variable 1	-0.53318	0.409947	-1.30062	0.211811	-1.40223	0.335863	-1.40223	0.335863
X Variable 2	0.107862	0.274138	0.39346	0.699173	-0.47328	0.689009	-0.47328	0.689009
X Variable 3	-0.20294	0.301241	-0.67369	0.510121	-0.84155	0.435657	-0.84155	0.435657

Interpretations

1. Price markdown is more significant in explaining the patronage to the store than quicker service and advertising frequency.
2. The R square(Rs) or coefficient of multiple determination is low, indicating a higher association between price markdown, quicker service and advertising frequency, but not store patronage.
3. The R square and the adjusted R square are not close, indicating that the addition of the other variables did not really make much contribution in explaining why they did not help in store patronage.

4. The F statistics is .617 which does not differ significantly from the adjusted R of .613. Also, the calculated F is less than the critical F (5.29). Therefore, the null hypothesis is accepted. None of the strategies applied by Mama-Me was indicated as the major reason for the increased patronage during the thanksgiving period.

Table 13-8c
Sales/Food Purchase And Store Strategies

Respondents	Food Purchase	Quicker Service	Price Markdown	Advertising Frequency
1	4	4	4	5
2	4	2	3	3
3	3	4	5	4
4	4	2	3	2
5	3	4	5	1
6	4	5	3	3
7	2	3	5	5
8	1	2	3	5
9	1	5	5	3
10	1	4	3	5
11	1	5	5	5
12	3	3	3	5
13	4	4	5	5
14	3	4	3	5
15	2	3	2	5
16	2	4	3	5
17	3	3	5	3
18	4	1	4	4
19	2	5	3	5
20	3	5	5	4

Y   (c10:c29)
X   (d10:d29):(e10:e29):(f10:f29)

Y (food purchase) = $a + b_1X_1 + b_2X_2 + b_3X_3 + b_4X_4$

Table 13-8d
Food Purchase and Store Strategies

SUMMARY OUTPUT   Food Purchase And Store Strategies

Regression Statistics	
Multiple R	0.442985
R Square	0.196235
Adjusted R Square	0.045529
Standard Error	1.102585
Observations	20

ANOVA

	df	SS	MS	F	Significance F
Regression	3	4.748896	1.582965	1.302108	0.308064101
Residual	16	19.4511	1.215694		
Total	19	24.2			

	Coefficients	Standard Error	t Stat	P-value	Lower 95%	Upper 95%	Lower 95.0%	Upper 95.0%
Intercept	4.869116	1.508908	3.226914	0.005271	1.670375302	8.067857	1.670375	8.067857
X Variable 1	-0.24283	0.226425	-1.07244	0.299434	-0.72282674	0.237174	-0.72283	0.237174
X Variable 2	-0.00189	0.264852	-0.00715	0.994382	-0.56335608	0.559568	-0.56336	0.559568
X Variable 3	-0.31406	0.2191	-1.43341	0.170992	-0.77853113	0.15041	-0.77853	0.15041

Interpretations

1. None of the strategies is significant in explaining the amount of food purchased by the customers during the period.
2. The R square(Rs) or coefficient of multiple determination is low, indicating a higher association between price markdown, quicker service and advertising frequency but not to amount of food purchased.

5. The R square and the adjusted R square are not close, indicating that the addition of the other variables did not really make much contribution in varying the food purchase.
6. The calculated F (1.30) is less than the critical F (5.29). Therefore, the null hypothesis is rejected. All of the strategies applied by Mama-Me were indicated as the major reason for the increase in food purchase during the thanksgiving period.

Queuing model

What is a queuing model?

Queuing or Waiting line model is used to determine the amount of time and the number of customers appropriate to wait in the customer lines to be served at different times of the day.

Why does a marketer need a queuing model?

1. It is used to determine the number of check out stands adequate to open in a store or at customer service line at the various times of operation.
2. It is used to determine the number of service outlets to keep open at the peak hours of operation.
3. It is used to determine the appropriate number of workers to assign at the check-out stand during the peak hours of operation.

How does a marketer use the queuing model?

Edmond International Airport Inc. is a large regional airport located in Edmond, NC. For security sake, the passengers' carry-on bags, and the passengers are inspected prior to boarding the airplanes. Both operations are conducted with electronic equipment and X-ray devices. In 2001, two major airlines relocated their central port to Edmond. The increase in traffic and passengers resulted in the problems of excessive delays and long waiting lines.

In order to find a solution to this problem, the airport decided to find out the adequate number of outlets for the security-screening operations. In order to develop a waiting-line model for

Photo 31: DIRECT JETCHARTER

the security-screening system, Edmond International Airport had to identify the arrival distribution of the passengers, the service-time distribution for the screening operation, and the waiting line or queue discipline of the passengers.

ARRIVAL DISTRIBUTION OF PASSENGERS

Due to the wide variety of flight schedules at Edmond International Airport, the arrival of passengers to the airport has a random pattern. A two-month study of passenger arrivals estimated an average of 10 arrivals per minute during the peak flight periods. At this mean arrival rate ($\wedge = 10$), the airport computed the probability of x passenger arrivals in a 1-minute period by using the **Poisson probability distribution.**

Poisson probability distribution $P(x) = \dfrac{\wedge^x e^{-\wedge}}{x!}$ for x = 0, 1, 2,.........

x = number of arrivals in a specific period of time
$\wedge$ = average, or expected number of arrivals for the specific period of time
e = 2.71828

$$x^{-10}$$

Thus, $P(x) = \dfrac{10\,e}{X!}$

A sample calculation for x = 0, x=1, x=2, x=3, x=4, x=5, x=6, x=7, x=8, x=9, x=10 passenger arrival during a 1-minute period are:

$$P(0) = \dfrac{10^{0}\ e^{-10}}{0!} =$$

Table 13-9
POISSON PROBABILITY DISTRIBUTION OF PASSENGER ARRIVALS

Estimate Arrival Per Minute	Probability of Occurrence
5	.037
6	.063
7	.090
8	.111
9	.125
10	.125
11	.113
12	.094
13	.073
14	.052
15	.035
16	.022
17	.013
18	.007
19	.003
20	.001

Interpretation of results

1. Edmond International Airport has a higher probability of .125 for 9 or 10 arrivals per minute.

Implication of the results

1. Edmond International Airport should invest to open more screening gates to accommodate the present rate of passenger flow as it seems to be the average.

Strategic Profit Model

What is a strategic profit model?

It is a technique that shows the mathematical relationship between the net profit, asset turnover, and financial leverage.

Why does a marketer need to know the strategic profit model?

1. It provides a marketer with a performance measure termed return on net worth, which is used to plan and control assets.

How does a marketer develop a strategic profit model?

Lagos Refrigeration Services Inc. sells, installs, and services commercial and industrial ice machines, coolers, and freezers. Located in Los Angeles, CA, the company serves more than sixty percent of the institutional and commercial refrigerator users like restaurants, convenience stores, offices, schools, and churches in the city.

The economy of scale that results from its large customer base gives Lagos Refrigeration Services the advantages of low price and high sales. The net sales in 2000 was $11.4m, and the net profit was $6.1m. The company invested a part of this profit to acquire assets as it has done since its beginning in 1978. It now has about $82m in assets and a total liability of $27.6m. Lagos Refrigeration Services needed to know how much to manipulate the market to achieve desired success levels. For example, how much increase in the return on net worth will result from given amounts of increases or decreases in the net profit margin, or asset turnover, or financial leverage? The company did the following.

Table 13-10
Lagos Refrigeration Services
Strategic Profile Model

a. Return on net worth = $\dfrac{\text{Net Profit}}{\text{Net Sales}}$ x $\dfrac{\text{Net Sales}}{\text{Total Assets}}$ x $\dfrac{\text{Total Assets}}{\text{Net worth}}$

$$= \frac{\$6,100,000}{\$11,400,000} \times \frac{\$11,400,000}{\$82,000,000} \times \frac{\$82,000,000}{\$54,400,000}$$

= Net Profit Margin x Asset Turnover x Financial Leverage
      .5351   .1390   1.5074

Return on Net Worth
= .1121 or 11.21%

b. To increase the RONW to 18.21% by using the net profit margin:

Furthermore, Lagos Refrigeration Services wanted to increase the return on net worth by 7% to 18.21%. It needed to know how much to increase the net profit margin, or asset turnover, or financial leverage in order to achieve an 18.21% return on net worth, by using the net profit margin.

RONW $= \dfrac{\$9,912,500}{\$11,400,000} \times \dfrac{\$11,400,000}{\$82,000,000} \times \dfrac{\$82,000,000}{\$54,400,000}$

$\quad\quad = \quad .8695 \quad\quad\quad \text{x} \quad .1390 \quad\quad\quad \text{x} \quad 1.5074$

$$= \quad .1821 \text{ or } 18.21\%$$

The increase in RONW from 11.21% to 18.21% is a 62.5 percent raise (18.21-11.21/11.21). Therefore an increase of 62.5% in the net profit from $6,100,000 to $9,912,500 is required in order to increase the net profit margin by 62.5% from .5351 to .8695.

c. To increase the RONW to 18.21% by using assets turnover:

$$\textbf{RONW} \quad = \quad \frac{\$6,100,000}{\$11,400,000} \text{ x } \frac{\$18,525,000}{\$82,000,000} \text{ x } \frac{\$82,000,000}{\$54,400,000}$$

$$= \quad .5351 \qquad \text{x} \quad .2259 \qquad \text{x} \quad 1.5074$$

$$= \quad .1821 \text{ or } 18.21\%$$

The increase in RONW from 11.21% to 18.21% is a 62.5 percent. Therefore an increase of 62.5% in the sales from $11,400,000 to $18,525,000 is required in order to increase the RONW by 62.5% or from .1390 to .2252, using the assets turnover.

d. To increase the RONW to 18.21% by using the financial leverage:

$$\text{RONW} \quad = \quad \frac{\$9,905,000}{\$11,400,000} \text{ x } \frac{\$11,400,000}{\$82,000,000} \text{ x } \frac{\$133,250,000}{\$54,400,000}$$

$$= \quad .5351 \qquad \text{x} \quad .1390 \qquad \text{x} \quad 2.4494$$

$$= \quad .1821 \text{ or } 18.21\%$$

The increase in RONW from 11.21% to 18.21% is a 62.5 percent. Therefore an increase of 62% in the total asset from $82,000,000 to $133,250,000 is required in order to increase the RONW by 62% or from 1.5074 to 2.4494, using the financial leverage.

Interpretation of the results.

1. Lagos Refrigeration Services had 11.21% return on net worth or $6,098,240 in 2000.
2. To increase RONW by 7% (18.21%-11.21% or 62.5%) using the net profit margin will require an increase in net profit margin to $3,812,500.
3. To increase the RONW by 7% using the asset turnover will require an additional $7,125,000 in sales.
4. To increase the RONW by 7% using the financial leverage will require an additional $51,250,000 in total asset.

Implications of the results.

1. If Lagos Refrigeration Services wants to increase RONW it could increase either the net profit margin, or asset turnover, or financial leverage.
2. Lagos Refrigeration Services could increase the net profit margin by increasing sales at a lower cost.
3. Lagos Refrigeration Services could increase the asset turnover by increasing sales at the same level of assets.
4. Lagos Refrigeration Services can increase financial leverage by increasing the total assets.

Calculation steps.

1. Determine the net profit margin by dividing the net profit with the net sales.
2. Determine the asset turnover by dividing the net sales with the total assets.
3. Determine the financial leverage by dividing the total assets with the net worth.
4. Determine the return on net worth by multiplying the net profit margin, the asset turnover, and the financial leverage.

CHAPTER 14

TARGET MARKETING

Lifetime Value of a Customer

What is the lifetime value of a customer?

It is a technique used to determine the worth of a customer by considering the customer's initial and estimated future purchases.

Why does a marketer need to know the lifetime value of a customer?

1. For marketers that use incentives to attract customer purchases, knowing the lifetime value of the customers allows them to determine the amount that could be profitably spent to acquire new customers or reactivate old ones.
2. The lifetime value of customers enables the marketer to estimate the potential value of customers on an annual basis.

How does a marketer determine the lifetime value of a customer?

Jon Thomas Hardwood Flooring Inc. has seven categories of customers ranging from none to six repeat purchases. Based on 2001 purchase data shown on Table 14-1, the company categorized the customers according to their repeat purchase habits. From this, Jon Thomas learned that the average customer repeated purchases 2.27 times in 2001, and made an average buy of $120 per customer. The average-contribution margin per buy is .60 or 60 percent of the sales, and the variable contribution margin is $66. The company's marketing objective is to acquire 5,000 new customers in 2002 by spending $200,000 in advertisement and $82,000 in sales promotion. This is at a total acquisition cost of $56.4 per customer ($200,000 +$82,000/5000). However, the company needed to know the lifetime value of each customer to assure that it could recover its acquisition costs, and it took the following steps.

Table 14-1
Jon Thomas Hardwood Flooring Purchase History 1999-2001
Lifetime Value
# of repeat purchases x % of your customers = Weighted Average Customer

# of repeat purchases	% of your customers	Weighted Average Customer
0	.19	0
1	.23	.23
2	.20	.40
3	.14	.42
4	.05	.20
5	.12	.60
6	.07	.42
	1.00	2.27

Lifetime Value of Customer = Av. # of repeats **x** Av. $ sale **x** Av.
Variable contribution margin +
Variable contribution margin on initial sale.
= 2.27 x $120 x .60 + $66 = $229.44

Interpretation of the results.

1. The lifetime value of each customer in 2002 was $229.44. This was far above the $56.4 it costs to attract one new customer.

Implication of the results.

1. The investment was wise and profitable.

Calculation steps.

1. Based on historical data, segment the buyers into similar characteristics, and indicate the percentage of repurchase by customers in each segment.
2. Add the percentage of repurchase by all the segments.
3. Calculate the weighted average of each segment by multiplying the number of repeat purchases by the percent of repurchase customers. Add all the segment weighted averages.
4. Multiply the average number of repeat purchases by the average sales and the average variable-contribution margin. Add this to the variable-contribution margin on initial sales to get the lifetime value of the customers.

PART SIX

THE FOUR Ps

CHAPTER 15

PRODUCT

Attribute Rating

What is attribute rating?

It is a technique used to determine which features or attributes of a product are the most important to the consumers.

Why does a marketer need to know the attribute rating?

1. It gives the marketer a knowledge of how the consumers perceive the make up of a merchandise compared to similar products.
2. It provides the marketer with the information to develop a perceptual mapping that groups markets according to similarity in characteristics.
3. A map of how the customers perceive or rate the characteristics of competing products or companies will assist the marketer to select the appropriate strategies.
4. To determine the brands of products to carry in the inventory.
5. To measure the degree of similarity or differences among brands of a product category.
6. To speculate consumers' brand choices.

How does a marketer determine the attribute rating?

Example 1

Nic's Health Foods Inc. is a natural foods retail store located in Bumdel, TN. It sells different types of natural foods, including herbs, vitamins, oils, and extracts. Since its opening in 1976, Nic's had been the leading natural food seller in the city. Regular customers included both the city and county residents. However, in the 1980's there was a challenge to Nic's. TNC and two other natural food retailers located stores in Bumdel. By the middle of the 1990's, the leadership was equally shared by Nic's Health Foods, TNC, CHELL, and Bumdel's Natural Life.

In order to remain competitive, Nic's resorted to using the results of marketing research as the basis for all marketing decisions made by the store. Although the store is conveniently located, the manager Mrs. Nicole Jugnut believed that the best way to determine the best foods to carry was to ask the customers. In 1995, the store randomly surveyed the customers and found that the four most important attributes to them were personal care, price discounting, wide brand assortments, and staff experience. Because of this, the store decided to base its plan and strategies on two key elements; (1) the customer ratings of Nic's on personal care, price discounting, brand assortments, and staff experience, and (2) the customer ratings of Nic's, TNC, CHELL, Bumdel's on personal care, price discounting, brand assortments, and staff experience. The rating form is shown in Figure 15-1 below.

Figure 15-1

CUSTOMER SURVEY
Please complete both section one and section two below.

Section 1: Please rate Nic's Health Foods on the four items below. 1=poor, 2=fair, 3=okay, 4=good, 5=execellent.

		1	2	3	4	5
1.	Personal care	—	—	—	—	—
2.	Price discounting	—	—	—	—	—
3.	Brand assortments	—	—	—	—	—
4.	Staff experience	—	—	—	—	—

Section 2: Please rate Nic's Health Foods and these three other natural food stores in Bumdel on the four items below. 1=poor, 2=fair, 3=okay, 4=good, 5= excellent.

RATING OF HEALTH FOODSTORES IN BUMDEL

	Nic's	TNC	CHELL	Bumdel's

Attributes:
1. Personal care ____ ____ ____ ____
2. Discounted Price ____ ____ ____ ____
3. Brand Assortments ____ ____ ____ ____
4. Staff experience ____ ____ ____ ____

In the first three months, one hundred and fifty forms were completed. The store added up the ratings for each item in section one, and divided the total by one hundred and fifty. Table 15-1 shows the items rated by their importance.

Table 15-1
NIC'S HEALTH FOOD
Attribute Rating

	IMPORTANCE
1. Staff experience	4.45
2. Brand Assortments	3.99
3. Personal care	3.55
4. Discounted price	3.50

The store added the ratings on the four items for the four stores in section two, and divided each total by one hundred and fifty. Table 15-2 shows the stores and their ratings.

Table 15-2
RATING FOR HEALTH FOODSTORES IN BUMDEL

	Nic's	TNC	CHELL	Bumdel's
Attributes				
1. Personal care	4.0	4.6	3.9	4.0
2. Discounted Price	3.7	4.1	3.8	4.3
3. Brand Assortments	4.6	4.5	3.5	3.2
4. Staff experience	4.7	3.9	3.1	2.9
Total	17.0	17.1	14.3	14.4

Interpretation of the results.

1. Staff experience is the most important attribute to Nic's Health Food customers, followed by brand assortments, personal, care, and discount price.
2. According to the simple compensatory rule (ranked by size), TNC is the most preferred store.
3. According to noncompensatory rules, Nic's Health Food is the most preferred store. It ranked highest on the two most important attributes (staff experience, and brand assortments).

Implications of the results.

1. Nic's Health Foods should devote most of its marketing budget on the activities that will increase staff experience, brand assortments, personal care, and discounted price.
2. While Nic's Health Food should endeavor to maintain leadership in the two most important attributes, it should also seek to capture leadership in the remaining two attributes.

Calculation steps.

1. Add the ratings for each attribute in section one.

2. Divide the total for each attribute by one hundred and fifty to get the average rating for each attribute.
3. Add ratings for each attribute for each store in section two.
4. Divide the total ratings for each of the four attributes by one hundred and fifty, and do this for each store.

Example 2:

How does a marketer determine the attribute rating?

Purple Cross Inc. is a non-profit humanitarian organization located in Imo State, Nigeria. The organization was created in 1966 as an apparatus to coordinate the relief and assistance for hopeless and dying war refugees during the Nigerian civil war. Purple Cross now competed with and complemented other humanitarian groups in the state such as the Red Cross, World Council of Churches, and the Group for World Relief. Because it was indigenous, foreign humanitarian groups relied and worked with Purple Cross for efficient, effective, and safe food distribution. When the foreign organizations reduced their operations after the war in 1970, Purple Cross kept its structures in order to provide free assistance to the people.

Purple Cross provides food, shelter, blood, and first aid to the people in times of emergency. The organization depended on donations from the people, businesses and the government for operations. Because of a prolong downturn in the economy, donations have greatly reduced. Purple Cross was always in a dire need for money, and the manager decided to find a more efficient way to make more impact on donors to donate more money. From past records and research, the manager classified donors into five segments or groups in terms of what motivated them to donate to Purple Cross. These were shelter-motivated, blood-motivated, disaster-motivated, politics-motivated, and mercy-donors.

In order to develop more effective promotion strategies to make optimum impact on the donors, Purple Cross had to know two things:

(a) how does each segment of donors perceive Purple Cross on six attributes: fast service, easy to reach, reliability, dependability, pleasant atmosphere, and stability?

(b) how does the society compare Purple Cross to the three top competitors on the six attributes?

Table 15-3 below presents the mean rating of the different donors' perception on attributes for Purple Cross. Table 15-4 presents the mean attribute ratings for Purple Cross and the competitors. A questionnaire with Likert scale of 1=lowest, and 7=highest was used, and one hundred and fifty questionnaires were returned, and Table 15-4 shows how the Purple Cross compares with the three other humanitarian organizations on the perceptions of the society on the same attributes.

Table 15-3
MEAN ATTRIBUTE RATINGS FOR PURPLE CROSS

Motivators

Attributes

	Shelter	Blood	Disaster	Politics	Mercy
Fast service	6.1	5.2	4.0	3.9	4.5
Easy to reach	4.3	4.8	6.5	6.0	5.9
Reliability	6.0	3.1	7.0	4.7	5.6
Dependabili ty	5.6	7.0	3.2	4.6	6.7
Pleasant atmosphere	4.9	5.7	4.9	3.9	4.8
Stability.	3.1	5.9	5.8	4.9	2.9

Table 15-4
<u>MEAN ATTRIBUTE RATINGS FOR ORGANIZATIONS</u>

Attributes	Purple Cross	Red Cross	WCC	GWR
Fast service	5.1	6.2	5.0	5.9
Easy to reach	6.3	3.8	5.5	6.0
Reliability	7.0	4.1	4.0	3.7
Dependabilit y	3.6	6.6	3.2	3.6
Pleasant atmosphere	4.5	4.7	4.9	3.9
Stability.	<u>3.2</u>	<u>5.9</u>	<u>5.8</u>	<u>4.9</u>
Total	29.7	31.3	28.4	28

Interpretation of the results.

1. The Shelter-motivated donors prefer mostly organizations that offer fast service.
2. The Blood-motivated donors prefer mostly organizations that are dependable.
3. The Disaster-motivated donors prefer mostly organizations that are reliable.
4. The Politics-motivated donors prefer mostly organizations that are easy to reach.
5. The Mercy-motivated donors prefer mostly organizations that are dependable.
6. According to the simple compensatory rule, Red Cross is the most preferred recipient followed by Purple Cross.

Implications of the results.

1. Purple Cross should highlight those areas that they are ranked highly, as they seek for donations.
2. Purple Cross should endeavor to improve on the areas that they are ranked low.

Calculation steps.

1. Add the ratings for each attribute in section one.
2. Divide #1 by the total number of respondents.

Brand Rating

What is brand rating?

It is a technique that evaluates the attributes or features of identical product brands and rank them according to their importance.

Why does a marketer need to know the brand rating?

1. It shows the marketer the brands that should use similar marketing strategy.

How does a marketer determine the brand rating?

Peoples Brewing Inc. is a national brewer of alcoholic beer. Their best selling premium brand Hype, competes against Milwaukee's Premium, Coors' Super, and Bud's Best. When it was introduced in 1993, Hype was well liked by beer drinkers who made it the top sellers in a six months period. Today, Peoples Brewing evaluates the brand attributes of the beers and uses the results to develop product and promotion strategies. Occasionally, it blind tests Hype and the other beers on two most preferred attributes: taste and potency. Table

15-5 shows the average ratings for the beers on a maximum rating of ten.

Table 15-5
BLIND-TEST RESULTS OF THE BEERS

Brands	Taste	Potency
a. Hype	5	9
b. Milwaukee Premium	9	6
c. Coors' Super	5	8
d. Bud's Best	8	4

In order to know how similar the beer brands are, Peoples Brewing decided to determine the perceived distance of the brands to beer drinkers.

Perceived Distance of Brands A & D$= (\text{Taste A} - \text{Taste D})^2 +$
$(\text{Potency A} - \text{Potency D})^2$

$$= (5 - 8)^2 + (9 - 4)^2 = 34$$

Table 15-6
PERCEIVED DISTANCE OF THE BRANDS

Brands	a Hype	b Milwaukee Premium	c Coors Super	d Bud's Best
a. Hype	—	—	—	—
b. Milwaukee's Premium	25	—	—	
c. Coors' Super	1	20	—	—
d. Bud's Best	34	5	25	

284

Note: The lower the number, the higher the similarity between the brands.

Interpretation of the results.

1. Hype is very similar to Coors' Super in taste and potency.
2. Hype is higher in potency than the other three beers.
3. Bud is very similar to Milwaukee's Premium in taste

Implications of the results.

1. The marketing strategies should focus on convincing drinkers to drink Hype in place of Coors' Super for taste and in place of all the three brands for potency.
2. The promotion should point out the best in Hype that makes it different from the other two brands.

Calculation steps.

1. Use a survey to rate drinkers' perceptions of the beers in taste and potency.
2. Use the perceived distance equation to determine the number that indicated how close or different the beers are to each other in taste and potency.

CHAPTER 16

PRICING

Break-even Point

What is a break-even point?

It is a technique that is used to find out how many units a business can sell at a given price in order to cover both its variable and fixed costs. It is the point where total revenue equals total cost.

Why does a marketer need to know the break-even point?

1. It is used to analyze the cost-revenue-profit relationships.
2. It is used to determine the initial price of a product.
3. It is used to determine how many units to sell in order to earn a certain profit.
4. It is used to make a price change decision.

How does a marketer use the break-even point?

Fantastic Tops Inc. is a residential roofing company located in Glumstown, TX. The company was started in 1999 by Mr. J. T. Pots, a retired city transit operator. The business plan for the first year had a total fixed cost of $300,000, including salaries, rents, utilities, and materials. Each house roofed had a variable cost of $2,500, including material and labor, and the average charge or selling price per replacement was $4,000.

In 2000, a total of 10,000 houses had their roofs replaced in the market area that included Glumstown. Because of the numerous hurricanes predicted for the area, the number of roof replacements was estimated to increase by 4% to a total of 10,400 in 2001.

In order to make better marketing decisions for the year, Mr. Pots wanted to know four things: (1) how many residential house roofs to replace in order to break-even or cover the costs? (2) how much sales

286

in dollar to make in order to break-even? (3) what share of the residential roofing market is needed to break-even, and (4) how many residential house roofs to replace in order to earn a profit of $40,000?

Table 16-1
Fantastic Tops Inc.
Break Even Point

BEP (sales units) =
Total fixed cost
Selling price per unit -Variable cost per unit

= Total fixed cost
Contribution per unit

TFC = $300,000
VC = $2,500
SP   = $4,000

1. BEP (sales units) = TFC = $300,000 -:- ($4,000-$2,500) =200
                                   SP-VC   houses

2. BEP (sales dollars) = Sales Units x Unit Price = (200 houses x
                                                                  $4,000) = $800,000

3. BEP (profit units) = (TFC + Expected Profit)/(SP-VC)
     = ($300,000 + $40,000) -:- ($4,000 - $2,500) = 227 houses

4. BEP (market share) = Profit Units/Estimate Sales increase
                  = (227 houses -:- 10,400 houses) = 2.18%

Interpretation of the results.

1. Fantastic Tops had to replace the roofs of 200 houses in order to cover the fixed and variable costs.

2. Fantastic Tops had to make $800,000 in sales in order to cover the fixed and variable costs.
3. Fantastic Tops had to replace the roofs of 227 houses in order to cover the fixed and variable costs, and make a profit of $40,000.
4. Fantastic Tops had to have a 2.18% share of the area's residential replacement roof market in order to cover the fixed and variable costs.

Implication of the results.

1. In order to make a profit, Fantastic Tops must set up a plan with activities and actions that should assure that it changes more than 200 house roofs.

Calculation steps.

1. To find the number of houses that should be re-roofed in order to cover the costs and begin to make a profit, subtract the VC from the SP, and divide by TFC.
2. To find the amount of dollars to make in order to cover the cost and begin to make a profit, multiply the number of houses to re-roof to make a profit by the sales price.
3. To find the number of houses to re-roof in order to earn a $40,000 profit, (a) add the total fixed cost to the desired profit($40,000), (b) subtract the variable cost from the sales price, and (c) divide (a) by (b).
4. To find the size of the market share to have in order to make enough sales to cover costs and begin to make a profit, divide the BEP profit units by the total number of roofs projected for replacement in the whole market.

Cost-plus Pricing

What is a cost-plus pricing?

It is a process by which a firm adds the fixed and variable costs of providing services to a desired profit margin to determine a selling price.

Why does a marketer need the cost-plus pricing?

1. It enables a firm to determine a price that covers the cost and produces a desired profit.
2. It is used to make price change decisions.

How does a marketer use the cost-plus pricing?

Usually, holidays and special occasions are busy and profitable periods for restaurants and hotels. It was the 2001 Fourth of July, and City Bar and Grills Inc. located in Marvelous Point, CA anticipated a weekend of heavy eating and drinking. To be competitive, the restaurant offered an all-you-can-eat grilled barbecue beef and chicken special. All patrons that were of drinking age and drank alcohol, were offered all-you-can-drink and a ride home. Also, telephones were mounted on each table so that customers could make calls within the city. City Bar and Grill estimated to feed a total of 350 customers during the three-day holiday period. The total fixed cost to acquire and provide the meals was $2,500. The variable cost per customer was $5, including the anticipated services to customers that will be drunk. The restaurant wanted to make a 30 percent profit margin from each customer, however the problem was to determine what price to charge per customer. So it did the following.

Table 16-2
City Bar and Grills
Cost-plus Pricing

1. Total Cost = TFC + (Total Expected Sales Units x Unit Variable cost)

= $2,500 + (350 x $5) = $4,250

2. Total Cost per Customer = TC/Total Sales Units = $4,250 -:- 350

=$12.14

3. Expected Profit per Customer = (% Profit Margin x TC)/Total Sales Unit)

= (.30 x $4,250)/350 = $3.64

or TC per Customer x. % Profit Margin

($12.14 x .30) = $3.64

4. Unit Selling price = Total Cost per Customer + Expected Profit Per Customer

= $12.14 + $3.64 = $15.78 per customer

5. Total Sales = Selling Price x Total Sales Units = $15.78 x 350

= $5,523

6. Total Expected Profit = Total Sales - Total Cost

= $5,523 - $4,250 = $1,273

Interpretation of the results.

1. The total cost to operate the event is $4,250.
2. The cost per customer is $12.14.
3. The expected profit from each customer is $3.64.
4. City Bar and Grills should charge $15.78 per customer in order to cover its cost and make a 30 percent profit.
5. City Bar & Grills will make a sales of $5,523.
6. City Bar & Grills will earn a total profit of $1, 273.

Implications of the results.

1. Any price lower than $15.78 will not attain the desired profit margin.

2. City Bar and Grills should emphasis the worth and benefits of the full package in the pre-sale advertisement.

Calculation steps.

1. Find the total cost by multiplying the variable cost of $5 by the expected number of customers, and adding it to the fixed cost of $2,500.
2. Find the total cost to serve each customer by dividing the total cost ($4,250) by the total number of customers (350).
3. Find the expected profit (at 30% profit margin) from each customer by multiplying the total cost to serve a customer by the percentage profit margin ($12.14 x .30).
4. Find the selling price by adding the cost to serve a customer ($12.14) to the expected profit per service ($3.64).

Markup at Retail or Cost (%)

What is a markup at retail or cost?

It is a pricing method that sets the price of a product or service by basing it on the desired selling price of a merchandise or at its cost.

Why does a marketer need to know the markup at retail or cost?

1. It is needed to determine the amount to increase the selling price of a product or service by expressing the increase as a percentage of sales or cost.

How does a marketer find the markup at retail or cost?

Cocks Chiropractic Center Inc. is a large treatment center in Cockscomb, NJ. Started in 1971, the center specialized in back, neck, and joint cares. Like most chiropractic centers, it attended to all kinds of neck pains, headaches, disc injuries, pinched nerves, arthritis, numbness, muscle spasms, tight muscles, and low back pains. In order to be competitive in pricing, Dr. Joan Cocks, the owner, tried not to

charge excessive prices by staying within the market price range. In 1980, the center resorted to using a markup percentage that was based on the cost of the service. For example, in that year the Center spent $80 an hour to provide treatment to a patient that had disc injuries.

Photo 32: Salama Chiropractic

Regardless of the type of treatment, the Center sought to have a 42% markup on retail selling price and needed to know the following:

1. The selling price of the service to the disc injury patients that costs $80 to provide at a desired mark up of 42%.
2. The maximum price to charge for a low back pain service that retails at $95 an hour with a 42% markup.

Table 16-3
Cocks Chiropractic Center
Markup at Retail or Cost (%)

1. Retail selling price for a disc injury patient:

    a. 0.42(Retail selling price) = Retail selling price-$80
    b. 0.58(Retail selling price) = $80
    Retail selling price = $80 / 0.58 = $137.93

2. % markup on retail = <u>Retail selling price - Merchandise cost</u>
                                    Retail selling price

$$= \frac{\$137.93 - \$80}{\$137.93} = 0.42$$

or $\quad \frac{\text{\% Markup on Cost}}{100\% + \text{\% Markup on Cost}}$

$$= \frac{72.4}{172.4} = 0.42$$

or $\quad (P-C)/P = M/P$

$$= \frac{137.93 - \$80}{137.93} = \frac{57.95}{137.93} = 0.42$$

3. % markup at cost = $\frac{\text{Retail Selling Price-Merchandise Cost}}{\text{Merchandise Cost}}$

$$= \frac{\$137.93 - \$80}{\$80} \quad 72.4\%$$

or $\quad \frac{\text{\% Markup on Retail selling price}}{100\% - \text{\% Markup on Retail selling price}}$

$$= \frac{42}{100-42} = 72.4\%$$

or $(P-C)/C = M/C$

$$\frac{\$133.93 - \$80}{\$80} = \frac{57.93}{\$80} \quad 72.4\%$$

4. What would be the merchandise cost for a back pain service that retailed at $95 per hour with a 42% markup?

% Markup on Retail selling price = $\frac{\$95 - \text{Merchandise cost}}{\$95}$

$$\$95 - \text{Merchandise cost} = (0.42)(\$95)$$
$$\$95 - \text{Merchandise cost} = \$39.90$$
$$\text{Merchandise cost} = \$95 - \$39.9$$
$$\textbf{Merchandise cost} = \$51.10$$

Interpretation of the results.

1. The Center should charge the disc injury patient a price of $137.93 in order to achieve a 42% markup at retail.
2. The Center should use a markup of 72.4% at the cost of the service in order to charge the same price as on retail.
3. The Center will incur a maximum cost of $51.10 in order to provide a back pain service at $95, which includes a 42% markup.

Implication of the results.

1. The Center should increase or decrease the markup percentage as it desires by either using the selling price or the cost approach.

Calculation steps.

1. To determine the retail selling price, multiply the cost by desired markup-100 percent.
2. To determine the percentage markup at retail, subtract the merchandise cost from the retail selling price, and divide by the retail selling price.
3. To determine the percentage markup at cost, subtract the merchandise cost from the retail selling price, and divide by the merchandise cost.
4. To determine the maximum cost to incur on a service, multiply the proposed retail price of the service by the desired markup percentage, and subtract the result from the proposed retail price.

Initial Mark-up Percentage

What is an initial mark-up percentage?

It is the markup placed on a merchandise after the store receives it and subtracts the costs and any discounts on the original retail value of the merchandise.

Why does a marketer need to know the initial mark-up percentage?

1. It is used to determine how much to markup a new product.

How does a marketer find the initial mark-up percentage?

Bush Discount Funeral Homes Inc. is one of the four funeral service homes in One Love, CA. It offers an array of services including a 24-hour service, 1,000 chapel seating capacity, ample parking, lines of caskets, cremations, burial, pre- and post burial counseling, family funeral flowers, and others. Bush Discount Funeral Homes uses a full-funeral package pricing as its competitive advantage. In 2000, a package cost Mr. Bush $1,859, and it sold for $2,999 (61% mark-up), which was competitive to the partial packages offered by the other funeral homes. The cost increased to $2,000 in 2001.

Bush Discount Funeral Homes forecasted a net sales of $2.0 million in 2001. This was projected to be reduced by: $40,000 for planned reductions or markdowns, $20,000 cash discount to employees, $40,000 for customer discounts, and $1,000 for stock shortages.

The estimated operating expense was $650,000. Mr. Bush, the proprietor, desired a profit of $100,000 and needed to know how much to markup a full-funeral package considering the new costs and reductions. He also needed to know the approximate number of packages to sell and the new selling price to attain the forecast. He did the following.

Table 16-4
Bush Discount Funeral Homes Inc.
Initial Markup Percentage

Initial Markup Percentage = (operating expenses + net profit
+markdowns + stock shortages + customer discounts –
employees cash discounts)/(net sales + markdowns + stock
shortages + employees cash discounts) x 100
or
Initial Markup Percentage = ($650,000 + $100,000 + $40,000
+$1,000 +$40,000 -$20,000)/($2,00,000 + $40,000 + $1,000 +
$20,000) = **39.34%**

Retail Selling Price = $\frac{Merchandise\ cost}{1\text{-}Markup}$ = $\frac{\$2,000}{1\text{-}0.3934}$ = **$3,297.06**

Number of full-funeral packages to be sold in 2001
= $\frac{\$2,000,000}{\$3,297.06}$ = **607 packages**.

Interpretation of the results.

1. Bush Discount Funeral Homes had to markup the price of a
   full-funeral package by 39.34% from $2,999 to $3,297.06 in
   2001 in order to achieve the profit goal.
2. Bush Discount Funeral Homes should sell 607 full-funeral
   package services in 2001 in order to achieve a sales of
   $2,000,000.

Implication of the result.

1. The initial or beginning markup percentage of the retail price
   of a product or service depends on the amount of retail
   expense to incur, the desired profits, any sales reductions, and
   the net sales desired.

Calculation steps.

1. To find the Initial Markup Percentage:
   a. add the operating expenses to net profit, markdowns, stock shortages, and customer discounts. Subtract any cash discounts.
   b. add net sales, markdowns, stock shortages, and employee cash discounts.
   c. divide #1 by #2.
2. To find the Retail Selling Price, divide the cost of the merchandise by one minus the initial percentage markup.
3. To find the number of full-funeral packages to be sold in 2001, divide the forecasted sales by the selling price.

Maintained Markup Percentage

What is a maintained or achieved markup percentage?

It is a markup on the actual or average selling price of a merchandise less the cost of the merchandise.

Why does a marketer need a maintained markup percentage?

1. It is used to reduce the price of a product or service from the original mark-up price in order to increase sales.

How does a marketer find the maintained markup percentage?

Smart & Associates Professional Center Inc. is a business center located in Youngstown, SC. Built in 1996 due to the city's

Photo 33: South Elm Center

downtown revitalization plan, the center was located on a major street that ran from the east to the west across the city. In order to entice developers, the city sold the land at a little or no price. In this case, Smart & Associates accepted to pay for laying the utility pipes and cables as the cost of the space. It used a $3m loan from the bank to develop the center.

In order to recover enough money for loan payments in the first five years, Smart and Associates assessed the space at $7 per square foot, and offered it to tenants at $16. This is a markup of 128.6% at cost. At the end of the first year, the Center noticed that only fifteen out of the forty-five or 33.3% of the spaces had been rented. In order to rent out the remaining spaces faster, Smith & Associates decided to reduce the price to $12 per square foot. All the remaining spaces were sold within six months at that price. Smith & Associates was told that that was a maintained markup approach, and they needed to know the percentage by doing the following.

Table 16-5
Smart & Associates Professional Center
Maintained Markup Percentage

1. *Maintained markup = (Actual retail price-Cost)/Actual retail price at retail*

$$= \frac{\$12 - \$7}{\$12} = 41.66\%$$

2. Original markup = $\frac{\$16 - \$7}{\$16}$ = 56.7%
   at retail

3. *Maintained markup % = (Actual retail price - Cost)/Cost*
   At cost $= \frac{\$12 - \$7}{\$7} = 71.4\%$

4. Original markup = $\frac{\$16 - \$7}{\$7}$ = 128.6%
   at cost

Interpretation of the results.

1. The maintained markup percentage on a space in the Smith & Associates Professional Center at retail was 41.66%, and the maintained markup percentage at cost was 71.4%. In other words, this is how much the $5 reduction of the original selling price was to the selling price and the cost.
2. Spaces in the Smith & Associates Professional Center were sold out at the price of $12 per square foot.

Implication of the results.

1. The percentage markup at cost is higher in figure than the percentage markup at selling price.

Calculation steps.

1. Subtract the actual price the merchandise sold for from the cost, and divide it by the actual retail price the merchandise sold for.

Additional Retail Markdown %

What is an additional retail markdown %?

The total dollar additional markdown as a percentage of net sales and profit.

Why do marketers have to know the additional Markdown %?

1. The techniques assist the retailer to make the right price adjustments.
2. They help the retailers to determine the correct unit sales required to achieve the sales goals.

How do marketers find the additional Markdown %?

Global Sports Inc. in Boulder, CO is a large sporting goods discount store that sells all lines of goods for all sporting occasions. Because of the heavy and prolonged snowfall forecasted in the winter 2001, Global Sports anticipated a high demand for snow related outdoor fun gadgets. It stocked up on snow clothing and equipment, snowboards, sleds and others.

Photo 34: acFITNESS

A large size snowboard costs $50. Global Sports marks it up by 54.5 percent at retail, for an original price of $110. Three hundred large snowboards were sold monthly for a total gross profit of $18,000 ($60 x 300). As the spring approached, Global Sports still had a lot of snowboards left. The store decided to reduce the price of the snowboards. However, it still loved to get the same amount of monthly gross profit that it made from snowboards during the winter, and it wanted to know how many snowboards to sell if the price was reduced to $89.99 in order to make the same gross profit. So it did the following.

Table 16-6
Global Sports Inc.
Additional Retail Markdown(%)

Unit Sales Required = $\dfrac{\text{Original Markup \% x Unit Sale}}{\text{Original Markup \% - Reduced selling price}}$

Unit sales required = $\dfrac{54.5}{54.5 - 20.01}$ x 300 = 1.5 x 300 = 450 snowboards
(at $89.99)

Part 11

Suppose that at the end of the season Global Sports decided to reduce the price further to $79.99 to sell the rest of the snowboards. It wants to know the markdown this was off the markdown price of $89.99.

Markdown off-original sales price (%)
= $\dfrac{\text{Original sales price-Reduced selling price}}{\text{Reduced selling price}} \times 100$

$= \dfrac{\$89.99\text{-}\$79.99}{\$79.99} \times 100 = \dfrac{\$10}{\$79.99} \times 100 = 12.5\%$

Interpretation of the results.

1. At the reduced price of $89.99, Global Sports sold 450 snowboards in order to make a sales of $40,495.5.
2. In order to make a $40,495.5 sales, Global Sports spent $22,500 on the snowboard and the $17,995.5 was the profit.
3. A price reduction from $89.99 to $79.99 is a 12.5% markdown.

Implication of the results.

1. Global Sports could check how increases or decreases in the prices of the items may affect total sales and profit prior to adopting them.

Calculation Steps.

1. Subtract the original markup percentage from the amount of price reduction.
2. Divide the original markup percentage by the result in #1.
3. Multiply the unit sale by the result in #2.

4. To find the percentage of markdown from the original sales price, subtract the reduced selling price from the original sales price, divide it by the reduced selling price, and multiply by 100.

Off-Retail Markdown Percentage

What is an off-retail markdown percentage?

It is a technique to determine how much the total dollar taken off or discounted from the retail price of an item or a merchandise category worths in percentage to the original price.

Why does a marketer need to know the off-retail markdown percentage?

1. It enables the marketer to know and compare the percentage of items that are marked down to those sold at the original price.

How does a marketer find the off-retail markdown percentage?

Jim's Hardware Inc. in Raleigh, NC sold an array of home improvement items, and appliances. In the anticipation of a good summer in 1987, and the usual craze for lawn mowers and other tools for outdoor endeavors, Mr. Jim Boyd acquired a great deal of inventory for resale, including two hundred medium sized push lawn mowers. At the beginning of summer, the store priced the lawn mowers at $289 each. Half of the lawn mowers were sold by the end of September. In order to sell more lawn mowers before the end of the season and to reduce the cost of inventory storage, Jim's Hardware reduced the price to $239.99 in October.

By the middle of November when the lawn mowers were put away, only twenty were left. The stores needed to know:
1. The off-retail markdown percentage,
2. The percentage of mowers sold at the markdown price, and

3. The total dollar made from the sales of the markdown mowers. It did the following.

Table 16-7
Jim's Hardware Inc.
Off-retail Markdown Percentage

1. Off-retail markdown percentage

= $\dfrac{\text{Original selling price-New selling price}}{\text{Original selling price}}$

= $\dfrac{289-239.99}{289}$ = .1695 or 16.95%

2. Percentage of lawn mowers sold at marked down price = 80/200
= 0.4 or 40%

3 .Total dollar markdown $289-$239.99 x 80 =$3,920.80

Interpretation of the results.

1. 16.95% was the reduction in the original price of the lawn mowers.
2. 40% of the lawn mowers were sold at the reduced price.
3. 80 lawn mowers were sold at a markdown for $3,920.80

Implication of the results.

1. The off-retail markdown was valuable.

Calculation steps.

1. To determine the off-retail markdown percentage, subtract the reduced price of $239 from the original price of $289, and divide the result by $239, and multiply by 100.

2. To determine the percentage of lawn mowers sold at the markdown price, divide the number sold at the discount price (80) by the total number of lawn mowers, and multiply by 100.

3. To determine the total dollar markdown, subtract the off-retail markdown from the original price and multiply it by the number of lawn mowers sold at the off-retail markdown price.

Sales Variance Analysis

What is a sales variance analysis?

It is a technique used to measure how much variation in sales result from a price change or price forecast error.

Why does a marketer need to know the sales variance analysis?

1. The technique enables the marketer to identify how much of the variation in the sales volume was due to price cut, and how much was because of the difference between the forecasted and actual sales.
2. To decide when to use low price to increase market share.
3. To understand how to use price to keep out potential competitors.
4. To know when to use selective price increases to discourage less profitable customers.

How does a marketer determine the sales variance analysis?

Audio Technology Systems Inc. is a stereo and Hi-Fi custom installer located in Pobline, NY. The firm was started in 1971 by Miss Chic White, an engineering student who fell in love with sound engineering as a hobby, and ended up discovering various ways to create marvelous customized home theatres, sound systems, surround sounds, and intercoms for residential and commercial users. By 2001, Audio Technology Systems was the largest dealer in the city.

Although the large market share benefited the company, the changing sales pattern posed some problems.

For one, Audio Technology Systems had difficulties knowing how to interpret the causes of the periodic sales decline which often left the company overstocked with parts and supplies. For example, in 2000, the company priced a custom installation of a home theatre at $3,500, and forecasted a sales volume of 970 units or $3,395,000. However, as competitors announced several kinds of price reductions, Audio Technology Systems decided to reduce its price for the home theatres to $3,200. By the year's end, the company had sold 854 units or $2,732,800. Ms. White wanted to know how much of the variation in the sales volume was due to the price cut and how much was because of the difference between the forecasted and actual sales. Therefore the company did the following.

Table 16-8
Audio Tech Systems Inc.
Sales Variance Analysis

Variance due to the price reduction
=($3,500-$3,200)(854)

= $256,200	38.7%

Variance due to the decline in sales volume
= ($3,500)(970-854)

= $406,000	61.3%
$662,200	100%

Interpretation of the results.

1. The inability to attain the forecasted sales volume accounted for 61.3% of the sales variance, while 38.7% of the variance was due to the reduction in the price.

Implications of the results.

1. In order to study the effects of wrong price, Audio Technology Systems should simulate its sales forecast at various price levels prior to adoption.
2. Audio Technology Systems should watch out for the failure of the market to grow as much and as fast as anticipated.
3. Audio Technology Systems should be mindful when pricing, of a sudden loss of market share to competitors.
4. Audio Technology System should also simulate the sales forecast at high prices.

Calculation steps.

1. To find the variance due to the price reduction, subtract the actual price from the forecasted price, and multiply by the actual number of units sold.
2. To find the variance due to the decline in sales volume, subtract the forecasted units from the actual number of units sold and multiply by the forecasted price.
3. Add the products of #1 and #2.
4. To find the percentage of the sales variance caused by the change in the price, divide the product of #1 by #3, and multiply by 100.
5. To find the percentage of the inability to achieve the sales volume that was due to the change in the units sold, divide the product of #2 by #3, and multiply by 100.

Price Elasticity

What is price elasticity?

It is a measure of how sensitive buyers are to price changes, in terms of the quantities they purchase.

Why does a marketer need to know of the price elasticity?

1. It helps the marketer to measure the impact of price change on revenue.
2. It shows the marketer how customers react to price increase or decrease.
3. It helps the marketer to monitor and control the quantity demanded by the customers.

How does a marketer determine the price elasticity?

Jane's All Seasons Inc. is a medium sized retail store located in Uptown Dallas, TX. Miss Jane Lawrence thought of how nice it would be to have stores that one can go and buy items to fit all seasonal events in the year. With this idea, she opened a store in 1981 and called it Jane's All Seasons. The All Seasons kept a weekly and monthly calendar of cultural, national, and religious events in America. In the period between mid-October to the day after the Christmas for example, All Seasons is filled with toys, gift items, wrappers, trees, lights, and other Christmas ornaments. These were in abundance at low prices. After the Christmas, the store was cleared and filled with firecrackers, rockets, hats, flags and other flashy and noisy merchandise for the New Year's celebration. This was repeated in June until after the fourth of July. Other events such as Valentine, Easter, Thanksgiving, and Memorial Day were also celebrated.

Miss Lawrence made sure that the inventory switching went smoothly at the end of every period. The spontaneous heavy traffic for season products assured high profitability. Whenever she wanted to know the price to charge for some few products such as the American flags that sold year round, she found the price elasticity. Table 16-9 shows how elastic or sensitive the units customers buy are to price changes on the flags.

Table 16-9
All Seasons Inc.
Price Elasticity

Price	x	Demand (000)	= Total Revenue (000)		Price Elasticity of Demand
$20		120	$2,400		
					1.68a
$17.50		150	$2,625		
					1.54b
$15		190	$2,850		
					.811c
$12.50		240	$3,000 I		
			I	Max Total	1.00d
$10		300	$3,000 I	Revenue	
					0.538e
$7.50		350	$2,625		
					0.27f
$5		390	$1,950g		

$$Price\ elasticity = \frac{\dfrac{Quantity\ 1 - Quantity\ 2}{Quantity\ 1 + Quantity\ 2}}{\dfrac{Price - Price\ 2}{Price\ 1 + Price2}}$$

a. *Price elasticity* $= \dfrac{\dfrac{120 - 150}{120 + 150} = \dfrac{30}{270} = \dfrac{0.111}{\_\_\_\_}}{\dfrac{\$20 - \$17.50}{\$20 + \$17.50} = \dfrac{\$2.50}{\$37.50} \quad 0.066} = 1.68$

b. *Price elasticity* $= \dfrac{\dfrac{150 - 190}{150 + 190} = \dfrac{40}{340} = \dfrac{0.117}{\_\_\_\_}}{\dfrac{\$17.50 - \$15}{\$17.50 + \$15} = \dfrac{\$2.50}{\$32.5} \quad 0.076} = 1.54$

c. *Price elasticity* $=$ $\dfrac{190 - 240}{190 + 240}$ $=\dfrac{50}{430}$ $= 0.116$

$\dfrac{\$15 - \$12.50}{\$15 + \$12.50}$ $=\dfrac{\$2.50}{\$27.50}$ $\dfrac{}{.09}$ $= 1.28$

d. *Price elasticity* $=$ $\dfrac{240 - 300}{240 + 300}$ $=\dfrac{60}{540}$ $= 0.111$

$\dfrac{\$12.50 - \$10}{\$12.50 + \$10}$ $=\dfrac{\$2.50}{\$22.50}$ $\dfrac{}{0.111}$ $= 1.00$

e. *Price elasticity* $=$ $\dfrac{300 - 350}{300 + 350}$ $=\dfrac{50}{650}$ $=0.077$

$\dfrac{\$10 - \$7.50}{\$10 + \$7.50}$ $=\dfrac{\$2.50}{\$17.50}$ $\dfrac{}{0.143}$ $= 0.538$

f. *Price elasticity* $=$ $\dfrac{350 - 390}{350 + 390}$ $=\dfrac{40}{740}$ $=0.054$

$\dfrac{\$7.50 - \$5}{\$7.50 + \$5}$ $=\dfrac{\$2.50}{\$12.50}$ $\dfrac{}{0.2}$ $= 0.27$

Interpretation of the results.

1. All Seasons makes a maximum revenue when the elasticity is equal to 1. At this point, which is between $10.00 and $12.50, the maximum item is between 300 and 240 units, and the maximum sale is $3,000.
2. The price caused the most change in demand when the price was reduced from $20 to $17.50.
3. According to this example, whenever the selling price was reduced by $2.50, the quantity demanded rose significantly, and the elasticity increased.

Implication of the results.

1. In order to make the highest revenue, All Seasons Inc. should sell more flags that are priced between $12.50 and $10.

Calculation steps.

1. Subtract the first quantity from the second quantity.
2. Add the first quantity to the second quantity.
3. Divide the product of #1 by the product of #2.
4. Subtract the first price from the second price.
5. Add the first price to the second price.
6. Divide the product of #4 by the product of #5.
7. Divide the product of #3 by the product of #6.

Retail-Based Pricing

What is a retail-based price?

It is a technique that is utilized to predict the expected demand for a store's merchandise at various price levels.

Why does a marketer need to know the retail-based price?

1. It is useful for forecasting the demand of the items for sale.

How does a marketer determine the retail-based price?

Adamma Quality-Used Computers Inc. retails used computers and accessories in Greensboro, NC. Since it began in 1999, the demand for used computer has remained high. The Zomoto models of computers were very popular and high in demand. The store sold the Zomoto models as fast as they could stock them. Unfortunately, the other brands were not selling as fast. In 2001, the store became concerned that it would not attain the projected revenue for the years, and may have to curtail operations in the future due to the diminishing capital.

The store owner Miss Adamma Chidomere considered making up for the revenue downturn by increasing the price of the popular Zomoto models from $800 to $900. A total unit of 84,000 of the

Zomoto computer models were sold by the distributors in the state in 2000. An anticipated downturn in the industry in 2001 and the following year left Adamma Quality-Used Computers unsure of its expected total sales for the year. In order to come up with a more reliable sales prediction, the store forecasted the sales for the Zomoto on three levels, from the best to the worst scenarios. It wanted to know the largest expected volume the store could sell at the new price level of $900. It also needed to know how elastic (changing) or (unchanging) the demand for the Zomoto computers would be when the price changed. Adamma Quality-Used Computer did the following.

Table 16-10
Adamma Quality-Used Computers
Retail-Based Pricing

Three Levels of forecast:

Optimistic estimate: 84,000 units
Pessimistic estimate: 60,000 units
Most likely estimate: 79,000 units

Largest Expected Vol. = $\dfrac{\text{Pessimistic Estimate} + 4(\text{Most likely}) + \text{Optimistic Estimate}}{6}$

$$= \frac{60,000 + 4(79,000) + (84,000)}{6}$$

$$= \frac{460,000}{6} = 76,667 \text{ units}$$

Price elasticity = $\dfrac{\dfrac{\text{Quantity 1} - \text{Quantity 2}}{\text{Quantity 1} + \text{Quantity 2}}}{\dfrac{\text{Price 1} - \text{Price 2}}{\text{Price 1} + \text{Price2}}}$

Elasticity (e) = $\dfrac{\dfrac{84,000-76,667}{84,000+76,667}}{\dfrac{800-900}{800+900}}$ = $\dfrac{\dfrac{7,333}{160,000}}{\dfrac{100}{1,700}}$ = $\dfrac{0.046}{0.059}$ = .78

Interpretation of the results.

1. A total of 76,667 units of Zomoto used computers were forecasted for sales in the state of North Carolina in 2001.
2. The demand for the Zomoto used computers was not very elastic. It was a .85, which is less than elastic.

Implications of the results.

1. Adamma Quality-Used Computer should be aware that a sizable change (9.5%) would occur in the quantity demanded.
2. Adamma Quality-Used Computers should note that the state forecast predicted a downturn in demand in 2001.
3. Enough promotion should be used to avoid a loss in the store's market share.

Calculation steps.

1. To determine the largest expected volume to sell, multiply the most likely estimate by 4, add it to the pessimistic estimate and the optimistic estimate, and divide by 6.
2. To determine the price elasticity of demand;
   a. Subtract the first quantity from the second quantity.
   b. Add the first quantity to the second quantity.
   c. Divide the product of (a) by the product of (b).
   d. Subtract the first price from the second price.
   e. Add the first price to the second price.
   f. Divide the product of (d) by the product of (e).
   g. Divide the product of (c) by the product of (f).

Target-Return Price

What is a target-return price?

It is a form of cost-oriented technique to set the price of a merchandise so as to yield a target rate of return on investment.

Why does a marketer need to know a target-return price?

1. It helps a business to find out the price to charge in order to recover cost.
2. Companies need this technique when they want to determine the profitable price to charge for a new or existing product or service.

How does a marketer find the target-return price?

Affordable Homes Inc. builds and sells single family homes in the Triad region of North Carolina. Started in 1972 by Mr. Alford Gables, the purpose of the company was to serve the people that wanted

small-sized houses with one or two bedrooms. Affordable Homes invested $2.5m to build one hundred homes at $25,000 per home in the southeast part of the region. The company wanted to know the price to sell each house

Freedom Homes

Photo   35:

in order to earn a *30 percent return on investment or $750,000. Therefore, it used a target-return pricing formula as follows.*

Table 16-10
Affordable Homes Inc.
Target-Return Pricing

Target-return per home =unit cost + Desired dollar return
$$\text{Unit sales}$$

$$=\frac{\$25,000 + (.30 \times \$2,500,000)}{100} = \$7,750$$

Target-return price per home = $25,000 + $7,750 = $32,750 per home

Interpretation of the results.

1. Affordable Homes Inc. should sell each home for $32,750 in order to achieve the 30% ROI or a $750,000 total profit.

Implication of the results.

1. Affordable homes could only attain the desired returns if it maintains the 30% return on investment, and sold all the homes.

Calculation steps.

1. To determine the target-return per home, multiply the invested capital by the desired percentage of return, add it to the unit cost, and divide by the unit sales.
2. To determine the target-return price per home, add the target-return per home to the cost of each home.

CHAPTER 17

RETAILING

Index of Retail Saturation (IRS)

What is an index of retail saturation?

It is a technique that measures how many similar stores to locate in an area to satisfy the needs of the population for such products or services.

Why does a marketer need to know the index of retail saturation?

1. To determine if existing store facilities in different market areas are utilized efficiently to meet customer needs.
2. To determine if the store should be closed, or become more aggressive.
3. To know the ratio of sales to other factors in the market area.
4. To determine if an area is under-saturated, saturated, or over-saturated with similar stores.

How does a marketer determine the index of retail saturation?

In 2001, Racquetball of Minnesota Inc. contemplated on adding more footage to either the huge racquetball centers in the city of Edmonds or the suburb of Redsville. According to the state's consumer guide, Edmonds had a total of 43,000 households that spent $89,000 at the center in 2000. The city of Redsville had a total of 51,000 households that spent $69,000 at the center in 2000. Altogether, Edmonds had 2,000 square feet of racquetball centers, and Redsville had 2,410 square feet of racquetball centers. The size of the proposed addition to a center was 1,500 square feet. Racquetball of Minnesota needed to know which city is the least saturated or has the least customers already commited to existing centers. As shown below, it found out the level of saturation of racquetball in the two

315

cities based on the number of households in the cities; the annual retail expenditures on racquetball in the cities; and the square feet of facilities in the centers.

Table 17-1
Racquetball of Minnesota
Index of Retail Saturation

	Edmonds	Redsville
Background Data		
Total racquetball sales	$89,000	$69,000
Total number of households	43,000	51,000
Total square footage on the centers	2,000	2,410

Retail Saturation Index (IRS) $= \dfrac{H \times RE}{FR}$

H = number of households in the area.

RE = annual retail expenditures for a particular line of trade per household in the area.

RF = square feet of retail facilities of a particular line of trade in the area (including square footage of proposed store).

1. Average sales per square foot:
   Edmonds: $89,000 -:- 3,500sqft.* = $25.43
   Redsville: $69,000 -:- 3,900sqft.* = $17.64

Note: 3,500sqft. = 2,000sqft. + 1,500sqft
3,910sqft. = 2,410sqft. + 1,500sqft.

2. IRS (Edmonds)
a. Original

$$\frac{43,000 \times 2.07}{2,000} = \frac{\$89,010}{2,000} = \$44.5$$

b. New

$$\frac{43,000 \times 2.07}{3,500} = \frac{\$89,010}{3,500} = \$25$$

3. IRS (Redsville)
a. Original
$$\frac{51{,}000 \times 1.35}{2{,}410} = \frac{68{,}850}{2{,}410} = \$28.56$$

b. New
$$\frac{51{,}000 \times 1.35}{3{,}910} = \frac{68{,}850}{3{,}910} = \$17.60$$

Interpretation of the results.

1. The average sales per square foot of a racquetball space in Edmonds is $25, and $17 in Redsville.
2. When racquetball playing is forecasted based on the total annual sales, the number of households, and the square footage of the centers, both in Edmonds and Redsville have gaps in demand, and both are unsaturated.
3. Edmond has a higher average sales and more gap in demand than Redsville.

Implication of the results.

1. Racquetball of Minnesota should expand in the city of Edmonds because it has a higher average sales and market potential.

Calculation steps.

1. To determine the average sales per square foot, divide the total sales in the store by the sum of the existing square footage and the proposed square footage.

2. To determine the retail saturation index, multiply the number of households by the annual sales, and divide the total by the sum of the existing square footage and the proposed square footage.

Retail Gravitation Model

What is a retail gravitation?

It is a gravity model that is used to measure the extent to which buyers are drawn to retail stores that are closer or more attractive than competitors.

Why does a marketer need to know the retail gravitation?

1. To find out the geographic breaking point between two cities or communities at which consumers will be indifferent or would not mind shopping at either city.
2. To consider the most appropriate areas to expand the promotional activities.
3. It is used to establish a trading area.

How does a marketer find the retail gravitation?

Dick's Used Autos Inc. is the largest used cars, vans, and trucks seller in Greensboro, North Carolina. Its size and numerous assortments give buyers the unique advantages of discounted prices and selection, and attract buyers from afar. The city of Winston-Salem is located 35 miles away from Greensboro on a major highway. The city of High Point is located 10 miles from Greensboro, and the city of Burlington is located 18 miles away from Greensboro. Greensboro has a population of 250,000 people, and Winston-Salem has a population of 140,000 people. Twenty miles from Greensboro on the highway is Kernersville, a smaller city that has no large used auto sellers, and therefore used car buyers often went to either Greensboro or Winston-Salem for better deals.

In 2001, Mr. Dick was contemplating on spending some of the advertisement budget in newspapers and rebates to potential used car buyers in Kernersville. He needed to know how wise such an investment was and the potential buyers to come. Two things had to happen. First, he had to find out the point or distance from which the customers would not mind to come to Greensboro to buy cars from his dealership. Second, he had to find out the point at which it does not make any difference to the customers whether they go to the dealership in Greensboro or Winston-Salem. So he used the model below to calculate that.

$$D_{ab} = \frac{d}{1 + \sqrt{P_b/P_a}}$$

D_{ab} = limit of city(community) A's trading area, measured in miles along the road to city (community) B.

d = distance in miles along the major highway between cities (community) A and B.

P_a = population of city A (larger in population).

P_b = population of city B.

Table 17-2
Dick's Used Autos Inc.
Retail Gravitation
Data From Surrounding Cities

Distance		Population
From Greensboro to:		
a. Greensboro	0miles	250,000
b. Winston-Salem	35miles	140,000
c. High Point	10miles	35,000
d. Reidsville	18miles	18,000
e. Kernersville	12miles	15,000

1. Greensboro-Winston-Salem

$$D_{ab} = \frac{35}{1 + \sqrt{140,000/250,000}} . \quad = 35/1.75 = 20 \text{ miles}$$

2. Greensboro-High Point

$$D_{ac} = \frac{10}{1+ \sqrt{35,000/250,000}} \quad = 10/1.37 = 7 \text{ miles}$$

3. Greensboro-Reidsville

$$D_{ad} = \frac{18}{1+ \sqrt{18,000/250,000}} \quad = 18/1.26 = 14 \text{ miles}$$

4. Greensboro-Kernersville

$$D_{ae} = \frac{12}{1+ \sqrt{15,000/250,000}} \quad = 35/1.24 = 9.6 \text{ miles}$$

a.

Greensboro	20miles		Winston-Salem
250,000		0	140,000
population	15miles		population

b.

Greensboro	7miles		High Point
250,000		0	35,000
population	3miles		population

c.

Greensboro	14miles		Reidsville
250,000		0	18,000
population	4miles		population

d.

Greensboro	9.6miles		Winston-Salem
250,000		0	250,000
population	2.4miles		population

Interpretation of the results.

1. Greensboro is able to attract people from 20 miles in the direction of Winston-Salem, and Winston-Salem is able to attract people from 15 miles in the direction of Greensboro.

2. Greensboro is able to attract people from 7 miles in the direction of High Point, and High Point is able to attract people from 3 miles in the direction of Greensboro.
3. Greensboro is able to attract people from 14 miles in the direction of Reidsville, and Reidsville is able to attract people from 4 miles in the direction of Greensboro.
4. Greensboro is able to attract people from 9.6 mile in the direction of Kernersville, and Kernersville is able to attract people from 2.4 miles in the direction of Greensboro.
5. "0" is the PI or point of indifference. This is the point where it does not matter to customers if they looked for cars in Greensboro or in the other city.

Implications of results.

1. Stores in a city with a larger population draw customers from a further distance than stores in a neighboring city with a smaller population.
2. Stores in the various cities should extend their advertisement to buyers within their market areas.

Calculation steps.

1. To find the distance buyers will come from city B to shop in city A, divide the population in city B by the population in city A, find the square of the answer, and add one to it. Use this number to divide the distance between cities A and B.
2. To find the distance buyers will come from city C to shop in city A, divide the population in city C by the population in city A, find the square of the answer, and add one to it. Use this number to divide the distance between cities A and C.
3. To find the distance buyers will come from city D to shop in city A, divide the population in city D by the population in city A, find the square of the answer, and add one to it. Use this number to divide the distance between cities A and D.

4. To find the distance buyers will come from city E to shop in city A, divide the population in city E by the population in city A, find the square of the answer, and add one to it. Use this number to divide the distance between cities A and E.

Retail Space Productivity Model

What is a retail space productivity model?

It is the model that is used to determine the amount of sales dollars contributed by each square foot in a retail store.

Why does a marketer need to know the retail space productivity model?

1. To determine how to use retail store space.

How does a marketer develop a retail space productivity model?

Davies Eatery Inc. is a convenience food store located in an old warehouse across the street from a large regional college in Johnny, Louisiana. Because of the large size of the building, Davies Eatery had difficulty utilizing the whole space. It considered dividing the space into two by using a divider. However, the building managers refused. The restaurant did not want to move from the building

because of its closeness to the campus. This offered a high traffic and an audience that is constantly hungry. Mrs. Rosy Davies, the owner, decided to use 1,230 square feet of the building for the eatery, including a kitchen, dining, storage space, and other related

Photo 36: Forsyth Seafood

cooking activities. The remaining 1,765 square feet was used to sell groceries.

In 2000, Davies Eatery had a net sale of $550,000 from cooked food and $350,000 from grocery. The cost of the cooked food was $200,000, and the cost of the groceries was $150,000. At the end of the year, Mrs. Davies wanted to know how productive the two spaces were, and she used the method below.

Table 17-3
Davies Eatery Inc.
Retail Space Productivity Model

Sales to Space

= *Sales Per Square   Gross Margin   Gross Margin Per*
   Foot of   x   *Percent*   =   *Square Feet of*
   Selling Space   *Selling Space*

Net Sales
  /
Average Inventory
  (At Cost)   = Net Sales   Gross Margin   =   Gross Margin
    x   /   x   /   /
Average Inventory   Square Feet of   Net Sales   Square Feet of
  (At Cost)   Selling Space   Selling Space
   /
Square Feet of Selling Space

For The Eatery Space

$\dfrac{\$550,000}{\$200,000}$ x $\dfrac{\$200,000}{1,230}$ = $\dfrac{\$550,000}{1,230}$ x $\dfrac{\$350,000}{\$550,000}$ = $\dfrac{\$350,000}{1,230}$

= $2.75 x $162.60   = $447.15 x $.64   = $284.5

Rowland Chidomere

For The Grocery Space

$$\frac{\$350,000}{\$150,000} \times \frac{\$150,000}{1,765} = \frac{\$350,000}{1,765} \times \frac{\$200,000}{\$350,000} = \frac{\$200,000}{1,765}$$

$$= \$2.33 \quad \times \quad \$84.98 = \$198.30 \quad \times \$.57 \quad = \$113.31$$

Interpretation of the results.

1. Davies Eatery made $284.5 for every square foot of space in the eatery.
2. Davies Eatery made $113.31 for every square foot of space in the grocery section.

Implication of the results.

1. Mrs. Davies should consider utilizing more of the space in the building for the eatery.

Calculation step

1. To find the sales per square foot; (a) divide the net sales by the average inventory at cost.
   (b) divide the average inventory at cost by the square feet of selling space.
2. Multiply 1a by 1b.

Retail Compatibility Model

What is retail compatibility?

It is a technique that is used to determine how much sales a store can generate by locating close to another store that sells similar or complementary products or services.

Why does a marketer need to know the retail compatibility?

1. To determine the appropriateness of a location.
2. To know the profitability of a location.

How does a marketer find the retail compatibility?

Tobeke Fabrics Inc. was started in 1990 as an importer of African designer fabrics and social wears. Due to the high quality and the uniqueness of the merchandise, there was a high demand for them. In order to accommodate the growing market, Tobeke Fabrics decided to relocate. It contemplated on locating in one of the two most popular shopping centers in the city.

Site A had a men's clothing store with a monthly average sales of 2,100 clothes or $84,000, and large discount clothing store with an average sales of $750,891 per month. Twenty percent of the buyers in the site interchanged between the two stores. Sixty-percent of the regular clothes buyers on the site purposefully shopped at the men's clothing store, and seventy-five percent of the discount clothes buyers purposefully shopped in that store. Site B had a large children apparel store with a monthly average sale of 300 apparel per day or 50,400 or $756,000 per month, and a sewing center with an average monthly sales of $32,000. Forty percent of the buyers in the site interchanged between the two stores. Eighty-percent of the children apparel store buyers purposefully shopped in that store while fifty-nine percent of the sewing center purposefully shopped in that store. In order to decide which shopping center to locate in, Tobeke Fabrics needed to know the site that will result in the most sales for imported designer fabrics. It used the following retail compatibility formula to find it.

$$V = I\{Vs(P_LVs + PsV_L)/V_L\}$$

V = site.

V_L = volume of larger store.

P_L = purposeful purchasing in larger store.

Vs = volume of smaller store.

Ps = purposeful purchasing in smaller store.

V = increase in total volume of two stores.

I = degree of interchange.

Table 17-4
Tobeke Fabrics Inc.
Retail Compatibility Model

Site A (increase in fabrics store sales)

= Degree of interchange{volume of the men's clothing store (purposeful purchasing in large discount clothing store **x** monthly sales of the men's clothing store + purposeful purchasing in men's clothing store x monthly sales in the large discount store)/monthly sales in the discount store).

Site A = $\dfrac{.20(\$84,000(.75 \times \$84,000 + .60 \times \$750,891)}{\$750,891}$

$\quad = \dfrac{.20(\$84,000(\$63,000 + \$450,534.60)}{\$750,891}$

$\quad = .20(\$84,000 \times .68)$

$\quad = .20(57,447)$

$\quad = \$11,489.53$

Site B (increase in fabric store sales)

= Degree of interchange { monthly sales in sewing center(purposeful purchasing in children's store **x** monthly sales in the sewing center + purposeful purchasing in the sewing center **x** monthly sales in the children's apparel store)/monthly sales in the children apparel store}.

$$\text{Site B} = .40\frac{(\$32,000(.80 \times \$32,000 + .59 \times \$756,000)}{\$756,000}$$

$$= .40\frac{(\$32,000(\$471,640)}{\$756,000}$$

$$= .40(\$32,000 \times .62)$$

$$= .40(19,964.8)$$

$$= \$7,985.92$$

Interpretation of the results.

1. Tobeke Fabrics Inc. will make an extra sales of $11,424 due to site interchange between it and the stores in Site A.
2. Tobeke Fabrics Inc. will make an extra sales of $7,936 due to site interchange between it and the stores in Site B.

Implication of the results.

1. Site A is more compatible to Tobeke Fabrics Inc. because it gives it more additional sales than site B.

Calculation steps.

1. Multiply the purposeful purchasing in the larger store by the volume of sales in the smaller store.
2. Multiply the purposeful purchasing in the smaller store by the volume of sales in the larger store.
3. Add #1 and #2, and divide by the volume of the larger store.

4. Multiply the result in #3 by the volume of sales in the smaller store.
5. Multiply the result in #4 by the degree of interchange.

Shopper Attraction Model

What is a shopper attraction model?

It is a model that calculates the size of the trading area in terms of the expected number of households that will be attracted to the retail site by looking at (1) the distance between consumers and competition, (2) the distance between consumers and a given site, and (3) the store image.

Why does a marketer need to know the shopper attraction model?

1. It is used to estimate the market size.
2. It enables the marketer to determine the trading areas on the basis of the product assortment carried at various shopping locations.
3. It enables the marketer to determine the trading areas on the basis of the travel times from the consumer's home to alternate shopping locations.
4. It enables the marketer to determine the trading areas on the basis of the sensitivity of the kind of shopping to travel time.

How does a marketer develop a shopper attraction model?

Adamma Reliable Fence Co. located in Adams Villa, NC. is considering relocating to three possible shopping spaces with 200, 300, and 500 total square feet of store space respectively to retail electric gate operators, wire partitions, guard rails, and portable dog cages. About 2,000 residents live in new residential developments that are respectively 10 minutes drive from the first location, 15 minutes from the second location, and 20 minutes from the third location. The company estimated that the effect of travel time is 3. The effect of the travel time was found by a previous research that studied how sensitive or willing the buyers were to spend that much time to travel such a distance to buy fences. Adamma Reliable Fence Co. needed to know the number of potential customers that may come from the new residential development to shop at the store. The company found the answer by using Table 17-5

$$P_{ij} = \frac{\dfrac{S_j}{(T_{ij})^\wedge}}{\displaystyle\sum_{j=1}^{n} \dfrac{S_i}{(T_{ij})^\wedge}}$$

P_{ij} = probability of a customer's traveling from home i to shopping location j.

S_j = square footage of selling space in shopping location j expected to be devoted to a particular product category.

T_{ij} = travel time from consumer's home i to shopping location j.

$\wedge$ = a parameter used to estimate the effect of travel time on different kinds of shopping trips.

n = number of different shopping locations.

Table 17-5
Adamma Reliable Fence Co
Shopper Attraction Model

Location 1 (P$_{i1}$) = $\dfrac{(200)/(10)^3}{(200)/(10)^3 + (300)/(15)^3 + (500)/(20)^3}$ or $\dfrac{0.2}{0.2 + 0.09 + .06} = \dfrac{0.2}{0.35} = 0.2 = 57\%$

Location 2 (P$_{i2}$) = $\dfrac{(300)/(15)^3}{(200)/(10)^3 + (300)/(15)^3 + (500)/(20)^3}$ or $\dfrac{.09}{0.2 + .09 + .06} = \dfrac{.09}{0.35} = .09 = 26\%$

329

Location 3 $(P_{i3}) = $ ___$(500)/(20)^{3}$___ or ___$.06$___ $= $ $\dfrac{.06}{0.35}$ $= 17\%$

$(200)/(10)^{3} + (300)/(15)^{3} + (500)/(20)^{3}$ $0.2 + 0.09 + 06$

Interpretation of the results.

1. Fifty-seven percent of the residents or 1140 people will likely come to shop at the first location.
2. Twenty-six percent of the residents or 520 people will likely come to shop at location two.
3. Seventeen percent of the residents or 340 people will likely come to shop at location three.

Implications of the results.

1. Adamma Reliable Fence Co. should locate at location one.
2. Adamma Reliable Fence Co. should avoid location three.

Calculation steps

1. To find the number of potential customers for location A;
    (i) divide the square footage in location one by the minutes of driving distance to location one, and multiply it by the effect of travel time.
    (ii) divide the answer in #1 by: (a) the square footage in location one divided by the minutes of driving distance to location one, multiplied by the effect of travel time, plus (b) the square footage of location two divided by the minutes of driving distance to location two, multiplied by the effect of travel time to location two, plus (c) the square footage in location three, divided by the minutes of driving distance to location three, multiplied by the effect of travel time.

2. To find the number of potential customers for location two;
    (i) divide the square footage in location two by the minutes of driving distance to location two, and multiply it by the effect of travel time.
    (ii) divide the answer in #1 by: (a) the square footage in location one divided by the minutes of driving distance to location one, multiplied by the effect of travel time, plus (b) the square footage of location two divided by the minutes of driving distance to location two, multiplied by the effect of travel time to location two, plus (c) the square footage in location three divided by the minutes of driving distance to location three, multiplied by the effect of travel time.

3. To find the number of potential customers for location three;
    (i) divide the square footage in location three by the minutes of driving distance to location three, and multiply it by the effect of travel time.
    (ii) divide the answer in #1 by: (a) the square footage in location one divided by the minutes of driving distance to location one, multiplied by the effect of travel time, plus (b) the square footage of location two divided by the minutes of driving distance to location two, multiplied by the effect of travel time to location two, plus (c) the square footage in location three divided by the minutes of driving distance to location three, multiplied by the effect of travel time.

CHAPTER 18

MARKETING COMMUNICATION

Advertising Reach

What is an advertising reach?

It is the percentage of a target audience that a business reaches with its advertisement message at least once every four weeks.

Why does a marketer need to know the advertising reach?

1. It is used to evaluate the effectiveness of the media in order to determine the best technique.
2. It provides the information a company uses to estimate sales in a market area.

How does a marketer find the advertising reach?

Homeland Fashions Inc. began in 1970 to import and wholesale African dresses, hats, postcards, foodstuff, and other items to retailers in the United States. In order to expose and pull customers to the retail stores, Homeland Fashions devoted a lot of its budget to promotion allowance and pull-in promotions. It ran national advertisement for the company's products on the television. In 2001 Homeland Fashions budgeted $1,000,000 for advertisement. According to its plan, the cost per thousand exposures was $100,000. Homeland Fashions wanted a frequency of 10 per year, and needed to know how many people it could reach at that frequency, and with the 2001 budget. It did the following.

Table 18-1
Homeland Fashions Inc.
Advertising Reach

$$\text{Reach} = \frac{\text{Advertisement budget } \times \text{ frequency} \times 1000}{\text{Cost Per Thousand Exposures}}$$

$$= \frac{\$1,000,000 \times 10 \times 1,000}{\$100,000} = 100,000 \text{ exposures per ad.}$$

At a frequency rate of 10 per year $= 100,000 \times 10 = 1,000,000$ total exposures.

Interpretation of the results.

1. With $1,000,000 in advertisement, and at $1,000 per thousand exposure, Homeland Fashion will get 1,000,000 exposures at a frequency rate of 10.

Implications of the results.

1. Homeland Fashion has a low advertisement reach and should not spend the budget on advertisement.
2. The cost per thousand is high.

Calculation steps.

1. Divide the advertising budget by the cost per thousand exposures to find the number of thousand exposures.
2. Multiply the number of the thousand exposures by 1000 to find the number of exposures or reaches per frequency.
3. Multiply the number of reaches per frequency by 10 to find the total number of times the people in the target were reached.

Advertising Frequency

What is an advertising frequency?

It is the average number of times a person in the target audience or group is exposed to the same advertisement message in a 4-week period.

Why does a marketer need to know the advertising frequency?

1. A marketer needs to know this in order to measure how effective or productive an advertising campaign is.

How does a marketer find the advertising frequency?

The Southeastern Women Center Inc. is a medium-size clinic located in New Way, AZ. It is operated as a partnership by four medical doctors. The clinic specializes in cancer detection and treatment, infertility, and gynecology. Because New Way had five large hospitals and numerous clinics and other medical offices, Southeastern Women Center had problems making its offerings known to the community. In 2002 the Center decided to devote a major part of its marketing budget to promotion. It ran advertisement on the Center 20 times on the radio, television, and in the newspaper during a four-week period. It reached 29% of the women in New Way and surrounding areas 5 times during the period with the radio, and 38% of the women 7 times with the television, and 24%

Photo 37: The Women's Hospital

334

of the women 8 times with the newspaper. However, it did not know how many women were reached and how many times they were reached during the period. The Center needed to determine how effective the advertisements were, and therefore decided to find out the average frequency of the advertisement by doing the following.

Table 18-2
Southern Women Center
Advertising Frequency

Advertising frequency
= $\dfrac{\text{Percentage of target audience reached x \# of times reached}}{\text{Total percentage of target audience reached}}$

$$\frac{(.29 \times 5) + (.38 \times 7) + (.24 \times 8)}{.91}$$

$$\frac{1.45 + 2.66 + 1.92}{.91} = \frac{6.03}{.91} = 6.62 \text{ times}$$

Interpretation of the results.

1. Ninety-one percent of the target audience were exposed to the Center's message on an average of 6.62 times during the four-weeks of advertisement period.

Implication of the results.

1. Southeastern Women Center should compare this frequency with those of competitors in order to decide if it is high enough.

Calculation steps.

1. Add the percentage of audience reached from all targets.
2. Multiply #1 by the number of times the audience is reached.
3. Divide #2 by #1.

Advertising Gross Impression

What is an advertising gross impression?

It is the total number or amount of advertisement that will have a marked effect on the mind and emotion of the viewers, and arouse their interest.

Why does a marketer need to know the advertising gross impression?

1. It enables the marketer to determine the extent of the advertisement necessary to effectively communicate the product or service to the target audience.
2. It helps in the make-up of the advertisement content.
3. It helps to decide on the advertisement frequency and budget of the advertisement.

How does a marketer find the advertising gross impression?

Don Dill Pottery Inc. is a regional clay and ceramic pottery factory located in Potgrove, North Carolina, a rural town with no television or radio stations. When Mr. Dill created his first pottery of a Carolina goose in a colored ceramic in 1960, he believed that it was the most beautiful goose that he had ever seen and that anyone who saw it would like to own one. He was proved

Photo 38: Old Time Pottery

right, and today Don Dill Pottery is the premier supplier of birds and various creatures in clay and ceramic pottery to stores around the nation.

To expose its products to wholesalers and retail stores and individuals around the nation, Don Dill Pottery advertised in local and national trade magazines. In 2001, one such magazine, Pottery World, a bi-monthly publication, had a circulation of 9,000,000. About 6,000,000 magazines were sold to retail stores in North Carolina, and the rest were sold to wholesalers around the country. Don Dill Pottery advertised in five issues of the magazine every year.

Also, in 2001, the company decided to split the ad budget with Internet advertising. It felt that advertisement on the Internet should reach everyone. It had 3,000,000 downloads of the magazine every two months (18m per year). Don Dill Pottery needed to know the gross impression of the magazine and the Internet in 2001. It did the following.

Table 18-3
Don Dill Pottery
Advertising Gross Impression

Gross impression

= # reached in target audience x # of times advertised

Magazine = National 9,000,000 x 5 = 45,000,000 impressions
              North Carolina = 6,000,000 x 5 = 30,000,000
Internet   = 3,000,000 x 6 = 18,000,000 impressions

Interpretation of the results.

1. The advertisement in the magazine was exposed to more people than the one on the Internet.

Implications of the results.

1. The magazine is more available and reachable than the Internet. The Internet is only available to those that have access to the computer.
2. Unlike the Internet, magazines are placed in offices, schools, libraries, and the other areas that non-subscribers are found.

Calculation steps.

1. Determine the number of people the advertisement reaches in the target audience.
2. Determine the number of issues in which the pottery is advertised.
3. Multiply number 1 by number 2 to determine the gross impression.

Advertising Rating Point

What is an advertising rating point?

It is the reach of an advertisement and the frequency of its reach.

Why does a marketer need to know the advertising rating point?

1. To find out how effective the advertisement that reaches the audience is.
2. To set the media goal.
3. To evaluate alternative vehicles or media schedule.

How does a marketer find the advertising rating point?

Uptown Investors Inc. is a financial investment company that deals in mutual funds, and investment advisement. It is located in Uptown, Texas, a city with approximately 2,000,000 people that are interested in mutual funds and other investments. Money Times, a financial investment magazine in the city had a total readership of 930,000, and with four issues during the year. In 2001, thirty-six percent of the subscribers were reached twice, 20 percent were reached three times, and 30 percent were reached four times. At the end of the year, Uptown needed to know the gross rating point of the advertisements in order to decide on the 2002 advertisement budget. It did the following.

Table 18-4a
Uptown Investors Inc.
Advertising Rating Point.

Frequency = $\frac{(.36 \times 2) + (.20 \times 3) + (.30 + 4)}{.86}$ = $\frac{2.52}{.86}$ = 2.9 times

Gross Rating Point = # reached in target audience x frequency of reach

86 x 2.9 = 249.4

Impressions = (36%) **334,800 x 2 = 669600**
(20%) **186,000 x 3 = 558,000**
(30%) **279,000 x 4 = 1,116, 000**
= **2,343,600 impressions**

Interpretation of the results.

1. Eighty six percent of the target population were exposed to the advertisement on an average of 2.9 times.
2. The gross rating point of all the advertisements is 249.4.

Example 2

A Ride of Elegance Inc. is a Limousine service located in Brucemate, Nevada, twenty miles south of Las Vegas. In order to reach the various celebrities that stay in Las Vegas, the company advertises on the radios, televisions, and newspapers. Radios reach 60 percent of the target audience 5 times in a week. Televisions reach 70 percent of the target audience 3 times in a week, and the newspapers reach 50 percent of the target audience with a frequency of 7 times a week. The company wanted to know which of the three media is the most effective, and it did the following to find the gross rating point.

Table 18-4b
A Ride Of Elegance Inc.
Advertising Rating Point

Gross Rating Point = *reach x frequency*
Radio   = 60 x 5 = 300points
Television   = 70 x 3 = 210points
Newspaper   = 50 x 7 = 350 points

Interpretation of the results.

1. The newspaper has the highest rating point, followed by radio, and television.

Implications of the results.

1. The gross rating point does not mean much unless it is compared to other rating points.
2. The newspaper with 350points rating is the most efficient of the three media.

Calculation steps.

1. Find out from the media the total percentage of the target audience reached.
2. Multiply the percentage of the target audience reached by the number of times they were reached.

Maximum Advertising Cost

What is a maximum advertising cost?

It is the most money a firm will spend on advertising in order to achieve an operating profit goal.

Why does a marketer need to know the maximum advertising cost?

1. To find out the breakeven point for advertising or the point at which advertising achieves a desired result or target.

How does a marketer find out the maximum advertising cost?

Rolly's Coaches and Campers Inc. wholesales sports coaches, van campers, and motor homes in Dog City, Wyoming. The company is setting up the next year's plan for the store. Their number one goal in 2002 was to increase the level of sales. The store believed that an aggressive advertisement would increase the sales by 15%, and it needed to know the amount that it had to spend on advertising in order to meet a target or operating profit goal of $1,150,000. Below is the projected marketing plan.

Table 18-5
Rolly's Coaches and Campers
Projected Marketing Plan for 2002

Sales	200,240 units
Selling Price (average)	$30 unit
Variable Production Cost	$18.00 unit
Fixed Production Cost	$800,960
Fixed Selling and Admin. Costs	$400,000
Store's normal capacity	250,000 units.

In order to find out the maximum amount to be spent on advertising, Rolly's Coaches and Campers did the following:

a. New Sales units = (200,240) x .15 + 200,240 = 230,276units.
b. VCM = $30 - $18 = $12.
c. Total Contribution for 230,276 units = $12 x 230,276 = $2,763,312.
d. Total Fixed Costs ($800960 + $400,000) =$1,200,960.

Total Contribution	$2,763,312
Total Fixed Cost	- $1,200,960
Income Before Ad.	$1,562,352
Target income	- $ 1,150,000
Avail for Ad.	$412,352

Interpretation of the results

1. In order to achieve a $1,150,000 profit, Rolly's Coaches and Campers should spend up to $412,352. in advertising.

Implication of the results.

1. Rolly's Coaches and Campers could have $649,040 available if it projects selling the store's normal capacity of 250,000 units.

Calculation steps.

1. Find the new sales units (230,276 units), by multiplying the old sales (200,240) by 15%, and adding the result to the old sales units.
2. Determine the variable contribution margin or VCM ($12) by subtracting the variable production ($18) from the selling price ($30).
3. Determine the total contribution ($2,763,312) by multiplying the VCM by the new sales unit.
4. Determine the total fixed costs ($1,200,960) by adding the fixed production cost to fixed selling and admin. costs.
5. Determine the amount to be spent on advertising ($412,352) by subtracting the total fixed cost ($1,200,960) from the contribution ($2,763,312) to get the income before the

advertisement ($1,562,352), and by subtracting the target profit ($,1,150,000).

Task and Objective Advertising Budget

What is a task and objective advertising budget?

It is a technique that is used to determine the budget by stating the objectives and tasks needed to achieve the goal.

Why does a marketer need to know the task and objective advertising budget?

1. It provides a more accurate and dependable estimate of advertising costs and spending.

How does a marketer develop a task and objective advertising budget?

CTS Clinical Lab Inc. provides DNA Paternity testing to parents and other individuals that are in dispute of paternal rights of children born out of wedlock. Because it is a new type of business, CTS Clinical Lab decided that it had to maximize its advertising efforts in order to penetrate the market. The three objectives it needed to achieve were: to reach every household in the city; to convince potential customers that are in doubt to give the

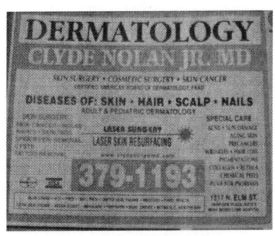

Photo 39: DERMATOLOGY

Lab a trial; and to inform the customers that it provided the necessary legal requirements.

In order to reach all the households, the Lab advertised on the television and the radio for an annual cost of $1,300,000 and $700,000 respectively. In order to convince potential customers, the Lab used actors to illustrate the value of DNA testing for $500,000 annually. Finally, in order to provide adequate legal services, the Lab contracted the service of a law firm at a $110,000 annual cost. CTS Clinical Lab determined the total task and objective budget as shown below.

Table 18-6
CTS Clinical Budget
Task and Objective Advertising Budget

Objectives	*Tasks*	*Estimated Cost*
Objective 1: To reach every household in the city		
Task A:	TV ads	$1,300,000 annual
Task B:	Radio ads	$700,000 annual
Objective 2: To convince the public to give the Lab a trial		
Task A:	Service of Actors	$500,000
Objective 3: To inform the public of the legal supports		
Task A:	Law firm	$110,000
Total advertising budget		**$2,610,000**

Interpretation of the results.

1. The total advertising budget is $2,610,000.

Implication of the results.

1. CTS Clinical could manipulate or change the estimated cost in order to attain different advertising budgets.

Calculation steps.

1. List each objective and the required tasks to accomplish it.
2. List the estimated cost of the required tasks to accomplish each objective.
3. Add all the estimated cost.

Recency/Frequency/Monetary Value Segmentation (1)

What is a Recency/Frequency/Monetary Value Segmentation (1)

It is a technique used to: (1) segment the customers in terms of how current they are in purchases.
(2) find the percentage of solicitations that results in an order.
(3) find the number of orders in some recent period of time.
(4) find the average order amount within some recent period of time.

Why does a marketer need a Recency/Frequency/Monetary Value Segmentation (1)

1. To estimate the response rates of customers in different segments to the marketing strategies.
2. To determine the buying practice or habit of customers in different customer segments in terms of recency, frequency, and order amount.

How does a marketer use a Recency/Frequency/Monetary Value Segmentation (1)

Carolyn's Marketing & Fundraiser Inc. is a full service fundraiser and candy distributor started in 1981 by Carolyn Chidomere to serve churches, schools, and other not-for-profit organizations in

345

fundraising events. The company has 20,000 customers on its mailing list. In order to have an accurate and reliable record on customers' buying habit, Carolyn's stored data on the customers' purchase history, including the frequency and the recency of purchase. In an effort to develop the 2002 marketing plan, the company needed an estimate of the sales revenue for the year, so it did the following.

Table 18-7
Carolyn's Marketing and Fundraising Inc.
Recency/Frequency/Monetary Value Segmentation (1)

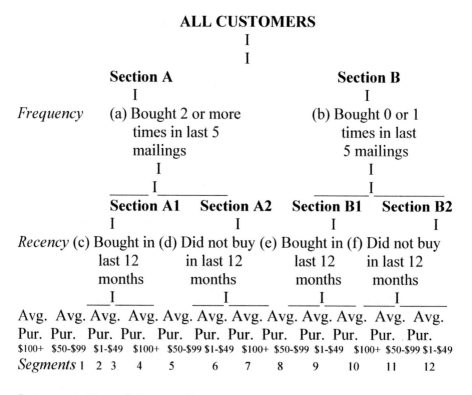

Interpretation of the results.

1. Carolyn added up the estimated purchase dollars from the 12 segments to arrive at the total sales estimate.

Implication of the results.

1. Recency and frequency of purchase vary by the ability of the customers to buy.

Calculation steps.

1. Frequency of purchase: Group the customers into A and B based on purchase frequency.
2. Recency of purchase: Group customer segment A into 1 and 2 and segment B into 1 and 2 based on their recency of purchase.
3. Purchase by segments: Divide A1 into segments 1, 2, and 3.
   Divide A2 into segments 4, 5, and 6.
   Divide B1 into segments 7, 8, and 9.
   Divide B2 into segments 10, 11, and 12, based on the amount of purchase.
4. Add the purchases in the 12 segments to find the total sales revenue.

Recency/Frequency/Monetary Value Segmentation (2)

What is Recency/Frequency/Monetary Value Segmentation (2)

It is a technique that: (1) makes a marketing strategy more efficient by increasing the rate of the customers' response to the strategy.

(2) segments the total market on recency, frequency and monetary value.

Why does a marketer need a Recency/Frequency/Monetary Value Segmentation(2)?

1. It shows the marketer what and how to communicate to the customers to make them buy more.
2. It acts as a tool to increase sales and meet the proposed budget.

How does a marketer use a Recency/Frequency/Monetary Value Segmentation(2)?

Modern Furniture Inc. is the second largest furniture department store in Washington, DC. Started in 1973 by Mrs. Leslie Jones, Modern furniture capitalizes on the great diversity of the city. It imports and resells fine quality furniture from all over the world. Today, Modern Furniture store composes of twelve departments comprising of twelve illustrations of how Leslie envisions the globe. Modern Furniture spends a lot of money to assure that buyers from each part of the world are kept up to date on the furniture fashion in their region.

In 2000, Modern Furniture spent $2.5m for promotion. This money was spent on catalogs with photos of furniture taken on sites and electronically transmitted to the store's catalog department in Washington DC. The twelve different catalogs for each part of the globe are made and updated. The catalogs are placed on the store's web site,

Photo 40: Southeastern FURNITURE

and the printed ones were sent to the 300,000 adults in the USA from different nationalities on the store's mailing list. Monthly changes in the furniture fashions in any part of the world are placed on the web, and printed on fliers that are inserted in city-wide newspapers and cultural publications, and inside ethnic businesses in and around Washington, DC.

In order to maximize the income from the promotion, Modern Furniture uses the Recency/Frequency/Monetary Value Segmentation (2) model to find out how many customers in each of the twelve world segments responded to its ad and how much they bought. The electronic zip codes and address data bank in the sales register classified each of the twelve customer segments into buying categories based on; how recent they are (R), how frequent they buy (F), and how much they spend (MV). As shown below on Table 18-18, the store grouped the customers into 12 segments that comprise of seven mixtures as follows; (1) High frequency (Hi F), or (2) Low frequency (Lo F), and on (3) High Recency (Hi R), or (4) Low Recency (Lo R), and on (5) High Monetary value (Hi MV), or (6) Medium Monetary Value (Me MV), or (7) Low Monetary Value (Lo MV). For each segment, the company determined the total customer size, the rate at which it responded to promotion, sales to the group in proportion to the total sale, and the average sales to the group.

Table 18-18
Recency/Frequency/Monetary Value Segmentation (2)
Sales: January-December 2000

Segments	Number of Customers	% of Total Customers (/300,000)	Response Rate (%)	Total Sales (000)	% of Total Sales (/10,604.5)	Av. Sales ($)
1 Hi F/ Hi R/ HiMV	36,000	12	.055	1,901	17.9	52.8
2. Hi F/ Hi R/ MeMV	20,000	6.7	.030	970	9.2	48.5
3. Hi F/ Hi R/ LoMV	16,000	5.3	.063	515	4.8	32.1
4. Hi F/ Lo R/ HiMV	34,000	11.3	.069	1,624	15.3	47.7
5. Hi F/ Lo R/ MeMV	14,000	4.7	.041	876	8.3	62.5

6. Hi F/ Lo R/ LoMV	26,500	8.8	.079	158.5	1.5	5.9
7. Lo F/ Hi R/ HiMV	12,000	4	.071	1,125	10.6	93.8
8. Lo F/ Hi R/ MeMV	20,500	6.8	.068	784	7.4	38.2
9. Lo F/ Hi R/ LoMV	12,500	4.2	.052	532	5	42.56
10. Lo F/ Lo R/ HiMV	59,000	19.7	.089	981	9.25	16.6
11. Lo F/ Lo R/MeMV	19,000	6.3	.045	643	6.05	33.8
12. Lo F/ Lo R/LoMV	30,500	10.2	.052	495	4.7	16.2
Total	300,000	100	.714	10,604.5	100	

Interpretations of the results.

1. In 2000, Modern Furniture had 300,000 customers on the mailing list, with a response rate of 71.4%, and a total sale of $10, 604.5m from the twelve segments.
2. Segment ten had 59,000 buyers that comprised of 19.7% of the total customers. The segment had $981,000 in sales or 9.25% of total sales. The average sales segment was $16.6, which was the ninth in the ranking.

Implications of the results.

1. Modern Furniture should encourage purchase in segments two, five, ten, and eleven where there are high monetary purchase values, but low sales in proportion to the total sales.
2. Modern Furniture's promotion strategy should include features that will encourage higher frequency and recency of buying in segments seven through twelve.
3. Modern Furniture should monitor the monthly reactions of each segment's customers to the stores promotion and use it as a guide to estimate promotion expenses, and the store's budget.
4. Modern Furniture could target only on the best segments (one, four, and seven) and on the second best segments (two, five, seven, and ten).

Calculation steps.

1. Segment the total customers in groups using geographic, demographic, psychographic or other factors.
2. Based on the buying habit, classify each segment into High Frequency (Hi F), or Low Frequency (Lo F), and on High Recency (Hi R), or Low Recency (Lo R), and on High Monetary value (Hi MV), or Medium Monetary Value (Me MV), or Low Monetary Value (Lo MV).
3. To determine the proportion of each segment in the total customer population, divide the number of customers in the segment by the total customers from all segments.
4. To determine the response rate of the customers in each segment to the promotion, divide the percentage of the individuals in the segment that bought furniture during a promotion period by the number of times the promotion was ran during the period.
5. To determine the percentage contribution of each segment to the total sales, divide the sales for each segment by the total sales for all segments, and multiply by 100.
6. To determine the average sale to individuals in each segment, divide the total sales for the segment by the number of customers in the segment.

Weighted Number of Exposures

What is a weighted number of exposure?

It is the amount or degree of impact that an advertisement makes on the viewers.

Why does a marketer need to know the weighted number of exposures?

1. To determine the efficiency of an advertisement campaign.
2. To determine the effectiveness of an advertisement campaign.

How does a marketer find the weighted number of exposures?

Four Seasons Roofing and Siding Inc. repairs and remodels roofs, vinyl sidings, garages, sunrooms, windows and stonework for residential and commercial customers. In order to reach the residential customers, the company advertises in the local newspapers, radio, and television. Advertisements to the commercial customers are made in the local trade magazines, trade shows, and by direct communication. In the middle of 2002, Four Seasons Roofing and Siding analyzed the promotion so far and discovered that for the residential customers, the advertisement reach was 75%, the frequency was 4, and the impact was 1.5, while the commercial customers had an advertisement reach of 61%, a frequency of 3.8, and an impact of 2.8. Four Seasons Roofing and Siding needed to know the weighted number of exposures for each segment, and they did the following.

Table 18-9
Four Seasons Roofing and Siding Inc.
Weighted Number of Exposures

1. Residential customer segment:

The weighted number of exposures is .75 x 4 x 1.5 = 4.50

2. Commercial customer segment:

The weighted number of exposures is .61 x 3.8 x 2.8 = 6.49

Interpretation of results

1. On a maximum impact level of 10, the effectiveness or impact of the advertisement by Four Seasons Roofing and Siding Inc. on residential customers is less than half of what was expected.

2. On a maximum impact level of 10, the effectiveness or impact of the advertisement by Four Seasons Roofing and Siding Inc. on commercial customers is more than half of what was expected

Implications of results

1. Four Seasons Roofing and Siding Inc. should re-examine the residential customer market base to make sure that home owners rather than renters are reached.
2. Four Seasons Roofing and Siding Inc. should create more appealing offers in its advertisement to both target markets.
3. Four Seasons Roofing and Siding Inc. should fortify its ground in the commercial market segment, and utilize more penetrating advertising strategies.

Calculation steps

1. To find the weighted number of exposures, multiply the reach by the frequency and the impact.

CHAPTER 19

MARKETING CHANNEL

Profitability of Indirect Channel Process

What is the profitability of indirect channel?

It is a process that estimates the sales productivity of a proposed new price or expenditure by using a sales benchmark.

Why does a marketer need to know the profitability of indirect channel?

1. To determine the total sales required to achieve a desired level of profitability.
2. To use industry standards or benchmarks to estimate how proposed price and marketing expenditure will affect the company's sales and profitability.

How does a marketer find the profitability of indirect channel?

Net Direct Inc. develops web sites and offers comprehensive online service to individual and business customers. Net Direct needed to estimate the sales productivity in 2002. It had served 5,208 customers in 2001. Each paid $40 per month for the services, amounting to approximately $2.5m (40x12x5,208) in annual sales. The total variable cost was $812,500 or $13 ($812,500/12/5,208) per service, and the VCM was $1,687,500 ($2.5m-$812,500) or $27.20 per service. The PVCM or the amount of sales required to cover the fixed cost and profit was .68 ($40-$13/$40). Thirty-five percent of the PVCM or $590,625 ($1,687,500 x .68) was used to cover direct and traceable costs. The target total contribution or the amount that the customers contributed each month through service payment to cover untraceable indirect cost and profit was $1,096,875 ($15.5 x 12 x 5,208). The untraceable fixed cost was $25,000.

In order to attract new customers in 2002, Net Direct needed to increase advertising and distribution, which are direct and traceable fixed costs by $150,000. It also intended to update the company's alarm system and soccer team, for a $75,000 addition to the untraceable fixed cost. However, Net Direct Inc. wanted to know the required sales, required units, and the required price to meet the past year's sales level in 2002 before making the decisions, so it did the following.

Table 19-1
Net Direct Inc.
Profitability of Indirect Channel Process

Total Required = $\dfrac{\text{Target total contribution} + \text{Untraceable fixed cost}}{\text{PVCM}}$
Sales ($)

2001: $\dfrac{\$1,096,875 + \$25,000}{.68} = \$1,649,816$ per annual

2002: $\dfrac{\$1,096,875 + \$100,000}{.68} = \$1,760,110$ per annual

Total Required = $\dfrac{\text{Target total contribution} + \text{Untraceable fixed cost}}{\text{PVCM per unit}}$
Sales (unit)
To achieve the profit
Level.

2001: $\dfrac{\$1,096,875 + \$25,000}{\$27.20} = 41,551$ service units per year

2002: $\dfrac{\$1,096,\ 875 + \$100,000}{\$27.20} = 44,329$ service units per year

Projected Price Per Unit = $\dfrac{\text{Total required sales in dollars}}{\text{Total required sales in units}}$

2001: $\dfrac{\$1{,}649{,}816}{41{,}551 \text{units}} = \$39.71$

2002: $\dfrac{\$1{,}760{,}110}{44{,}329} = \$39.71$

Interpretation of the results.

1. In order to achieve a similar return as in 2001, Net Direct should make at least $1,572,058.8 in sales, sell at least 2,757 service units, and charge 25 cents less in 2002 than in 2001.
2. Net direct should have sales of at least $1,649,816 in 2001 and $1,760,110 in 2002 in order to have a high sales productivity.
3. Net Direct should sell 41,551 service units in 2001, and 44,329 service units in 2002 in order to have a high sales productivity.
4. Net Direct should maintain the same price in both years. However, more promotion efficiency is required in the 2002 to maintain high productivity at the same cost.

Implications of the results.

1. More sales in dollars and units must be achieved in 2002.
2. Although $39.71 seems to be the equilibrium price, Net Direct Inc. could advertise this as a price reduction to attract more customers in 2002.

Calculation steps.

1. To find the total required sales in dollar, add the target total contribution to the untraceable fixed cost and divide by the PVCM.
2. To find the total required sales in units, add the target total contribution to the total direct or traceable cost and divide by VCM per service.

3. To determine the projected price per unit, divide the total required sales in dollar by the total required sales in units.

Additional Inventory Cost

What is the additional inventory cost?

It is a process used to find out the cost of maintaining a higher inventory level needed to meet the increase in demand.

Why does a marketer need to know the additional inventory cost?

1. It helps to provide the right amount of product assortments for sales.
2. It increases customers satisfaction by reducing stock-out.

How does a marketer find out the additional inventory cost?

Spiffy Looks Inc. sells outdoor wears for teenage girls. Due to its popularity and the large size of the market in See World, Jumpy Cove and Man-made cities where eight Spiffy Looks' chains are located, the company faced a high demand every spring and summer. The demand was so much in some summers that some stores ran out of some styles on a frequent basis. Miss Jenny Kat, the owner of the chain stores desperately wanted a way to maintain a higher inventory level in all stores and styles. Presently, the Spiffy chain maintains a 30-days inventory at a cost of $13,789,000 for goods, transportation and storage. Miss Kat wanted to increase the inventory level to a more accurate period of 45 days during the spring and summer months. The interest rate for the additional capital to keep the inventory is 18%. Miss Kat projected that her action would increase the next year's sales from $280million to $310million, and she wanted to know the additional cost of keeping an additional fifteen days' inventory. She did the following.

Table 19-2
Spiffy Looks Inc.
Additional Inventory Cost

$$\text{Additional Inventory Cost} = \frac{\text{Sales x Interest rate}}{(365/\text{Inventory Period})}.$$

$$= \frac{\$310,000,000 \times .18}{365/45} = \$6,875,000$$

Interpretation of the results.

1. The additional 15 days increase in the inventory level will cost Spiffy an additional $6,875,000 in goods, transportation and storage.
2. An increase of $6,875,000 in the inventory cost yielded an increase of $30million in sales, a ratio of 1:4.4.

Implication of the results.

1. Spiffy Looks did not specify how much the increase in sales was from the previous years. Therefore, it is not possible to know the ratio of the increase in sales to the increase in the inventory.

Calculation steps.

1. Multiply the projected sales by the interest rate to borrow the money for the additional inventory.
2. Divide 365 days by the number of days in the inventory period.
3. To arrive at the new and old inventory costs, divide #1 by #2 for the number of days before, and divide #1 by #2 for the proposed new days of inventory level.
4. Subtract the cost to keep the old inventory level from the cost of the new inventory level, to find the increase in the inventory costs.

Average Inventory Investment

What is an average inventory investment?

It is a technique used to determine the amount of money that a firm spends to buy adequate level of inventory each week for a period of time.

Why does a marketer need to know the average inventory investment?

1. To develop a more accurate plan for the inventory.
2. To develop a more accurate budget and profitability.

How does a marketer find the average inventory investment?

Bob's Quality Autos Inc. buys, sells, and trades used auto bikes, cars, vans, and trucks. A competitive advantage for Bob's Quality Autos is that it is always well stocked. Because of that, most potential used car buyers in the area go to Bob's Quality Autos first before going to any other used car dealerships. In January 2001, Bob's Quality Auto planned to purchase $8million worth of cars. It expected to sell the merchandise in fifty weeks at a retail value of $20million, without any markdowns. Normally, Bob's had an inventory turnover for autos of fifty weeks annually. It wanted to know the amount of money to spend in order to buy enough cars for the year and it did the following.

Table 19-3
Bob's Quality Autos Inc.
Average Inventory Investment

Average inventory investment = {(Beginning inventory + Ending inventory)/2)}(Inventory turnover in weeks/52 weeks)

Average inventory investment = {($8,000,000 + 0)/2)}(50/52)
(4,000,000)(.96)
= $3,846,153

Interpretation of the results.

1. Bob's Quality Autos should invest an average of $3,846,153 per annual on cars in 2001.

Implication of the results.

1. Bob's Quality Autos should have at least $3,846,153 for inventory for fifty weeks in 2001.

Photo 41: BILL HARVEY AUTO SERVICE

Calculation steps.

1. Add the beginning inventory to the ending inventory, and divide by two.
2. Divide the inventory turnover rate by fifty-two.
3. Multiply #1 by #2 .

Closing Inventory at Cost

What is a closing inventory at cost?

It is a technique that is used to determine the value of the goods unsold at the end of a period by basing their value on their cost price.

Why does a marketer need to know the closing inventory at cost?

1. It gives the marketer an idea of the value of the unsold goods based on the cost price.

How does a marketer find the closing inventory at cost?

King's Groceries Inc. is a neighborhood convenience store that

retails frozen food and some non-food items. Because it is the only such store in the area, King's Groceries is busy both days and nights. At the end of each month, Mr. Tom King, the owner, had difficulties determining the amount of goods he sold in each product category, and

Photo 42: Lowe's Foods

the value of the unsold items. In 2000, Mr. King's son, Sunny King who was studying accounting at a local college volunteered to assist him to determine the value of the inventory left at the end of the year, by using the cost of the inventory. That year, the adjusted ending book value of inventory at retail was $69,500. The cost complement or the part of the retail sales that would be used to pay for the merchandise cost was .488. Mr. King, Jr. wanted to know how much the unsold groceries was by basing it on how much it costs them, so he did as follows.

Table 19-4
Kings Groceries Inc.
Closing Inventory at Cost

Closing Inventory at Cost = Adjusted Retail Book Inventory x
Cost Complement
= $69,500 x .488
Closing inventory value at cost in 2000 = $33,916

Interpretation of the results.

1. The value of the remaining inventory is $69,500 at the selling price.
2. The value of the remaining inventory is $33,916 at the cost price.

Implication of the results.

1. When compared to one another, the value of the inventory at retail is more than twice of that of cost.

Calculation steps.

1. Determine the adjusted retail book value of the inventory.
2. Determine the cost complement or how much of the retail sales consists of merchandise cost.

Inventory cost

What is an inventory cost?

It is the cost that a marketer incurs to buy and keep adequate inventory.

Why does a marketer need to know the inventory cost?

1. It is necessary to understand how the cost of the inventory impacts the marketing strategy.

How does a marketer find out the inventory cost?

JJ Handy Homes Inc. was started in 1969, to produce and sell utility houses for storage and alternative living in the Brutman City, Ohio. The components of the inventory plan in 2001 are shown on Table 19-5. JJ Handy Homes was highly profitable until in 2001 when a severe recession and high competition adversely affected the market for utility homes in the area. JJ Handy Homes considered how to remain profitable in the coming years in light of the growing bad economy. In 2001, the President, Mrs. Gladys Johnson considered several options, and chose to reduce the cost of operating the business without losing the market leadership, and without reducing the employees' benefits. She decided to reduce the cost of building and maintaining the homes from 45.5% to 40.5% of sales in 2002. She expected no change in sales, and an inventory turnover of 8 times during the year, and she wanted to know how much effect the reduction in the inventory cost will have on the operation cost. She used the following method.

Inventory cost = $\dfrac{\text{annual sales}}{\text{Inventory turnover}}$ x inventory carrying cost

Table 19-5
2001 Inventory Expenses for JJ Handy Homes

1. Annual sale in 2001   = $10,332,000.
2. Annual building costs   = $4m
3. Transportation of homes   =$90, 460
4. Average display time before sale   = 20 days
5. Cost of display   = $80,890
6. Administrative cost   = $230,980
7. Loss and removal of obsolete homes = $23,765
8. Sales and promotion appeals   = $278,231 $4,704,326
9. Profit $5,627,674

Inventory cost in 2001

$=\dfrac{\$10,332,000}{8} \times .455 = \$587,632.5$ inventory cost per turnover period.

Inventory cost in 2002 (with 5% reduction)

$\dfrac{\$10,332,000}{8} \times .405 = \$523,057.5$ inventory cost per turnover period.

Inventory cost at 45.5% per turnover period = $587,632.5
Inventory cost at 40.5% per turnover period = $523,057.5
Reduction in cost per turnover period $ 64,575

Interpretation of the results.

1. The inventory carrying cost per turnover period in 2001 was $587,632.5.
2. The inventory carrying cost per turnover period in 2002 is $523,057.5.
3. By reducing the inventory cost from 45.5 % to 40.5%, JJ Handy Homes lowered the cost by $64,575 per inventory period.

Implication of the results.

1. JJ Handy Homes should look at the reduction of the inventory carrying cost as a viable option to reduce costs.

Calculation steps.

1. Estimate the annual sales.
2. Multiply the annual sales by the percentage of inventory carrying cost.
3. Divide the result in #2 by the inventory turnover.

Inventory Carrying Cost

What is an inventory carrying cost?

It is the amount of money a business spends to keep enough inventory to meet customers demand.

Why does a marketer need to know the inventory carrying cost?

1. It is necessary to know the cost of increasing the inventory in the effort to satisfy the customer.

How does a marketer find the inventory carrying cost?

Joe's Fine Shoes Inc. is a wholesale distributor of men and women dress shoes to shoe stores in the eastern and southern United States. Sales in 1999 was $10 million, with a variable contribution cost of

Photo 43: THE SHOE MARKET

25%. Recently, some of the stores located in the shopping malls demanded for guaranteed 2 days delivery on all rain check orders from their existing wholesalers, or that they will switch to faster distributors. Rain check orders accounted for 15% of all in-mall store sales. In order to meet the 2 days delivery demand, Joe's Fine Shoes had to increase the inventory level at the central warehouse from $5 million to $8 million. The cost of carrying the inventory is 20% of the average inventory. The company wanted to know the total increase in the carrying cost, so it did the following.

Table 19-6
Joe' Fine Shoes Inc.
Inventory Carrying Cost

1. Loss from rain checks (15% x $10 million)   = $1.5 million
2. Loss VCM on rain check (25% x $1.5million)   = $.38m
3. Cost of carrying current inventory level ($5million x .20) =
$1million annual cost
4. Cost of carrying increasing inventory level ($8 million x .20)=
$1.6 million annual cost

New carrying cost = $1.6 million
Old carrying cost = $1 million
Total increase $. 6million

Interpretation of the results.

1. Increasing the level of the inventory in the central warehouse from $5million to $8million will result in an increase of $.6million in the cost of maintaining the inventory.
2. Joe's Fine Shoes will have a higher loss ($1.5m rather than $.6m) if the company decides not to meet the requests for reduced rain check time.

Implication of the results.

1. The marketer may consider the amount of loss due to non-response to customer requests and the cost of meeting the requests.

Calculation steps.

1. Determine the possible amount of loss if the request is not met by multiplying the total sale by the percentage of customers that made the request.
2. Calculate the variable contribution margin (VCM) lost by multiplying the possible amount of loss if the request is not met by the variable contribution cost.
3. Calculate the present cost of carrying the inventory by multiplying the current level of inventory by the carrying cost.
4. Calculate the future cost of carrying the inventory after the increase by multiplying the new inventory level by the carrying cost.
5. Subtract # 4 from #3 to get the additional carrying cost due to the increase in the inventory.

Inventory costing - First in First out (FIFO) and Last in First out (LIFO)

What is a first in first out, and a last in first out inventory costing?

The *first in first out* process is used to determine the cost of the ending inventory by assuming that the oldest merchandise is sold before the recently purchased merchandise.

The *last in first out* process is used to determine the cost of the ending inventory by assuming that the most recent merchandise is sold before the oldest merchandise.

Why does a marketer need to know the FIFO or LIFO inventory costing?

1. To accurately cost the items and properly determine the correct prices for the products.
2. To determine the value of the available or sold products.

How does a marketer find the cost of the inventory by FIFO and LIFO approaches?

Carl's Car Mart Inc. was started by Mr. Carl Martin to retail repossessed cars and utility vans he bought from local banks. After the end of the year sales in 1998, Carl ran out of inventory, and had to buy 17 cars at $4,000 each on December 30th. Carl's Car Mart began in 1999 with $68,000 ($4000 x 17) worth of stocks. In July, Carl bought two cars at $4,950 each for a total cost of $9,900. In November, he bought five more cars at $3,750 for a total cost of $18,750. During the year, he sold 21 cars at $8,450 each for a total sales of $177,450. At the end of 1999, Carl's Car Mart had three cars in stock. Mr. Martin wanted to know the value of the remaining cars by using both first in first out (FIFO), and the last-in first-out (LIFO) inventory valuation methods. He also wanted to know how the two approaches can affect gross margin, so he did the following.

Table 19-7
Carl's Car Mart Inc.
1999 Inventory Valuation
FIFO and LIFO

FIFO

Net sales		$177,450
Less: Cost of Good sold		
Beginning inventory (17cars)	$68,000	
Purchases (7cars)	$28,650	
Goods available (24 cars)	$96,650	
Ending inventory (3 cars x $3750) $11,250		
Cost of Goods Sold		$85,400
Gross Margin		**$92,050**

LIFO

Net sales		$177,450
Less: Cost of Good sold		
Beginning inventory (17cars)	$68,000	
Purchases (7cars)	$28,650	
Goods available (24 cars)	$96,650	
Ending inventory (3 cars x $4000) $12,000		
Cost of Goods Sold		$84,650
Gross Margin		**$92,800**

Interpretation of the results.

1. Under the FIFO methods, the three cars that remained were valued at $11,250 or $3,750 each. They were among the five cars that were bought last. The first cars were sold first.
2. Under the LIFO methods, the three cars that remained were valued at $12,000 or $4000 each. They were among the cars that came in first. The last cars were sold first.
3. The higher the value of the ending inventory, the less the gross margin.
4. The LIFO method resulted in a higher gross margin.

Implication of the results.

1. The purchase sequence of the inventory affects the value of the ending inventories and also the gross margin.
2. The amount of the gross margin varies in each case, depending on the price of the inventory.

Calculation steps.

1. Determine the net sales by multiplying the total units sold by the price.
2. Determine the cost-of-goods-sold by adding the beginning inventory, purchases and goods available, and subtracting the ending inventory.
3. Determine the gross margin by subtracting the cost-of-good-sold from the net sales.

Inventory Reorder Point

What is an inventory reorder point?

It is the level of inventory at which new orders must be placed.

Why does a marketer need to know the inventory reorder point?

1. So as not to run out of stock.
2. In order to maintain customer satisfaction through product availability.

How does a marketer find out the inventory reorder point?

A Tough Walk Inc. is a retailer of sporting goods located in Swamp Town, FL. A Tough Walk sells mostly steelwork shoes, and insulated and waterproof hunting shoes to hunters and rough riders. The lifestyle in Florida encourages the use of these kinds of shoes.

The insulated and waterproofed hunting shoes were so popular that A Tough Walk was not able to maintain adequate inventory to meet the annual demand. The manufacturers of the shoes are located out of state. It took 6 days lead time for the order of the shoes to be placed, received, checked, and displayed in the store. A Tough Walk opens every day, and sold an average of 10 pairs of the insulated and waterproofed hunting shoes daily or 70 pairs per week. A Tough Walk had to keep at least 80 pairs of shoes as a safety stock at all times, and needed to know how many pairs of shoes should remain before the store reorders so as not to run out. It calculated that as follows.

Table 19-8
A Tough Walk Inc.
Inventory Reorder Point

Reorder point = (Order lead time x Usage rate) +(Safety stock)

= 6days x 10 pairs + 80 pairs =140 pairs

Interpretation of the results.

1. In order to maintain an adequate number of the insulated and waterproofed hunting shoes, Tough Walk must re-order whenever there are 140 pairs left in stock.

Implication of the results.

1. A Tough Walk should adhere to the reorder point or risk running out of stock.

Calculation steps.

1. Determine the lead-time or the time from when the order is placed to when the merchandise is displayed in the store.
2. Determine the usage rate.

3. Determine the safety stock.
4. Multiply the lead time by the usage rate, and add this to the safety stock.

Inventory Shortage or Overage

What is an inventory shortage or overage?

It is the amount or number by which the items for sales are either more or less than the number needed for sales.

Why does a marketer need to know the inventory shortage or overage?

1. To find out if inventory shortage may exist at the end of the inventory period.
2. To find out if inventory overage may exist at the end of the inventory period.

How does a marketer find out the inventory shortage or overage?

Jack's Industrial Containers Inc. is a manufacturer of corrugated boxes for shipping and moving supplies. On December 31st, 1999 the book value of inventory at retail was $85,550. However, after a physical count, the company found the actual value of the inventory to be $76,695. It needed to know the stock shortage or overage at the retail value. Jack found the shortage as follows.

Table 19-9
Jack's Industrial Containers Inc.
Inventory Shortage or Overage

Ending book value of inventory at retail	$85,550
Physical inventory (at retail)	$76,695
Stock shortages	$8,855

Adjusted ending book value of inventory at retail = $76,695

Interpretation of the results.

1. Jack's Industrial Containers had a stock shortage of $8,855.
2. The ending book value is adjusted to $76,695.

Implication of the results.

1. Jack needs to investigate for the shortage or overage in the inventory on a regular basis so as not to have a constant shortage.

Calculation steps.

1. Determine the ending book value of inventory at retail.
2. Do a physical count of the inventory.
3. Subtract the physical count from the ending book value.

Inventory Turnover

What is an inventory turnover?

It is a technique that is used to measure the rate at which the inventory is sold.

Why does a marketer need to know the inventory turnover?

1. It is used to determine whether the company is managing its inventory well. For example, does it have an excess or inadequate inventory compared to the industry average?
2. It is used to determine the efficiency at which the inventory is managed.
3. It shows the marketer how fast the inventory is sold.
4. It shows the marketer how long the inventory was held before resale.

How does a marketer find the inventory turnover?

High Roads Tires Inc. retails and wholesales auto and bicycles

tires to businesses and individuals. As shown on Table 19-10, the company had net sales of $4.1m and $4.8m in 1996 and 1997 respectively. High Roads Tires bought inventory once a year

Photo 44: Discount Tires

for distribution. The beginning inventories on January 1, 1996 and 1997 were $1.2m and $1.4m respectively. The closing inventories on December 31, 1996 and 1997 were $800,790 and $902,200 respectively. In order to plan for the 1998 sales, High Roads Tires needed to know if the inventory turnover or the number of merchandise they had for sale in the past two years was adequate or inadequate. They also needed to know the average days it took to sell each merchandise. They obtained this information by using the methods below.

Table 19-10
High Roads Tires Inc.
Inventory Turnover

	1996	1997
Sales	$4,100,000	$4,800,000
Inventories:		
January 1	$1,200,000	$1,400,000
December 31	$800,790	$902,200
Average (beg + ending /2)	$1,000,395	$1,151,100

(a) Inventory Turnover = $\dfrac{sales}{Average\ Inventory\ for\ the\ Period}$

1996 $= \dfrac{\$4,100,000}{\$1,000,395}$ $= \dfrac{\$4,100,000}{\$1,000,395}$ = 4.1 times

1997 $= \dfrac{\$4,800,000}{\$1,151,100}$ $= \dfrac{\$4,800,000}{\$1,151,100}$ = 4.2 times

(b) Average number of days' sales in inventory
$= \dfrac{number\ of\ days\ in\ a\ period}{Inventory\ turnover}$

1996 $= \dfrac{365\ days}{4.1}$ = 89 days

1997 $= \dfrac{365\ days}{4.2}$ = 87 days

Interpretation of the results.

1. High Roads Tires Inc. increased its inventory turnover from 4.1 in 1996 to 4.2 times in 1997.
2. The little increase in the inventory turnover in 1997 had the effect of reducing the average number of days to sell the inventory from 89 days in 1996 to 87 days in 1997.

Implications of the results.

1. In 1996 and 1997, High Roads Tires Inc. had relatively low inventory turnover compared to the industry average. Therefore, too much money was tied down as working capital-inventory rather than being used to earn a higher return.
2. The company should increase promotional efforts in order to accelerate the rate at which the tires are sold.
3. The number of days sales in inventory is relatively high compared to the industry.
4. High Roads Tires Inc. should reduce the number of days to sell the tires by using more effective marketing strategies such as better tires, better promotion, better pricing, and better distribution.

Calculation steps.

1. Determine the sales.
2. Determine the beginning and ending inventories.
3. Add the beginning and the ending inventory, and divide by two to find the average inventory.
4. Determine the inventory turnover by dividing the net sales by the average inventory.
5. Determine the number of days' sale in inventory by dividing 365 days by the inventory turnover.

Stock Turnover Rate

What is a stock turnover rate?

It is a technique used to determine the number of times during a specific period, usually one year, that the average inventory on hand is sold.

Why does a marketer need to know the stock turnover rate?

1. To maintain an adequate inventory at all times.
2. In order not to lose sales.
3. To determine which products sell better.

How does a marketer use a stock turnover rate?

Air Power Tech. Inc. is a producer of aircraft and aviation equipment and supplies located in Happy Home, TN. At the end of 1999, Air Power Tech had a net sales of $865,900 of aircraft engines. According to the sales records, the company began the year with an aircraft engine inventory of $76,780, and ended with $35,980. According to the purchase records, Air Power Tech began the year with an air craft engine inventory of $31,987 and ended with $41,870. The total cost of the goods sold in 1999 was $345,786. The company wanted to know how many times it sold the average engine inventory based on the sales price and based on the purchase cost, and so it did the following.

Table 19-11
Air Power Tech Inc.
Stock Turnover Rate

__Sales method__ Net sales (in $) = $865,900
       Average Inventory (in sales $)/   ($76,780+$35,980)/2
       (beg + ending/2)
        = $865,900 = 15.4 times
          56,380

__Cost method__ Cost of goods sold = $345,786
       Average inventory (at cost)/   ($31,987+$41,870)/2
       (beg + ending/2)

        = 345,786 = 9.4 times
          36,929

Interpretation of the results.

1. Based on the selling price, the company turned over the inventory 15.4 times during the year.
2. Based on the purchase price or cost, the company turned over the inventory 9.4 times during the year.

Implication of the results.

1. The rate of the stock turnover should use the sales method because it is faster.

Calculation steps.

Sales Method:
1. Determine the net sales in dollars.
2. Determine the average inventory sold (in dollars) by adding the beginning inventory to the ending inventory, and dividing by two.
3. Divide step #1 by step #2.

Cost Method:
1. Determine the total cost of goods sold.
2. Determine the average inventory purchased by adding the beginning inventory to the ending inventory and dividing by two.
3. Divide step #1 by step #2.

Reductions in Inventory Value

What is a reduction in inventory value?

It is the amount by which the book value of the inventory should be reduced in order to give a more accurate worth or value of the inventory.

Why does a marketer need to know the reductions in inventory value?

1. It enables the marketer to determine the correct value or worth of the remaining inventory by taking into consideration the various discounts and markdowns used during the period.

How does a marketer find the reductions in inventory value?

Lovem Flowers and Baskets Inc. sells fruit baskets, and flowers for all occasions. Mrs. Flowers makes the fruit baskets with both season and non-season fruits. The baskets are beautifully decorated and are often used as containers for other items after the fruits are eaten. Mrs. Flowers also created flowers for different occasions including church services, graduation ceremonies, weddings, birthdays and other occasions.

Due to the intensive competition in the flower market in the city of Harmony, Lovem Flowers and Baskets used low price as a major strategy. Lovem Flowers took low prices into consideration whenever it purchased the inventory. In May 1998, Lovem Flowers and Baskets had an inventory available for sale of $8,400. It made sales of $6,550, with $500 in markdowns, and $500 in discounts. At the end of the month Lovem Flowers needed to know the ending book value of the inventory, and it did the following;

Table 19-12
Lovem Flowers and Baskets Inc.
Reduction In Inventory Value

Inventory available for sale at retail		$8,400
Less reductions:		
Sales	$6,550	
Markdowns	$500	
Discounts	$500	
Total reductions	$7,550	
Ending book value of inventory at retail		$850

Interpretation of the results.

1. The value of the inventory remaining at the end of May 1998 was $850.

Implications of the results.

1. In order to maximize profit, Lovem Flowers should consider pricing the baskets higher. This will reduce the impact of the discounts or markdowns.
2. Lovem Flowers may consider reducing or eliminating the discounts or markdowns during some periods.

Calculation steps

1. Determine the inventory available for sale.
2. Subtract the sales, markdowns, and discounts from the inventory available for sales.

CHAPTER 20

SALES

Size of Sales Force Model

What is the size of sales force model?

It is a systematic approach that is used to determine the size of the sales force that a firm needs by considering the number of customers or prospects and their requirements.

Why does a marketer need to know the size of sales force model?

1. It enables marketers to determine the number of salespeople that will be needed.
2. It enables marketers that employ sales force to estimate the salaries and travel expenses necessary to support them.

How does a marketer determine the size of the sales force?

Derrick's Alarm Systems Inc. was started in 1994 by Mr. Derrick Chidomere, a computer-engineering graduate that founded a way to outfit homes and businesses with security systems that are installed and manned with orbital satellites. There is no visible structure, rather, the building's position, the doors, the windows, and the DNA of the occupants are placed in a computer system that is fed to the satellites. The residents used remote control to communicate with the satellite before the doors and windows are locked or unlocked. These functions would not occur without a match of DNA.

As the demand for Derrick's Alarm Systems increased, the need arose to employ additional salespeople to call on customers, make sales, and offer services. For a maximum efficiency, the company decided to maintain three types of sales force; residential, commercial, and industrial. They estimated to have 1,000; 750; and 845 residential, commercial, and industrial accounts respectively in

2001. Each residential account required 2 calls per year, each commercial account required 4 calls per year, and each industrial account required 6 calls per year. The company planned that each residential salesperson should make at least 100 calls per year, each commercial salesperson should make at least 150 calls per year, while each industrial salesperson should make up to 195 calls per year. Derrick needed to know how many salespersons to hire in each category and did the following.

Table 20-1
Derrick's Alarm System
Size of Salesforce

Size of sales force =

# of accounts in target market x required # of calls per year per account
number of calls each salesperson can make.

A. *Size of residential sales force.*

$$\frac{1000 \times 2}{100} = 20 \text{ salespersons}$$

B. *Size of commercial sales force.*

$$\frac{750 \times 4}{150} = 20 \text{ salespersons}$$

C. *Size of industrial sales force.*

$$\frac{845 \times 6}{195} = 26 \text{ salespersons}$$

Interpretation of the results.

1. Derrick's Alarm Systems should hire 20 salespersons for the residential market, 20 salespersons for the commercial market, and 26 salespersons for the industrial market.
2. Fewer number of calls were used to reach the customers in the residential area.

Implications of the results.

1. The company should need more funds to maintain an adequate industrial sales force.
2. Residential is the most cost efficient. Lower number of calls and salespersons were used.

Calculation steps.

1. To find the size of the sales force, multiply the estimated accounts by the required number of calls per account, and divide by the total number of accounts required in a year.

Required Level of Sales (RLS)

What is the required level of sales?

It is a technique used to determine the amount of sales needed to achieve a minimum desired level of each dollar contribution to indirect cost and profit. It uses the VCM and the PVCM as tools to find out the margins and the percentages that the variable cost leaves in total sales to cover any indirect costs and make profit.

Why does a marketer need to know the required level of sales?

1. It guides the marketer to determine if a benchmark or an average level of sales could be achieved at a given cost.

2. It helps the marketer to determine the level of sales required to achieve a minimum acceptable target contribution for a budget.

How does a marketer find the required level of sales?

Rolly Upholstery Inc. wholesales toilet seat covers to small general stores in Indiana. It had a sales of $250,000 in 2000. However, as the competition increased in 2002, the company considered lowering the selling price from $4.80 to $4.20 per unit. It estimated a variable manufacturing cost of $2.40 per seat cover, and a marketing cost of 10% of the sales price. The direct wholesale and marketing costs were $55,000 in 2000. The industry sales forecast for toilet seat covers in the state for 2002 was $1,450,190. Rolly Upholstery needed to find out the required level of sales in dollar and in units needed to achieve a minimum level of dollar contribution or $100,000 and to cover indirect cost and profit at the selling price of $4.20. The company took the following steps.

Required dollar sales =
   ($)

Target total contribution + total direct or traceable fixed cost
──
PVCM

Required unit sales =
   (#)

Target total contribution + total direct or traceable fixed cost
──
PVCM per unit

Table 20-2
Rolly Upholstery
Required Dollar and Units Sales

PVCM for old price

1st   Old Selling Price   = \$4.80
    Variable cost:
       Mfg.   = \$2.40
       Mkt.   =   .48 \$2.88
    VCM   \$1.92

$$\text{PVCM} = \frac{1.92}{\$4.80} \times 100 = 40\%$$

Contribution to Fixed Cost

3rd   \$250,000 Annual Sales
    x   .40 PVCM
    \$100,000 Total VCM
    - \$55,000 Last Year's DFC
    \$45,000 Cont. to IFC

PVCM for new price

2nd New Selling Price = \$4.20
    Variable cost:
       Mfg.   = \$2.40
       Mkt.   =   .42 \$2.82
    VCM   \$1.38

PVCM   = $\frac{1.38}{\$4.20}$ x 100 = 33%

Required level of sales

4th Required Level of Sales =
$$\frac{\$55,000 + \$45,000}{\text{PVCM (New Selling Price-VC)}}$$
New Selling Price

$$\text{RLS} = \frac{\$100,000}{.33} = \$303,030$$

$$\text{RLS} = \frac{\$303,030}{\$4.20} = 72,150 \text{ units}$$

(b) Required market share

$$\text{Required Market Share} = \frac{\text{Required level of sales}}{\text{Industry sales forecast}}$$

$$\frac{\$303,030}{\$1,450,190} = .2089 \text{ or } 20.89\% \text{ or } 21\%$$

Interpretation of the results.

1. The amount left to cover the cost and profit as well as margin and percentage decreased at the new price level from a VCM of $1.92 to $1.38, and PVCM of 40% to 33%.
2. At the new selling price of $4.20, Rolly Upholstery should sell 72,150 seat covers in order to achieve 33% of sales level of dollar contribution to indirect cost and profit.
3. At the selling price of $4.20, Rolly Upholstery should make $303,030 in sales in order to make $100,000 for indirect cost and profit.
4. Rolly Upholstery should have 21% of the toilet seat cover buyers' market in the state of Indiana in order to achieve a minimum level of contribution when the selling price is reduced to $4.20.
5. The PVCM of 40% left $100,000 and the PVCM of 33% at the new price and sales levels also left $100,000 to cover indirect cost and profit.

Implications of the results.

1. The percentage variable contribution margin (PVCM) or the amount of profit contributed by each seat cover is less at a lower price.
2. Rolly Upholstery can increase its profit by increasing the PVCM.
3. The PVCM increases as the variable cost decreases. The less the variable cost the more it leaves for or contributes to profit. (Sales-VC =VCM)

Calculation steps.

1. To find the percentage variable contribution margin (PVCM), subtract variable costs from the selling price to get the variable contribution margin (VCM), divide the VCM by the selling price, and multiply by 100.

2. To find the contribution to indirect fixed cost, multiply the annual sales by the old percentage variable cost margin, and subtract last year's direct fixed cost.

Example 2

Bettie's Live Baits Inc. makes and distributes fishing equipment. The company wanted to run a one-month coupon promotion in 2003 to attract new market for the flying fish tackles. However,

Photo 45: Kim's Grocery

the manager did not know the required sales volume to offset the lower contribution margin in profit due to price reduction, nor did she know how much the cost of sales will increase as a result of the promotion. Bettie's Live Baits used the information below to find the required level of sales in dollars and in units.

Pricing Information:

Regular Price Per dozen = $2.50
Variable product costs Per dozen = $1.25
Estimated sales vol. (units) for June (without coupons) =1m dozens
Number of coupons distributed before June =10 million
Consumer savings from each coupon =$ .20
Redemption costs per coupon =$ .05
Redemption rate (likely new customers) =10%
Redemption by regular customers =20%

Required Level of Sales =
        (dollar)

Target total contribution + total direct or traceable fixed cost
                    PVCM

Required Level of Sales
(units)

= Target total contribution + total direct or traceable fixed cost
                    PVCM per unit

Table 20-3
Bettie's Live Baits
Required Level of Sales

Old PVCM per unit   = $\dfrac{\$2.50 - \$1.25}{2.50}$ = .50

VCM $2,500,000-$1,250,000 = $1,250,000 or $1.25 per unit

New PVCM per unit = $\dfrac{(\$2.50 - .20) - (\$1.25 + .05)}{2.30}$ =.435

Required Level of sales (RLS)
(dollar)

= $\dfrac{\$1,250,000 + \$100,000}{.435}$ = $3,103,448

Required Level of sales (RLS) = $\dfrac{\$3,103,448}{\$2.30}$ 1,349,325 units
(unit)

Expected Total Contribution from Coupons

1. 2 million coupons redeemed by regular customers (10m x 20%)
2. 1 million coupons redeemed by new customers (10m x 10%)
3. $3,000,000 Total Contribution (3m x ($2.50-($1.25 + .20c + .05c)
4. $200,000 reduction for new customers (1m x .20c)
5. $400,000 reduction for regular customers (2m x .20c)
   $600,000 Displaced sales

Interpretation of the results.

1. Fifty percent of the regular price of $2.50 or $1.25 is contributed to profit.
2. At the estimated sales of 1 million dozens of baits, the variable contribution margin (VCM) is $1,250,000 ($2,500,000-$1,250,000) or $1.25 per unit.
3. At the discounted price, approximately forty-five percent of the $2.50 contributed to profit.
4. The company had a displaced sales of $600,000 ($200,000 from new customers, and $400,000 from regular customers).

Implications of the results.

1. Superior Live Bait should make a sales of $3,103,448 in order to offset the lower contribution margin and increased cost that resulted from the promotion.
2. Superior Live Bait should sell 1,349,225 dozens of flying fish tackles to offset the lower contribution margin and increased cost that resulted from the promotion.
3. Superior Live Bait will forgo $600,000, in order to make the required sales.

Calculation steps.

1. To find the old percentage variable contribution margin (PVCM) per dozen, subtract the variable product cost from the regular price, and divide by the regular price.
2. To find the variable contribution margin (VCM) multiply the regular price and the variable cost by 1 million or the estimated sales volume (units) for June (without coupons). Subtract the total of the variable cost from the total of the regular price.
3. To find the new percentage variable contribution margin (PVCM) per unit, (a) subtract the consumer savings from each coupon from the regular price of the coupon, (b) subtract the redemption cost per unit from the variable product cost, and (c) subtract *b* from *a,* and divide by *a.*
4. To find the required level of sales in dollar, divide the total VCM $1,250,000 plus the total for distributing the coupons by the PVCM .435.
5. To find the required sales in units, divide the required level of sales $2,873,563 by the new selling price of $2.30.
6. To find the total contribution from the coupons, multiply the number of redeemed coupons (10m x 202%) by the difference between the regular price and the variable product cost, consumer saving per coupon, and the redemption cost per coupon (3m x (2.50-(1.25 + .20 + .05)).
7. To find the total displaced sales, add the expected redemption by new customers (1m x .20) to the expected redemption by regular customers (2m x .20).

Example 3

Pleasure Bookstore Inc. was considering running a two months coupon promotion in November and December 1979 to attract owners of old Bible editions to trade them in for new versions. The retail margin for each new bible was 15%, and it sold at $15 per Bible. The variable cost per Bible was $5. Pleasure Bookstore expected to sell 1,000,000 units in one month and needed to know how much to increase the sales volume to offset the lower contribution margin and increased cost resulting from the promotion. With the following information, Pleasure Bookstore found the answer as shown on Table 20-3b

Photo 46: BORDERS

Pricing Information:

5m coupons to be distributed for $100,000
$.50 consumer savings from each coupon.
$.10 redemption cost per unit
15% redemption rate
25% of redemption are made by regular customers.

$$\text{Required Sales} = \frac{\text{Current Total contribution} + \text{Current Direct costs} + \text{Increase in Direct costs}}{\text{New \% of PVCM}}$$

Table 20-3b
Pleasure Bookstore Inc.
Required Level of Sales

Old PVCM per unit $= \dfrac{\$12.75 - \$5}{\$12.75} = .61$

VCM $\$12,750,000-\$5,000,000 = \$7,750,000$ or $\$7.75$ per unit

New PVCM per unit $= \dfrac{(\$12.75 - .50) - (\$5 + .10)}{\$12.25} = \dfrac{7.15}{12.25} = .58$

RLS ($) $= \dfrac{7,750,000 + 100,000}{.58} = \$13,534,483$

RLS (Units) $= \dfrac{\$13,534,483}{\$12.75} = 1,061,528$

Interpretation of the results.

1. The company has a lower contribution of $784,483 (from $12,750,000 to $13,534,483).
2. The company should sell an additional 61,528 units in order to offset the lower contribution.

Implication of the results.

1. Pleasure Bookstore should only embark on the promotion if they are sure to increase the sales in dollars and in units as shown above.

Calculation steps.

1. To find the regular price, multiply $15 by 15% ($2.25), and subtract from $15.
2. To find the old percentage variable contribution margin (PVCM) per unit, subtract the variable product cost per bible

($5) from the regular price ($12.75), and divide by the regular price.

3. To find the total variable contribution margin (VCM); (a) multiply the regular price ($12.75) by the expected number of sales per month (1m), (b) multiply the variable cost ($5) by the expected number of sales per month. Subtract *a* from *b*.

4. To find the new percentage variable cost margin (PVCM) per unit, (a) subtract the consumer savings from each coupon from the regular price, (b) subtract the redemption cost per unit from the variable product cost, (c) subtract *b* from *a*, and divide by *a*.

5. To find the required level of sales in dollar, add the total VCM to the distribution cost, and divide by the new PVCM (.58).

6. To find the required sales in units, add expected sales $13,534,483 to the new selling price ($12.25).

Sales Efficiency Ratio (%)

What is the sales efficiency ratio?

It is a technique that compares the sales output with the cost incurred to achieve such a sales level.

Why does a marketer need to know the sales efficiency ratio?

1. It shows the marketer how productive he/she was in making a given sales level.
2. It shows the marketer how wasteful or resourceful he/she was in achieving a target sales level.
3. It compares the net sales with the gross sales.

How does a marketer determine the sales efficiency ratio?

Yours Truly Exotics Cars Inc. buys American cars that were made prior to 1960, remodels them, repaints them with aesthetically pleasant designs and colors, outfits them with different hydraulic gadgets that control them to make different movements, and immaculately cleans the inside. These cars were targeted mostly to people that cherished high quality antiques and glamorous lifestyles. Yours Truly made a gross sales of $3.24m in 1998, and after deducting the expenses and taxes, the net sales was $2.12m. However, Yours Truly needed to know how costly it was to make that net sales, and it did the following.

Table 20-4
Yours Truly Exotics Cars Inc.
Sales Efficiency Ratio

$$Sales\ efficiency\ ratio = \frac{Net\ sales}{Gross\ Sales} = \frac{\$2,120,000}{\$3,240,000} = 65\%$$

Interpretation of the results.

1. At an industry efficiency level of 100, Yours Truly used 35% to pay sales expenses and taxes, and the remaining 65% was the net sales.

Implication of the results.

1. The cost of selling which is 35c for every dollar sales is high, and could be reduced.

Calculation steps.

1. To find the sales efficiency ratio, divide the net sales by the gross sales.

Sales Per Square Foot

What is sales per square foot?

It is a technique that marketers use to determine the ratio of products sold to the amount of selling space used for the sales.

Why does a marketer need to know the sales per square foot?

1. It measures the space productivity, or how productive the selling space is.
2. It measures how much a store yields by looking at how much sales are made at each area of a store.

Photo 47: World Market

How does a marketer determine the sales per square foot?

Earthly Foods Inc. started in Washington, DC. in the late 1970's, due to the high demand by Americans for foods to stay healthy and for good shape. It sold fresh herbs, fresh fruits,

and packaged condiments from different parts of the world. The store was segmented into seven sections as follows; 30,000sqft to display condiments from Europe, 35,000sqft for condiments from Asia, 21,000sqft for condiments from Africa, 24,000sqft for condiments from South America, 27,000sqft for condiments from Australia, and 60,000sqft for condiments from North America. The entrance and the aisles covering about 9,000sqft were used to display fresh fruits, vegetables, and herbs from all over the world.

By 2001, Earthly Foods had fifteen chains stores in three states, with a total sales of $9.7m. The Washington, DC's. store had a total sales of $3.1m that was contributed as follows: Europe $300,000, Asia $1.1m, Africa $300,000, South America $300,000, Australia $400,000, and North America $500,000. Lastly, $200,000 sales came from the entrance and the aisles displays. It needed to know how productive the continental sections were in terms of the amount of sales that came from each space. It did the following:

Table 20-5
Earthly Foods Inc.
Sales Per Square Foot

Sales per square foot = $\dfrac{\text{sales}}{\text{Square feet of selling space}}$.

1. Sales per square foot for condiments from Europe.

$300,000/30,000sqft. = $10

2. Sales per square foot for condiments from Asia

$1,100,000/35,000sqft. = $31.42

3. Sales per square foot for condiments from Africa

$300,000/21,000sqft. = $14.29

4. Sales per square foot for condiments from South America

$300,000/24,000sqft. = $12.50

5. Sales per square foot for condiments from Australia

$400,000/27,000sqft = $14.80

6. Sales per square foot for condiments from North America

$500,000/60,000sq.ft. = $8.33

7. Sales per square foot for fresh fruits, vegetables and herbs .

$200,000/9,000sqft. = $22.22

Interpretation of the results.

1. Sales per square foot was the highest for condiments from Asia, followed by the fresh goods, and condiments from Australia, Africa, South America, Europe, and North America.

Photo 48: 5 STAR International Market

Implication of the results.

1. Earthly Foods should make better use of the spaces in particularly the North American and European sections.

Calculation steps.

1. Divide the total sales from each section of the store by the square footage of space available in the section.

<u>Gross-Margin Return Per Square Foot</u>

What is a gross-margin return per square foot?

It is a technique to determine how much gross profit is generated by each square foot of a store.

Why does a marketer need to know the gross-margin return per square foot?

1. To determine the relationship between the gross margin and the amount of selling space used.

How does a marketer find the gross-margin return per square foot?

Lane Cargoes Inc. is a freight company that provides air shipment services to US firms that sell to clients overseas. Located in Tornado Lane, Oklahoma, the company operates ten cargo aircrafts that fly daily all night, transporting machinery, computers, and educational software to distributors in the Middle east and Europe. In 2001 Lane Cargoes leased 5 big warehouses with an average size of 1,781,000square feet, at $120,000,000 per warehouse. The total annual income was $963m at $108.14 sales per square foot ($963m/8,905,000sqft). A total of $250m was spent on renovating the warehouses. At the end of the year, the company wanted to know how much each square foot in the warehouses contributed to the gross margin, and it did the following.

Table 20-6
Lanes Cargoes Inc.
Return Per Square Foot

Gross-margin return per square foot =

Gross margin % x sales per square foot/Sales
$$= \frac{\$713,000,000}{\$963,000,000} \times \$108.14 = \$80$$

Interpretation of the results.

1. Lane Cargoes made a gross profit margin return of $80 per square foot in the warehouses.

Implications of the results.

1. Lane Cargoes had a gross profit margin of 75 percent. This is high.
2. The benefit of a high gross profit margin is realized if the direct and indirect cost are kept low.

Calculation step.

1. To find the gross-margin return per square foot, multiply the sales per square foot by the gross profit margin percentage.

GLOSSARY

Accounts Receivable Turnover A measure of the average times it takes for a business to receive the money for the sales it made on credit.

Additional Inventory Cost A process used to find out the cost of maintaining a higher inventory level needed to meet the increase in demand.

Additional Inventory Investment A technique used to determine the amount of money that a firm spends to buy adequate level of inventory each week for a period of time.

Additional Retail Markdown Percentage The total dollar additional markdown as a percentage of net sales and profit.

Advertising Frequency The average number of times a person in the target audience or group is exposed to the same advertisement message in a four-week period.

Advertising Gross Impression The total number or amount of advertisement that will have a marked effect on the mind and emotion of the watchers, and arouse their interest.

Advertising Rating Point The reach of an advertisement and the frequency of its reach.

Advertising Reach The percentage of a target audience that a business reaches with its advertisement message at least once every four weeks.

Attitude Toward Behavior A technique that determines how a person feels toward an action or behavior of an object rather than a person's feeling toward the object itself.

Attitude Toward A Product A measure of how a customer or a person feels toward the use of a product or a service line and the specific brands.

Attribute Rating A technique that determines which features or attributes of a product are the most important to the customers.

Analysis of Variance A measure of the difference between the means or average of two or more groups of activities.

Average Collection Period The average length of time a business could wait after making a credit sale before it receives the payment without having a cash shortage.

Average Inventory Investment The amount of money that a firm spends to buy an adequate level of inventory each week for a period of time.

Brand Development Index An index or number that shows the gaps in the selective demand or demand for similar brands in different geographic market territories.

Brand Rating An evaluation of the attributes or features of products brands in order to classify them based on similarities in attributes.

Break-even Analysis A technique that is used to find out how many units a business can sell at a given price in order to cover both its variable and fixed costs. It is the point where total revenue equals total cost.

Buying Power Index The potential sales opportunity of a trading area based on three factors: the effective buying index, the retail sales, and the area's population.

Cash Budget A financial marketing tool that presents the expected cash receipt from sales, and the disbursement in a period of time.

Cash Discount The reduction in price of an item to a buyer for paying for the product or service in time.

Cash-flow Per Share A measure of the discretionary funds over and above the business expenses that are available for the business to use as it wants.

Category Development Index An index or figure that shows the gap that exists in the demand for one product category in different geographic market territories.

Closing Inventory at Cost A technique used to determine the value of the goods unsold at the end of a period by basing their value on their cost price.

Cluster Analysis A technique used to divide or classify people or objects into homogeneous or similar groups based on selected variables.

Conjoint Analysis A technique used to determine the relative importance the consumers attach to the service a company offers, and the level of utilities they get from it.

Correlation Analysis A measure of the strength of association or relationship between two variables.

Cost Complement A financial marketing measure that shows how much of the retail price covers the merchandise cost.

Cost of Credit Sales A quantitative tool used to determine the cost of offering credit to customers.

Cost of Forecast Error The amount of money a company will lose from making a wrong sales forecast.

Cost of Goods Sold Ratio A financial tool that shows the portion of the net sales that covers the money used to make or buy the goods sold.

Cost Per Thousand (CPM) How much it costs for an advertisement to reach one thousand people.

Cost-plus Pricing A process that adds the fixed and variable costs of providing services to a desired profit margin to determine a selling price.

Cost-Volume Profit Analysis A measure of how the cost and the profit of a product or service will change as the volume of sales changes.

Credit Impact on Profitability The effect of credit or delayed payment on the amount of profit a business would make.

Cross Elasticity Budgeting A technique used to forecast or project sales in units or in dollars for one product or service by basing it on the demand estimate for a related major product or service.

Current Ratio The amount of cash or near cash assets that a business has to be able to pay short-term bills as they due.

Debt-to-Assets Ratio The measure of the extent to which a marketer operates the activities with borrowed money.

Debt-to-Equity A comparison of the amount of operation funds that is borrowed to the amount that is provided by the stockholders or owners.

Direct Product Productivity A method of planning variable markup that finds the profitability of a category or unit of merchandise by finding the adjusted per -unit gross margin and assigning direct product costs.

Discriminant Analysis A classification of customers or objects into two or more categories in order to find out the variables responsible for success or failure in the different categories.

Distribution Cost Analysis A process used to determine the amount of money spent to generate a given level of sale.

Dividend Yield on Common Stock A pro-rated distribution of money or additional shares to common shareholders.

Dividend Yield on Preferred Stock The percentage of the profit paid out to preferred stockholders.

Earning Per Share The amount of the earnings available to the owner of each share of the common or preferred stock in the business.

Factor Analysis An interdependent technique that reduces a large number of variables into a manageable level by examining the relationship among the sets of variables and representing them by a few underlying factors.

Fixed Assets Turnover A measure of sales productivity of assets or how efficient a business utilizes its plants and equipment in selling.

Fixed-Charge Coverage A measure of the ability of a business to meet all of its fixed-charge obligations.

Fixed-Cost Per Unit The cost that remains the same regardless of the volume, for example, salaries and electricity bills.

Functional Process Development A step-by-step method that incorporates customer needs into the design of new products and/or in the augmentation of existing products.

Gross Margin on Inventory Investment A measure of the profit return on the amount invested to buy an inventory.

Gross Margin on Return Per Square Foot The gross profit margin percentage that results attribute to sales in each square foot of the selling space.

Gross Margin Ratio The proportion of the net sale that is allocated to operating expenses and net profit.

Gross Profit Margin The margin or difference between the sales price and the cost of a product or service before deducting other operating expenses such as salary, rent, and utility.

Income Statement (Profit and Loss Statement) A financial tool used to determine how much income is available for marketing and other operations.

Index of Retail Saturation A measure of how many stores located in an area sell similar goods and services to satisfy the population's needs.

Initial Markup Percentage The markup placed on a merchandise as soon as the store receives it.

Inventory Carrying Cost The amount of money a business spends to keep enough inventory to meet the customers' demand.

Inventory Cost The cost that a marketer incurs to buy and keep adequate inventory.

Inventory Costing (LIFO) A process that is used to determine the cost of the ending inventory by assuming that the most recent merchandise is sold before the oldest merchandise.

Inventory Costing (FIFO) A process that is used to determine the cost of the ending inventory by assuming that the oldest merchandise is sold before recently purchased merchandise.

Inventory Reorder Point The level of inventory at which new orders must be placed.

Inventory Shortage or Overage The amount or number by which the items for sale are either more or less than the number needed for sale.

Inventory-to-Net Working Capital Ratio A measure of the extent to which a company's working capital or operation funds are tied up in the inventory.

Inventory Turnover A measure of the rate or how many times the whole inventory is sold.

Investment Turnover Ratio The dollar sales generated by each dollar invested in the business.

Lifetime Value of a Customer The net worth of acquiring a new customer based on the initial purchases and an estimate of future purchases by the customer.

Maintained Markup Percentage A markup on the actual or average selling price of a merchandise less the cost of the merchandise.

Market Potential - Consumer Market The number of possible users of a consumer product or service, and their maximum rate of purchase.

Market Potential - Industrial Market The number of possible users of an industrial product or service, and their maximum rate of purchase.

Marketing Budget - Direct Approach A technique used to estimate the productivity of proposed price and marketing expenditure levels in generating a company's sales by specifying the specific estimate of the sales.

Marketing Budget - Indirect Approach A technique used to estimate the productivity of a proposed price and marketing expenditure level in generating a company's sales by using a benchmark rather than a specific estimate of sales.

Markup at Retail or Cost A pricing method that sets the price of a product or service by basing it on the going selling price of a merchandise or at its cost.

Maximum Advertising Cost The most money a firm will spend on advertising in order to achieve an operating profit goal.

Merchandise Budget A process that determines the correct number of products or services a reseller should have available at a given period to meet customers' demand.

Merchandise Planning - Basic Stock Method A process used by a retailer to determine the base(lowest) level of inventory investment or the unit of merchandise to carry regardless of the predicted sales volume for every month in the year.

Merchandise Planning - Percentage Variation Method A technique that determines the amount of inventory to carry to face fluctuations in sales without having a set or given level of inventory at all times.

Merchandise Planning - Stock-to-Sales method A technique used to determine how much inventory is needed at the beginning of each month to support that month's estimated sales.

Merchandise Planning -Weekly Supply Method A technique for planning inventory on a weekly basis for retailers whose sales do not fluctuate substantially, by setting it at a predetermined number of supplies.

Multidimensional Scaling A class of techniques for representing perceptions and preferences of buyers in spaces by using visual displays.

Multiple Regression A technique that determines if there is any relationship or association between two or more independent variables or occurrences and an interval-scaled dependent variable.

Net Profit Margin The portion of each sales dollar that is left as profit after costs, taxes and interests are deducted.

Net Return on Sales The portion of each sales dollar that is left as profit after costs, taxes and interests are deducted.

Non-traceable Variable Contribution Margin The amount each unit of product or service sold contributes to cover those costs of operating the company that are non-traceable to particular units or jobs such as company security and yard maintenance.

Off-Retail Markdown Percentage A technique to determine how much the total dollar taken off or discounted from the retail price of an item or a merchandise category amounts in percentage to the original price.

Operating Expense Ratio The percentage of each sales dollar that is used to pay for marketing operations.

Opportunity Cost   The foregone revenue for not using an optimal marketing mix or a combination of marketing mix that maximizes the profit.

Optimal Marketing Mix   A combination of marketing mix that maximizes the profit.

Part-worth Utility   A process that estimates the utility or values of the attributes of a product or service.

Percentage Variable Contribution Margin (PVCM)   A measure of the percentage of each sales dollar that is available to cover fixed cost, and make profit.

Price-Earning Ratio   A comparison of a company's market price per share and the earning per share.

Price Elasticity   A measure of how sensitive buyers are to price changes in terms of the quantities they purchase.

Product Survival Rate   The rate at which products survive the wear and tear of customers' usage or obsolescence.

Profit Impact of Customer Satisfaction   The relationship between an increase in the type and amount of customers service and the change in profit.

Profit Impact of Quantity Discount   An indication of how profit is affected by a reduction in the cost of items based on the size of the order.

Profitability of Indirect Channel   A process that estimates the sales productivity of a proposed new price or expenditure by using a sales benchmark.

Queuing Model(Waiting Line Model)   A model that determines the amount of time and the number of customers appropriate to wait in the customer lines to be served at different times of the day.

Quick Ratio   A measure of a business' ability to pay short-term bills in times of real crises without relying on the sales of inventory.

Recency/Frequency and Monetary Value Segmentation1   It is a technique used to: (1) segment the customers in terms of how current they are in purchases, (2) find the percentage of solicitations that results in an order, (3) find the number of orders in some recent period of time, and (4) find the average order amount within some recent period of time.

Recency/Frequency and Monetary Value Segmentation2 It is a technique that: (1) makes a marketing strategy more efficient by increasing the rate of the customer's response to the strategy, and (2) segments the total market on recency, frequency and monetary value.

Reduction in Inventory Value The amount by which the book value of the inventory should be reduced in order to give a more accurate worth or value of the inventory.

Relative Market Potential - Single Index Approach The percentage of the market potential in the different parts of the market that a firm sells its products or services.

Replacement Potential An estimate of the quantity of a brand of a product to produce in a period of time by studying customers' historical rate of scrapping or getting rid of the brand.

Required Increase in Customer Satisfaction A state where the buying and using of the product or service meet or exceed users expectations.

Required Level of Sales A technique used to determine the amount of sales needed to achieve a minimum level of each dollar contribution to indirect cost and profit.

Required Market Share (RMS) The number of customers that a firm requires to reach a target contribution margin or to make enough money from individual product or service to cover the indirect and fixed costs, and make profit.

Required Total Dollar Sales The amount of sales in dollars that is necessary to achieve the minimum dollar contribution to cover cost and make profit.

Required Total Unit Sales The amount of sales in units that is required in the budget to achieve the minimum dollar contribution to cover cost and make profit.

Retail Based Pricing A technique that determines the expected demand for a merchandise at various price levels.

Retail Compatibility A measure that determines how much sales a store can generate by locating close to another store that sells products or services used by the same target market or products and services that complement the store's.

Retail Gravitation A gravity model that is used to measure the extent to which buyers are drawn to retail stores that are closer and more attractive than competitors'.

Retail Space Productivity Model A model that determines the amount of money resulting from sales in each retail space.

Return on Investment Percentage The percentage of the dollar profit generated by each dollar invested in the business.

Return on Investment Model A model that finds out the percentage of profit that a business makes for the owners by using information from the balance sheet and income statement.

Return on Total Assets A measure of how productive a company's assets are.

Sales Cost/Ratio Analysis A process used to determine the cost difference between using your own sales force and using a sales agency to sell your products or services.

Sales Efficiency Ratio A measure that compares the sales output with the cost incurred to achieve such a sales level.

Sales Forecasting - Exponential Smoothing A forecasting technique that uses a weighted average of past time series of sales values to forecast future sales.

Sales Forecasting - Moving Average A forecasting technique that uses the average sales in a specific period in the past to predict the sales for a future period.

Sales Forecasting - Straight Line A forecasting technique that determines the "best fitting line" or the curve that closely approximates the historical trend, and forecasts sales by projecting the same line or curve into the future.

Sales Per Square Foot A technique that determines the ratio of a product's sales to the amount of selling space used to display the product.

Sales Variance Analysis A technique that measures the effectiveness of the prices of merchandise.

Selling Price on Profit The effect of a change in the selling price of a product on its profitability.

Semi Fixed Cost-effect The cost that does not change automatically with an additional unit, but may change if substantial increase occurs in volume, for example, a new production plant, additional air route, hire a lot of supervisors in a season.

Shopper Attraction Model A model used to calculate the size of the trading area in terms of the expected number of households that will be attracted to the retail site by looking at (1) the distance between the site and its consumers, (2) the distance between the site and its competitors, and (3) the site's image.

Size of Sales force Model A systematic approach to determine the size of the sales force that a firm needs by considering the number of customers or prospects and their requirements.

Size of Trading Area A measure of how many stores located in an area sell similar goods and services to satisfy the population's needs.

Stock Turnover Ratio The number of times during a specific period, usually one year, that the average inventory on hand is sold.

Strategic Profit Model A tool that shows the mathematical relationship among net profit, asset turnover, and financial leverage.

Target Market Profile A form of cost-oriented approach to set the price of a merchandise in order to yield a target rate of return on investment.

Target Return Pricing A form of cost-oriented technique to set the price of a merchandise so as to yield a target rate of return on investment.

Task and Objective Advertising Budget A technique that determines a budget by stating the objectives and tasks needed to achieve the goals.

Territory Performance Measure A measure of the performance of a sales territory by using the rate of return on assets to stockholders and creditors.

Time-interest Earned Ratio A measure of how low a business profits can decline without the business becoming unable to pay annual interest cost.

Total Assets Turnover The overall measure of how effectively a company's assets are used during a period of time.

Total Market Potential The sum of the sales that is possible to come from a given market area.

Total Market Potential - Combined Market A total market potential determined by using the value of shipment or the value of the production output in the market area.

Trade Discount A reduction in the supplier's list price granted to either a wholesaler or retailer who performs functions such as storage, transportation and others that are normally the responsibility of the supplier.

Trend Analysis A technique that develops the forecasts of future sales by analyzing the historical relationship between sales and time.

Variable Contribution Margin (VCM) The sum or percentage remaining from sales after a business deducts all the variable costs such as sales commissions, materials, labor, and packaging.

Weighted Number of Exposures The amount or degree of impact that an advertisement makes on the viewers.

SUBJECT INDEX

A

A Comfort World Inc. 81
A Man and A Pan Inc. 119
A Ride of Elegance Inc.340
A Tough Walk Inc. 371
A World of Pets Inc. 129
Accounting 3
Accounts receivable turnover 75
Adamma Quality Computers Inc. 311
Adamma Reliable Fence Co. Inc. 329
Additional assets turnover 70
Additional inventory cost 358
Additional retail markdown percentage 300
Adults Pleasure Inc. 89
Advanced Home Security Inc. 96
Advanced Vinyl Siding Inc. 121
Advertising frequency 335
Adverting gross impression 337
Advertising rating point 339
Advertising reach 333
Affordable Homes Inc. 314
Air Power Tech. Inc. 378
All Season Farm Supplies Inc. 21
Allied Facsimile Inc. 49
Alternative marketing mix 42
American Koast-to-Koast Inc. 123
American Nail Care & Tan Inc.163
American Toilet Supplies Inc. 131
Amity Termites Kontrol Inc. 125
Analysis of variance (ANOVA) 197
Annual yield per share 103
Asset turnover 142
Attitude 65
    -toward behavior 68

-toward a product 65
Attribute 225
 -rating 248, 277, 282
Audio Technology Systems Inc. 305
Average collection period 77
Average income per job 138
Average inventory investment 360

 B

Basic Stock 186
Beginning inventory 22, 370
Beginning of the month merchandise (BOM) 186, 189
Bettie's Live Baits Inc. 388
Behavioral belief 70
Bill & Sons Foods Inc. 149
Bob's Quality Auto Inc. 360
Body & Soul Inc. 177
Body & Soul Recreational Inc. 246
Brand Development Index (BDI) 160
Brand rating 284
Break-even point 287
Budgeting 10
Bush Discount Funeral Homes Inc. 296
Buying Power Index 162

 C

CTS Clinical Laboratory Inc. 344
Carl's Car Mart Inc. 369
Carolina Standard Bank Inc. 170
Carolyn's Marketing & Fundraiser Inc. 346
Category Means 199
Cash Budget 3
Cash Discount 46
Cash-flow Per Share 83
Category Development Index (CDI) 157

Children's Heaven Inc. 37
City Bar & Grill Inc. 290
Classic Windows Inc. 39
Clayburn Florist Inc. 3
Closing Inventory at Cost 362
Club Jam 'O' Jam Inc. 238
Club Kool 239
Cluster Analysis 205
Cocks Chiropractic Center Inc. 292
Collection period 78
Come & "C" Used Appliances Inc. 75
Consumer behavior 57
Customer Attitude 65
Conjoint Analysis 233
Correlation Analysis 231
   -product moment 231
Cost 21
   -complement 21
   -benefit ratio 35
   -of credit sales 23
   -of forecast error 26
   -of goods sold 28
   -of goods sold ratio 28
   -per thousand (CPM) 29, 31
   -plus pricing 290
   -volume profit analysis 101
Credit impact on profitability 48
Credit sales 46
Cross elasticity budgeting 10
Cruise-For-Fun Inc. 185
Current asset 95, 97
Current liability 95, 97
Current market price per share 128
Current ratio 94
Customer satisfaction 59, 61

D

Davis Eatery Inc. 323
Debt-to-assets ratio 87
Debt-to-equity ratio 89
Derrick's Alarm Systems Inc. 382
Dick's Fruit Basket Inc. 112
Dick's Used Autos Inc. 319
Disbursement 14
Discriminant analysis 238
Distribution cost analysis 34
Dividend pay out ratio 106
Dividend yield on common stock or equity 103
Dividend yield on preferred stock or equity 104
Dollar contribution margin per unit 52
Dollar merchandise planning 145
Don Dill Pottery Inc. 337

E

Earning per share 107
Earning per common share 103
    -preferred share 104
Earthly Foods Inc. 396
Edmond International Airport Inc. 265
Elegance Mall Inc. 197, 201
Elm Street Antiques Inc. 191
Estimated market potential 121
Evaluation component 66, 70
Exclusive marketing 42
Expected cash receipt 14
Expected profit per customer 200
Expected total contribution 272

F

Factor analysis 246

Fantastic Tops Inc. 287
Fixed assets turnover 79
Fixed-charge coverage 85
Fixed-cost per unit 39, 40
Four P's 275
Four Season's Roofing and Siding Inc., 353
Frequency 237
Fresh Choice Juice Inc 253
Fresh For 'U" Inc. 206
Functional fees 54

G

Gents 30
Genuine Wears Inc. 51
Global Computers Inc. 10
Global Foods Inc. 162
Global Sports Inc. 301
Golf-4-You 30
Good Views Inc. 179
Goodlife Christian Bookstore Inc. 83
Greenstown Sheet Metal Inc. 7
Gross margin on inventory investment 112
    -per week 113
    -per month 113
    -per year 113
Gross margin on return per square foot 115, 399
Gross margin ratio 119
Gross profit margin 117
Gross profit per job 111
Gross rating point 340
Gross sales 17
Gunminos Handguns Inc. 107, 133

H

Had-I-Known Inc. 87

Happy Homes Funerals Inc. 109
High Roads Tires Inc. 375
Home-Boy Fashion Inc. 30
Home Land Fashions Inc. 333
Hu-Nose-Tomorrow Inc. 173

I

I Hear "U" Inc. 232
Ideal Rent & Own Inc. 44
Impressions 340
Income statement (Profit and Loss Statement) 6
Income tax expense 17
Index of retail saturation 316
Industry sales forecast 15, 178
Initial markup percentage 296
Internal channel of distribution 40
Inventory carrying cost 366
Inventory cost 364
Inventory costing (LIFO) 368
Inventory costing (FIFO) 368
Inventory Reorder Point 371
Inventory shortage or Overage 373
Inventory-to-net working capital ratio 96
Inventory turnover 374
Investment turnover ratio 121

J

JJ Handy Homes Inc. 364
J&J Blueprints and Supplies Inc. 183
JR Robotics Inc. 127
Jack's Industrial Containers Inc. 373
Jane's All Season Inc. 308
Jim's Hardware Inc. 303
Jimbus Xmas Shoppe Inc. 28
Joe's Fine Shoes Inc. 366

Jokey's Products Inc. 155
Jo-Jo Utensils Inc. 188
Jon Thomas Hardware Flooring Inc. 272

K

Kic-Jim-Kic Karate Inc. 117
King's Groceries Inc. 362
KompuAmerica Inc. 165

L

Lagos Refrigeration Services Inc. 268
Lane Cargoes Inc 399
Lifetime Value of a Customer 272
Little Heaven Retirement Inc. 115
LizTex Check Printing Services Inc. 101
Long-term debt-to-equity ratio 90
Lovem Flowers and Baskets Inc. 380
LuvNest Bridal Inc. 92

M

Maintained markup percentage 298
    -at cost 299
    -at retail 299
Mama-Me Foods Inc. 259
Markdown off-original sales (%) 302
Market activity ratio 75
Market attractiveness 145
Market forecast 179
Market leverage ratio 85
Market liquidity ratio 94
Market potential 147
    - Consumer market 147
    - Industrial market 149
Market profitability/productivity ratios 101

Marketing Budget - Direct Approach 14
Marketing Budget - Indirect Approach 17
Marketing channel 355
Marketing communication 333
Marketing cost 14
Marketing ratios 73
Marketing research 197
Marketing strategy 195
Markup at Retail or Cost 292
Mass marketing 42
Maximum Advertising Cost 342
Meats "R" Us Inc. 46
Merchandise Planning 184
 - Basic Stock Method 184
 - Percentage Variation Method 188
 -Weekly Supply Method 191, 192
MeriAnn Chinaware Inc. 107
Modern Furniture Inc. 349
Modern Interior Inc. 14
Monthly credit cost 50
Multidimensional Scaling 252
Multiple regression 258

N

Net Direct Inc. 355
Net profit before tax 17
Net profit margin 123
Net return on sales 123
Nic's Health Foods Inc. 277
Non-traceable cost contribution margin 139
Non-traceable unit cost 140
Non-traceable variable contribution margin 139
NorthWest Discount Furniture Inc. 99

O

Ordinary least squares 226
Off-retail markdown percentage 303
Operating expense 43
Operating expense ratio 45
Operating profit 17
Opportunity cost 41
Optimal marketing mix 41
Original markup 298
   -at retail 299
   -at cost 299

P

Pave-It-4-U Inc. 137, 140
Percentage value contribution margin (PVCM) 12, 17, 25, 125, 171
Percentage variation method 189
Perceived distance of brands 285
Perfect Dentures Inc. 153
Perfect Shapes Inc. 147
Peoples Brewing Inc. 284
Pets Import Inc. 32
Pleasure Bookstore Inc. 391
Poisson probability distribution 267
Price-earning ratio 127
Price elasticity 307
Pricing 287
Priority One Drives Supplies 34
Product 277
Product survival rate 164
Productivity 101
Profit impact of customer satisfaction 61
Profit impact of quantity discount 50
Profitability of indirect channel process 355

Projected Marketing Plan 239
Purple Cross Inc. 281

Q

Quality Import Cars Inc. 151
Quality Mobile X-ray Services Inc. 69
Quality Sealed Air Inc. 167
Queuing Model(Waiting Line Model) 268
Quick Ratio 98

R

Racquetball of Minnesota Inc. 316
Reach 333
Recency/Frequency and Monetary Value Segmentation1 346
Recency/Frequency and Monetary Value Segmentation2 348
Reduction in inventory value 379
Relative market potential - Single index approach 150
Reliable Office Furniture Inc. 18
Reorder point 371
Replacement potential 166
Required increase in customer satisfaction 59
Required level of sales 384, 388, 391
Required market share (RMS) 176
Required total dollar sales 169
Required total unit sales 172
Retail based pricing 311
Retail compatibility model 326
Retail gravitation 319
Retail Saturation Index (IRS) 221
Retail space productivity model 323
Retailing 316
Returns and allowances 17
Return on investment 131
Return on investment percentage 129
Return on investment model 133

Return on net worth 269
Return on total assets 129
Return per footage 116
Rolly's Coaches and Campers Inc. 342
Rolly Upholstery Inc. 385

S

Sales budget 20
Sales cost/ratio analysis 32
Sales efficiency ratio 394
Sales forecasting
    -exponential smoothing 179
    -moving average 183
Sales per square foot 396
Sales variance analysis 305
Selling price on profit 109
Semi fixed cost-effect 36
Serv-Em-UP Inc. 85
Serve "U" Fast Inc. 158
Selective marketing 42
Shields Glue & Adhesives Inc. 79
Shopper attraction model 329
Simply Unbeatable Inc. 42
Sit-In-Comfort Inc. 103
Size of sales force model 382
Smart & Associates Professional Cent Inc. 298
Spiffy Looks Inc. 358
Southeastern Women Center Inc 335
Southland Flags and Poles Inc. 26
Standard Error 27
Star Locks Inc. 24
Stock turnover ratio 377
Strategic profit model 268
Substitution effect 12
Suki Soki Orthopedic Inc. 53

T

TCI Agric. Inc. 224
Target marketing 272
Target return pricing 314
Task and objective advertising budget 344
Tecks-Com Wireless 160
Territory performance measure 144
The Southeastern Women Center Inc. 124, 125
Time-interest earned ratio 91
Tobeke Fabrics Inc. 326
Total assets turnover 81
Total contribution 15
    -per dollar sale 39
Total current asset 95, 97
Total current liabilities 95, 97
Total debt-to-equity ratio 90
Total dollar markdown 210
Total market potential 153
    -Combined Market 155
Total order cost 52
Traceable fixed cost 25, 26
Trade discount 52

U

Unique Web Works Inc. 62
UP Tiles Company Inc. 65
Uptown Investors Inc. 339

V

Value of shipment 151
Variable contribution 35
Variable Contribution Margin (VCM) 17, 15, 25, 136, 171
Variable cost per job 110

W

Web "R" Us Inc. 59
Weighted Number of Exposures 352
Wesley & Wise Law Office 77
Whoz-UP Fashions Inc. 141
Whuman Genetics Inc. 105
Woods Pro Inc. 94

Y

Yours Truly Exotic Cars Inc. 394

REFERENCES

PART ONE: MARKETING COST

CHAPTER 1   ACCOUNTING

1. Stickney, Clyde P. and Roman L. Well *Financial Accounting: An Introduction to Concepts, Methods, and Uses.* Fort Worth, TX: The Dryden Press, 1994.
2. Horngren, Charles and Tom Harrison, *Principles of Accounting,* 4th ed. Englewood, N.J Prenctice Hall, Inc. 2001.
3. Huff, Lois A. "Restructuring Correct Problems with Fixed Assets" *Chain Age Executive,* August 1993, pp. 19A-23A.
4. Tergen, Anne "The Ins and Outs of Cash Flow," *Business Week,* Jan. 22 2001, p.102

CHAPTER 2   BUDGETING

1. Little, John D. C. Models and Managers: The Concept of a Decision Calculus," *Management Science,* April 1970, pp. B-466 –B-485.
2. Piercy, Nigel "The Marketing Budgeting Process: MarketingtManagement Implications," *Journal of Marketing,* October 1987, pp. 45-59

CHAPTER 3   COST

1. Adelman, Philip and Alan Marks *Entrepreneurial Finance*, New Jersey: Prentice Hall, 20001
2. "How Much Is a Customer Worth?" *Sales and Marketing Management*. May 1989, p.23
3. Siropolis, Nicholas *Small Business Management 6th* Ed. Boston: Houghton Mifflin Company 1997.

4. Saporito, Bill, "The High Cost of Second Best," *Fortune,* July 26, 1993, pp. 99-102.

CHAPTER 4   CREDIT SALES

1. Anderson, Erin, "The Salesperson as Outside Agent or Employee: A Transaction Cost Analysis," Marketing Science, Summer 1985, pp 234-254.
2. Monahan, James P. "A Quantity Discount Pricing Model to Increase Vendor Profits," Management Science, June 1984, pp. 720-726
3. Rao, Ashak "Quantity Discounts in Today's Marketing," Journal of Marketing, Fall 1980, pp. 44-51.

PART 2   CUSTOMER DECISION

CHAPTER 5   CUSTOMER SATISFACTION

1. Engel, James Roger Blackwell and Paul Miniard ConsumerBehavior 5th ed. Chicago: The Dryden Press 1986
2. Dawkins, Peter and Frederick Reichheld, "Customer Retention as a Competitive Weapon." Directors and Boards, Summer 1990, pp41-47.

CHAPTER 6   CONSUMER BEHAVIOR

1. Fishbein, Martin. "A Behavioral Theory Approach to the Relations between Beliefs about an Object and the Attitude toward the Object" in Readings in *Attitude Theory and Measurement,* ed. Martinn Fishbein, New York: Wiley, 1967, p. 389-400
2. Schiffman, Leonard and Kanuk L, *Consumer Behavior 6th ed.* New Jersey: Prentice Hall 1997.

PART 3   MARKETING RATIOS

CHAPTER 7   MARKET ACTIVITY RATIOS

1. Berman, Barry, *Retail Management: A Strategic Approach,* 6th ed. Englewood Cliffs, NJ: Prentice Hall, 1995.
2. *Industry Norms and Key Ratios: Desk-top Edition,* 1992-1993, New York: Dun & Bradstreet, 1993, pp. v-vi.

CHAPTER 8   MARKET LEVERAGE RATIOS

1. Berman, Barry, *Retail Management: A Strategic Approach,* 6th ed. Englewood Cliffs, NJ: Prentice Hall, 1995.
2 *Industry Norms and Key Ratios: Desk-top Edition,* 1992-1993, New York: Dun & Bradstreet, 1993, pp. v-vi.

CHAPTER 9   MARKET LIQUIDITY RATIOS

1. Berman, Barry, *Retail Management: A Strategic Approach,* 6th ed. Englewood Cliffs, NJ: Prentice Hall, 1995.
2. *Industry Norms and Key Ratios: Desk-top Edition,* 1992-1993, New York: Dun & Bradstreet, 1993, pp. v-vi.

CHAPTER 10   MARKET PROFITABILITY/PRODUCTIVITY RATIOS

1. Berman, Barry, *Retail Management: A Strategic Approach,* 6th ed. Englewood Cliffs, NJ: Prentice Hall, 1995.
2. Berss, Marcia, "High Noon," *Forbes,* December 20, pp.44-45 Douglas, Lambert M. and Jay U. Sterling, "What Types of Profitability Reports Do Marketing Managers Receive?" *Industrial Marketing Management,* Nov. 1987, pp.289-304.

3. Grant, Alan W.H., and Leonard A. Schlesinger, "Realize Your Customers Full Profit Potential," *Harvard Business Review,* September-October 1955, pp. 59-72
4. *Industry Norms and Key Ratios: Desk-top Edition,* 1992-1993, New York: Dun & Bradstreet, 1993, pp. v-vi.
5. Coopers & Lybrand, "Utilizing Inventory Information for Enhanced" *Supply Chain Management,* p.4
6. Jackson, Donald, and Lonnie Ostrom, "Grouping Segments for Profitability Analysis'" *Business Topics,* Spring 1980. pp. 39-44.

PART 4   MARKET ATTRACTIVENESS

CHAPTER 11   MARKET POTENTIAL

1. Ennis, Beavin F. *Marketing Norms for Product Managers,* Association of National Advertisers, New York 1985.
2. Geurts Michael and David Whitlark, "Forecasting Market Share" *Journal of Business Forecasting,* Winter 1992-1993
3. "How to Construct a Customer BPI." *Sales and Marketing Management.* October. 28, 1994. p. 9
4. Szymanski, David M., Sundar G. Bharadwaj, and P. Rajan Vardarajan, "An Analysis of the Market Share-Profitability Relationship" *Journal of Marketing,* July 1993, 991-18.

CHAPTER 12   MARKET FORECAST

1. Proctor, R. A. "A Different Approach to Sales Forecasting: Using a Spreadsheet" *European Management Journal.* Winter 1992-1993.

PART 5   MARKETING STRATEGY

CHAPTER 13 MARKETING RESEARCH

1. Carrol, Douglas and Paul E. Green "Psychometric Methods in Marketing Research: Part 1, Conjoint Analysis" Journal of Marketing Research, vol. XXXII, November 1995
2. Evans, James R *Applied Production and Operations Management,* Minneapolis/St. Paul: West Publishing Company. 1993.
3. Ferrell, O.C., George Lucas and David Luck *Strategic Marketing Management,* Cincinnati: South-Western Publishing Co. 1994.
4. Green, Paul and Yoram wind, "New Way to Measure Consumers' Judgments," *Harvard Business Review,* July-August 1975.
5. Geurts, Michael and David Whitlark, "Forecasting Market Share," *Journal of Business Forecasting,* Winter 1992-1993, pp.17-22.
6. Malhotra, Naresh *Marketing Research: An Applied Orientation,* New Jersey: Prentice-Hall 1993.
7. Mentzer John T.and Kenneth B. Kahn, "Forecasting Familiarity, Satisfaction, usage, and Application," *Journal of Forecasting,* vol. 14, 1995, pp 465-476
8. Microsoft Excel 1985-1999, 2000. Microsoft Corporation.
9. SPSS for Windows, SPSS Inc. 1989-1999, 2002.
10. Wang, George C.S "What You Should Know about Regression Based-Forecasting" *The Journal of Business Forecasting,* Winter 1993-1994.

CHAPTER 14   TARGET MARKETING

1. Hughes, Arthur *The Complete Database Marketer*, Probus Publishing, 1991.

PART 6   THE FOUR P's

CHAPTER 15   PRODUCT

1. Guiltinan, Joseph, Gordon Paul and Thomas Madden *Marketing Management: Strategic and Programs* Boston 6th ed. McGraw Hill Inc. 1997.

CHAPTER 16   PRICING

1. Anderson Carol and Julian Vincze *Strategic Marketing Management: Meeting the Global Marketing Challenge.* Boston: Houghton Mifflin Company 2000.
2. Burston, William. *A Checklist of 38 Ways of Controlling Markdowns,* New York: National Retail Federation, n.d.
3. Daft, Richard *Management 2nd ed.* Chicago: The Dryden Press 1991.
4. Mason, Barry and Hazel Ezell *Marketing Management* New York: Macmillan Publishing Company, 1993
5. Guiltinan, Joseph, Gordon Paul and Thomas Madden *Marketing Management: Strategic and Programs* New York: McGraw Hill Inc. 1991.

CHAPTER 17   RETAILING

1. Benavent, Christophe, Marc Thomas, and Anne Bergue, "Application of Gravity Models for the Analysis of RetailPotential," *Journal of Targeting Measurement, and Analysis for Marketing,* Vol. 1 Winter 1992-1993, pp.305-315
2. Berman, Barry, *Retail Management: A Strategic Approach,* 6th ed. Englewood Cliffs, NJ: Prentice Hall, 1995.

3. Craig, Avijit Ghosh, and Sara McLafferty, "Models of the Retail Location Process: A Review," *Journal of Retailing,* Vol. 60, Spring 1984, pp. 5-36.
4. Huff, David L. "Defining and Estimating a Trading Area," *Journal of Marketing,* Vol. 28, July 1964, pp. 34-38.
5. ___ and Larry Blue *A Programmed Solution for Estimating Retail Sales Potential,* Lawrence: University of Kansas, 1966.
6. Gautschi, David A. "Specification of Patronage Models for Retail Center Choice," *Journal of Marketing Research,* Vol. 18, May 1981, pp. 162-174.
7. Ghosh, Avijit, *"The Value of a Mall and Other Insights from a Revised Central Place Model," Journal of Retailing,* Vol. 62 Spring 1986, pp. 79-97.
8. LeBlang, Paul. "A Theoretical Approach for Predicting Sales at a New Department Store Location Via Lifestyles," *Direct Marketing,* Vol. 7, Autumn 1993, pp. 70-74.
9. Nelson, Richard L. *The Selection of Retail Locations* New York: F.W. Dodge, 1959 p. 149
10. Reilly, William, *Method for the Study of Retail Relationships,* Research Monograph No. 4. Austin: University of Texas Press,t1929, University of Texas Bulletin No. 2944
11. Weisbrod, Glen E., Robert J. Parcells, and Clifford Kern, "A Disaggregate Model for Predicting Shopping Area Market Attraction," *Journal of Retailing,* Vol. 60, Spring 1984, pp. 65-83.
12. Young, Mark R. and Roger J. Calantone, "Advances in Spatial Interaction Modeling of Consumer-Retailer Interaction" in William Bearden, Rohit Despande, and Thomas J. Madden, et al. (Editor), 1990 *AMA Educators' Proceedings* Chicago: American Marketing Association, 1990, pp. 264-267.

CHAPTER 18 MARKETING COMMUNICATION

1. Donahue, George "Evaluating Services" Part II," *Marketing Communications,* April 1982, p.61
2. Gensch, *Advertising Planning: Mathematical Models in Advertising Media Planning,* Elsevier Scientific, Amsterdam, 1973.

3. Lavidge and Gary a. Steiner, "A Model for Predictive Measurements of Adverting Effectiveness," *Journal of Marketing,* October 1961. p.61.
4. Mandese, Joe "Revisiting Ad Reach Frequency" *Advertising Age,* vol. 66 November 27, 1995, p.46. *Marketers Guide To Media,* Spring-Summer 95, Adweek Publishing
5. Patti, Charles H. and Charles F. Frazer, *Advertising: A Decision-Making Approach.* Hinsdale, Ill.: Dryden Press, 1988.
6. Roberts, Mary Lou and Paul Berger, *Direct Marketing Management,* Prentice-Hall, Englewood Cliffs, NJ., 1989, pp.105-107.
7. Shimp, Terrence A, *Marketing Communications: Managing of Advertising and Promotions,* 4th ed Fort Worth, Texas: HBJ/Dryden 1996.
8. Young, James Webb "What is Advertising, What Does It Do?" *Adverting Age,* November 21, 1973. p.12

CHAPTER 19 CHANNEL INVENTORY

1. Coopers & Lybrand, "Inventory Management for Improved Profitability," *Chain Store Age Executive,* December 1992, Section two.
2. Berman, Barry, *Retail Management: A Strategic Approach,* 6th ed. Englewood Cliffs, NJ: Prentice Hall, 1995.

CHAPTER 20   SALES

1. Futrell, Charles *Sales Management* Fort Worth: The Dryden Press 1994.
2. Dalrymple, Douglas and Hans B. Thorelli "Sales Force Budgeting" *Business Horizon 27* July-August 1984
3. Gates, Michael, "New Measures of Sales Performance,"*Incentive,* November 1988, pp. 45-52
4. Laforge, Raymond and David Cravens, "A Marketing Response Model for Sales Management Decision Making," *Journal of*

Personal Selling and Sales Management, Fall/Winter, 1981-1982, pp. 10-16

5. Lodish, Leonard "A User-Oriented Model for Sales Force Product, and Market Allocation Decisions," *Journal of Marketing,* Summer 1980, pp. 70-78,

6. "Vaguely Right Approach to Sales Force Allocation," *Harvard Business Review,* January-February 1974. pp. 199-214

7. Pearson, Ray, "Space Management From Product to Store," *Progressive Grocer,* December 1993, pp. 31-32.

8. Schiff, J. S., "Evaluating the sales Force as a Business," *Industrial Marketing Management,* April 1983, pp. 131-137.

A Handbook of Marketing Mathematics
with automatic spreadsheets for Quantitative Marketing

435

PHOTO CREDITS

Chapters	Photo Number Companies	Location
1	1 Sledgefield Florist & Gifts	Greensboro, NC.
	2 Southside Metals	"
2.	3 COMPUSA	"
	4 Rhodes Furniture	"
3.	5 Southern States	"
	6 Blumenthal's	"
	7 COZY COUNTRY KENNELS	Liberty, NC
	8 Academy of Spoiled Babies	Greensboro, NC
	9 RAC Rent-A-Center	"
4.	10 ANN's TRIAD MEATS	"
	11 Carolina Office Machines Inc.	"
	12 Orthopaidic Center	"
5.	13 WebBuilder	"
7.	14 Priority One	"
	15 Barron & Berry L.L.P	"
	16 Bed Bath & Beyond	"
	17 Special Occasions	"
8.	18 Skip's Hot Dogs	"
	19 Harper's Cabaret	Winston-Salem, NC
9.	20 Burchette & Burchette Hardwood Floors	Elkin, NC.
10.	21 Community Funeral Homes	Greensboro, NC.
	22 Central Carolina Home Improvement	"
11.	23 Krush Kutz Barber shop	Winston-Salem, NC.
	24 Chicken & Honey	"
	25 Bank of America	Greensboro, NC.
12	26 Camera Corner	"
	27 TRIAD MARINE	"
	28 Greensboro Antiques	"
13.	29 Lost Dimension	"
	30 May Flower	"
	31 DIRECT JETCHARTER	"
15.	32 Salama Chiropractic	"

16	33 South Elm Center	"
	34 acFITNESS	"
	35 Freedom Homes	"
17.	36 Forsyth Seafood	Winston-Salem, NC.
18.	37 The Women's Hospital	Greensboro, NC.
	38 Old Time Pottery	Atlanta, GA.
	39 DERMATOLOGY	Greensboro, NC.
	40 Southeastern Furniture	"
19.	41 Bill Harvey's Auto	"
	42 Lowe's Food	"
	43 The Shoe Market	"
	44 Discount Tires	"
20.	45 Kim's Grocery	"
	46 Border	"
	47 World Market	"
	48 5 STAR	Winston-Salem, NC

ABOUT THE AUTHOR

Dr. Rowland Chidomere is an Associate Professor of Marketing at Winston-Salem State University in Winston-Salem, North Carolina. He holds a Ph.D. from the University of Oklahoma and an MBA and BBA from the University of Central Oklahoma. Dr. Chidomere has taught several marketing subjects including the Principles of marketing, Marketing management, Salesmanship, Retailing, Marketing research, and International marketing courses since 1984. He won Teaching Excellence Awards in 1987 and 1999 at Winston-Salem State University.

Dr. Chidomere's research and publications have focused primarily on marketing management and marketing education with articles published in the *Journal of Marketing Education, Journal of Advanced Management, and Ideas in Marketing.* His presentations are published in the *Atlantic Marketing Proceeding and SAM International Management Proceeding.* Dr. Chidomere has been involved in several professional development projects, including Distance Learning, Internet marketing, and ways to utilize technology such as Microsoft Excel to create mathematical functions and models to use in marketing. He is a frequent contributor and reviewer for marketing and management journals and proceedings. His marketing knowledge is vast, and he has taught and researched in different areas of marketing in the past nineteen years.

Printed in the United States
20809LVS00002B/105